ON THE ROAD
IN TRUMP'S AMERICA

A JOURNEY INTO THE HEART
OF A DIVIDED NATION

DANIEL ALLOTT

REPUBLIC
BOOK PUBLISHERS

ISBN 9781645720188 (Hardcover) 9781645720195 (ebook)

For inquiries about volume orders, please contact:

Republic Book Publishers

501 Slaters Lane #206

Alexandria VA 22314

editor@republicbookpublishers.com

Published in the United States by Republic Book Publishers

Distributed by Independent Publishers Group

www.ipgbook.com

Book designed by Mark Karis

Printed in the United States of America

To the memory of my beloved mother, Leslie Allott.

CONTENTS

INTRODUCTION

AN ESSENTIAL PART of a journalist's responsibility is to listen, observe, ask good questions, and then listen some more. For too long, too few journalists have taken this responsibility seriously. This has been particularly true in the Trump era. Most political journalists failed to anticipate Donald Trump's rise because they were utterly unable to understand his appeal. From the start, they treated Trumpism as a pathology. They dismissed his voters as being guided by bigotry, ignorance, and fear. Needless to say, this has skewed their coverage.

Worst of all, no one seems to have learned anything. The media malpractice that characterized the 2016 presidential campaign has arguably become even worse during the Trump presidency. Most of the media have remained unwilling or unable to understand and objectively report on the people and places that put Trump in the White House. That's partly because most political journalists disagree with Trump's politics. It's also because most live and work in large coastal cities, geographically and culturally removed from the rural communities and Rust Belt towns that delivered the election to Trump. The Washington media is a small, isolated, and insular club whose members talk to and about one another. They are largely oblivious to what happens elsewhere around the country.

When reporters do venture into "Trump's America," they typically parachute in for only a few hours in search of evidence to confirm their pre-written narratives. As Jill Abramson, former executive editor of the *New York Times,* wrote in 2019, in most of the news media "there is little evidence that reporters have fulfilled their pledge to report on and reflect the interests and values of the people who voted for (Trump). There have been some good dispatches from the heartland, but too often what is published amounts to the proverbial 'toe touch in Appalachia.'"[1]

This book's purpose is to provide some balance by taking a different approach. In spring 2017, I left my position at a Washington, DC, political magazine and began reporting from across the country. I spent most of the following three years living in and reporting from nine counties that were crucial to understanding the 2016 election; they will be equally crucial to determining who will win in 2020. The nine counties are scattered across nine states—in Florida and North Carolina, through Appalachia, the industrial heartland, and across the Upper Midwest, to the western states of Utah and California. The counties differ widely, ranging from two-stoplight Howard County, Iowa, to sprawling Orange County, California, whose population exceeds that of twenty states; from majority-minority Robeson County, North Carolina, to rural Grant County, West Virginia, where 99 percent of residents are white. I selected each county with one idea in mind: Each had to reveal something important and interesting about the Trump phenomenon or politics in the Trump era.

This book is not just a study of Trump voters. I spoke with as many people as I could, regardless of their politics. My one preference was for "switchers"—people who voted one way in 2016 and have subsequently changed their minds ahead of the 2020 election. I discovered that these voters are like an endangered species in Trump's America. I interviewed farmers and professors; congressmen and homeless people; refugees and drug addicts; students and retirees; progressives, conservatives, and people with no discernible or consistent political ideology.

Six of the nine counties are Obama-Trump counties, meaning they voted for Barack Obama for president before switching to Trump; one is a historically Republican county, and two are formerly Republican counties that are now trending Democratic. I entered these counties with no agenda other than to listen, learn, and report. To do this, I spent weeks at a time in each, returning to them again and again. I hope and believe that my consistent presence, my thoughtful questions, my willingness to listen, and my desire to understand helped me to develop a deep level of trust and goodwill with many of the people I met. And because I returned numerous times, I was able to track how my subjects' views, priorities, and circumstances changed over the course of Trump's first term in office. When people noticed that I was staying in their community for long stretches and returning, it communicated to them that I was committed to understanding. On numerous occasions, I heard comments to the effect that, "I'm so glad you'll be here two weeks instead of just a day."

This account includes tales of job loss and gain; of social alienation and reconciliation; of addiction, recovery, and relapse; and of relationships strained or torn apart over arguments about Donald Trump. I recorded my interviews whenever I could. This allowed me to maintain eye contact and read body language, and to convey with mine that I was interested and really listening. I learned that people opened up to me when I signaled a sincere interest in what they had to say. Spending more time with them allowed me to move beyond politics to explore intimate subjects of values, family, and loss.

Just as revealing as the hundreds of formal interviews I conducted were the thousands of informal encounters and impressions and observations I gathered while on the road. Some people were reluctant to meet with me—understandable, given the deep distrust of the media that exists in America today. Others, such as retired manufacturing worker

Allen Ewanick, simply wondered why I was interested in learning their opinion at all.

"I was a little reluctant to meet with you," Ewanick confessed as he pulled a chair up across from me at the outdoor seating area of a gastropub on the outskirts of Erie, Pennsylvania. "I was like, 'Why does he want to meet with me? I don't have any pearls of wisdom, or earth-shattering viewpoint.' But I didn't want to be closed-minded. I think it's important for people to see other people's viewpoints—the average working guy or whatever." I felt it was particularly important to visit rural places, where people have felt especially neglected and misunderstood.

One frigid February night in 2018, I drove Mike Gooder home in his car after watching President Trump deliver his first State of the Union address. Mike had helped me convene a group of a dozen or so local people for a watch party at The Pub, a bar in Cresco, a small city in Howard County, Iowa. I was feeling somewhat dejected at the time, questioning whether I should continue my research. But as would often happen during this three-year journey, something occurred that buoyed my spirits enough to keep me going. In this case it was Mike, a few drinks in him, telling me how much he appreciated my attempts to understand his community. "We're just some dumb-fucks from rural Iowa to most of the media," he said. "But you're making an effort to get to know this place and to tell its story. Regardless of how we are portrayed, at least you're giving us a voice. I appreciate that."

I didn't just visit the diners and campaign events beyond which political reporters rarely venture. The point of my journey was to get to know my subjects personally by sharing in their lives and even staying in their homes.

I was often surprised by how people reacted to being interviewed. Many became emotional. And I realized early on that for many people I spoke with, it was the first time they had ever talked at length about their political opinions, values, hopes, dreams, and regrets. This level of intimacy offered both benefits and challenges. It invited people to open up and lower their guard. But it also produced the challenge of accurately reporting on people I'd initially encountered as interview subjects but come to know and appreciate as friends.

When I arrived at Volusia County, Florida, resident Sandi Hodgden's Halloween party in 2018, she wanted to know whether I had come as a friend or as a reporter. I was initially interested in getting to know Sandi as an interview subject. She's a Midwest transplant and former Obama voter who had embraced Trump with the zeal of a religious convert. But I'd also grown quite fond of Sandi, and thought of her as a friend.

"Both," I said.

"But which one more?" she asked.

"Sandi, of course, as your friend," I replied, at which point she introduced me to her husband, Dave, who was suffering from late-stage dementia. He would die only a few months later. But I was fortunate to glimpse the beautiful love that Sandi and Dave had shared for more than forty years.

"I'm glad you got to meet Dave," Sandi texted me later. I was too.

This book began as a reporting project undertaken with my brother, Jordan Allott, for the *Washington Examiner* called "The Race to 2020." In 2018, I started reporting independently, authoring freelance columns for the *Washington Examiner*, *National Review Online*, and other outlets. I have incorporated some of those pieces into this book.

I visited each county at least four times. My visits lasted anywhere from a couple of days to five weeks. In all, I drove 70,000 miles, including a cross-country trip that started in Miami and ended in Huntington Beach, California, with stops in all nine counties in between. I boarded dozens of planes and spent nights in hundreds of hotels, Airbnbs, and friends' homes.

My goal wasn't simply to learn why people had voted the way they did in 2016, or to predict how they might vote in 2020. It was also to chart how their lives and circumstances changed over the course of Trump's first term in office, and how the values and priorities that inform their political views might have changed. In short, my goal was to explain these people and places—not to explain them away. My hope is that the following account will challenge preconceived ideas about who the people in these places are, what motivates their decisions, and what animates their lives.

1

HOWARD COUNTY, IOWA

AFTER EIGHT YEARS of displeasure with Barack Obama's presidency, Carla Johnson was ready for a drastic change. The forty-five-year-old lab technician from Cresco, Iowa, fell for Donald Trump very early on in the 2016 primary season. She loved what she called his "take-no-shit" style, his conservative stances on gun control and immigration, his defense of traditional religion, and all that winning he promised to do on the economy. "I was a huge Trump supporter from the beginning," she said. "Huge. I love the man. He was my first choice all the way through."

A year-and-a-half into Trump's presidency, Johnson was so pleased with Trump that she couldn't envision not voting for him again in 2020. "It would have to be something catastrophic," she said of what it would take for her to cast her ballot for somebody else. What's remarkable about Johnson's support for Trump is that not long before he came along, she had been a lifelong Democrat, and she had once voted for Barack Obama. It's a vote she clearly regrets.

"When Obama first ran, he preached change, and it sounded fantastic," Johnson told me in the summer of 2018, when we spoke near the county courthouse in downtown Cresco. "I bought into the hope and change, which is terrible because he didn't do any of that."

"Did he do any good?" I asked.

"No. I don't like him—at all. I think he lied. I think he lied when he campaigned, and I have no time for lying. What did he bring us? Segregation."

Johnson is so bitter that she now entertains the conspiracy theory, at times championed by Trump, that Obama was born in Kenya and thus was ineligible to run for president. "I believe that he honestly somewhat supported the Muslims and terrorist ways," she said. "I don't think he had the country's best interests at heart."

Johnson's political evolution underscores several of this book's core themes, including how thoroughly the disease of tribalism has spread through America's body politic.

Howard County, Iowa, is the only county in America that voted for Obama by more than 20 points in 2012 and then for Trump by more than 20 points in 2016.[1] I first traveled to Howard County in the summer of 2017 to find out what had prompted such a dramatic reversal. I spoke at great length and on multiple occasions with more than two-dozen voters. Not all of the Trump supporters I met were as harsh as Johnson in their criticism of Obama, nor were most as effusive in their praise of Trump. But even the more restrained assessments conveyed roughly the same sentiment. At the top of their list was a complaint about the Democratic Party's abrupt leftward shift. It has alienated the culturally conservative Democrats who populate much of the rural Midwest. Perhaps that merely confirms the conventional wisdom. But the question I arrived with during a ten-day trip the following year was whether Howard County's vote for the maverick Republican was a fit of pique or the sign of a permanent political shift.

My first stop was the Mighty Howard County Fair in Cresco, where I poked my head into the Moo Mobile malt truck to say hello to Joe

Wacha. Like Johnson, Wacha had been a lifelong Democrat and an Obama voter before switching to Trump. At the fair the year before, Wacha told me his vote for Trump was prompted by the Democrats' leftward drift and preoccupation with identity politics. "The reason I didn't vote as a Democrat, and I am a registered Democrat, was I felt like they're no longer the party they were thirty years ago," he told me in 2017 as we strolled around the fairgrounds. Today's Republican Party "is more like the way the Democratic Party was thirty or forty years ago," Wacha, who is in his early sixties, added.

I was curious to know how Wacha was feeling a year and a half into Trump's presidency. I had spent enough time around Wacha to know him to be kind, gracious, and unfailingly polite. So I half expected him to tell me that Trump's boorish behavior was making him regret his vote. I was wrong. He felt no such regret. Wacha told me he was pleased with Trump's performance thus far. In fact, the media's and Democrats' unflinching opposition to everything Trump was doing had only hardened his support for the president. And he told me he was planning to change his voter registration to Republican the following week.

Later that day, I sat down with Lee and Larry Walter and Ernie Martin, three elderly brothers who had instructed me to meet them at the Cresco Wildlife Club, an indoor shooting range inside the fairground's main exhibition hall. For weeks prior to our interview, Ernie had peppered me with emails containing facts about Howard County that often started with "People have NO IDEA that …" or "Your readers

Joe Wacha at the Howard County Fair in Cresco in 2017. (Jordan Allott)

9

will be surprised to know that ..." The emails were meant to underscore how remote and disconnected this two-stoplight county really is. "We're so behind here," Lee and Ernie each told me separately, "that we don't get the *Today Show* until tomorrow."

Like most people in rural areas, Ernie and his brothers regarded their hometown's cultural and geographic distance from America's cities as a point of pride. This stands in contrast to the disdain with which Hillary Clinton seemed to regard rural places, depicting them as backward and out of step with the times. Ernie, Lee, and Larry had come to my attention on a previous visit when I walked past Lee's home in Cresco and saw three billboard-sized pro-Trump, anti-Clinton signs displayed in his front yard. One of the signs simply read, "Lock the bitch up." I had a feeling it wouldn't be hard to get these guys to open up.

I asked them for their thoughts on why Howard County had swung so far from Obama to Trump. Lee said it was because Clinton had pledged to "take away all the guns and abolish the Second Amendment. Your readers should know that everyone here owns at least two ARs and dozens of shotguns and long guns and two handguns."

All three brothers complained about the opposition Trump was receiving from the media, Democrats, and even some Republicans. "We didn't vote for Obama, but after the election we supported Obama," Ernie said. "I'm seventy-two. I've seen a lot of national elections. I've never seen one like this, with people upset, so upset they want to kill Trump for a year-and-a-half."

Then Ernie slid into the familiar conservative refrain about voter fraud:

> Hillary spent millions rigging that last election, we know that. There were all kinds of foreigners that voted in California. The dead voted in Chicago. Illegal foreigners voted in New York by the busload. Not only did they vote once, they voted two or three times. There are lots of precincts where they have gone through and checked and found out that they had more people vote than the people who live there.

Ernie Martin and Lee and Larry Walter at the Cresco Wildlife Club in 2018. (Daniel Allott)

"Where did you hear that?" I asked.

"I have read that in the Republican news," Ernie responded. "And … ah … Rush Limbaugh talked about it. He's the only news source we can trust."

What struck me in speaking with Ernie Martin and his brothers, as well as other Trump voters, was not their loyalty to the president. That I had expected. It was their eagerness to defend policies that Washington pundits were sure would cause his voters to abandon him. For instance, I found little sympathy for immigrants affected by the administration's policy of separating migrant families who crossed into the US illegally and detaining children without their parents. At the time, a "zero tolerance" policy had resulted in thousands of separations, drawing rebukes even from some pro-Trump Republican lawmakers. But every Trump supporter I met offered some variation of "Nobody wants to see children separated from their mothers" before launching into a full defense of a policy that had sent Trump's opponents into fits of rage.

"I don't want to see people suffer, but they're putting themselves in that situation," said Chris Chilson of nearby Lime Springs, a city of 485 people located a couple of miles south of the Minnesota border. "There's a legal way to come to this country, and they're not doing it. And we're supposed to put out all the stops? We have twenty-two veterans a day committing suicide, probably because they can't get proper care at the VA. But yet, we're supposed to take in everybody who gets across the border and breaks the law? That doesn't make any sense to me."

"We need to quit worrying about everybody else first, and we need to focus here," Chris's wife, Sandy, a registered Democrat who voted for Trump, added. "It's fine to help other people, but we need to have our house in order first. We can't let every Tom, Dick, and Harry just come in because they want to. There's a process and there always has been a process, and that process works because people do it and become naturalized citizens, so I don't think we need to open those gates wide open."

The Walter brothers were similarly unmoved. "Those children who are locked up in those cages, they've got three meals a day, they've got fans, televisions, they've got gymnasiums, games," Lee Walter said. "They've got more benefits in them jails they're keeping them in than they ever had from where they came from. And the Democrats are screaming how terrible it is? B.S.!"

The brothers then fantasized about what they'd do if the president asked for armed volunteers to guard the border. "Bring your own gun and ammunition. You give me my fifty feet, then I'll go protect it," Ernie mused.

"I'll take more than fifty feet," Larry said.

"With Larry and me, we could at least protect half a mile real easy," Lee added. "Real easy, with our scopes, oh yeah. The first shot would be a warning shot. That's it. They don't belong here. They know they don't belong here. There is a legal way to get here. Let's do it."

"Do you feel animosity toward immigrants here in Cresco?" I asked.

"The ones here have green cards, and by God they work twenty-four hours a day. That's hard work," Lee said. "When we see them we smile and have a fine time. We don't have a hatred for these people."

"We just want them to do it the right way," Ernie said.

Coastal liberals tend to conflate legal and illegal immigration, while most conservatives consider the distinction crucial. Ernie Martin and his brothers' emphasis on immigrants doing things "the right way" underscores a core value that informs conservatives' policy positions—a deeply ingrained sense of fairness. The feeling that certain people—immigrants, welfare recipients, foreign governments—are not doing things the right way, that they're exploiting the system, jumping the line, or otherwise getting away with something, is pervasive in Howard County and places like it. So pervasive, in fact, that it was making Todd Mensink seriously consider moving away.

"I firmly believe that if you give everybody an opportunity to do their best, the vast majority of people are going to use that opportunity to the best of their abilities," said Mensink, who lives a few doors down from the Chilsons in Lime Springs. "Other people have the ideology that if you give someone that opportunity, they will just take advantage of it." As we sat in deck chairs beside the Lime Springs Municipal Swimming Pool on a sweltering day, I asked Mensink, a sociology professor and Bernie Sanders supporter, whether he felt that ideology prevailed in Howard County.

"Absolutely I do," he said. "That everyone's out to milk the system, which is unfortunate because these communities are exactly the ones that need these programs. What happens if the student loan program is done away with? What's going to happen to this area, where the average household income is thirty-some thousand dollars? That's the one thing that bugs me, is that I see people voting against their own self-interests."

Mensink was repeating Thomas Frank's standard critique of Heartland and Rust Belt residents who vote for Republican candidates opposed to government programs that could benefit them.[2] But this critique has its limitations. Political scientists have found that self-interest is a very poor predictor of policy preferences and political attitudes.[3] One reason is that one's interests, translated to align with a particular candidate or policy, can be highly subjective. Are one's "interests" defined only by the economic benefits one accrues from a particular policy? Or, can those interests also be related to some social good, system of belief, or higher principle? Shouldn't we commend those who vote out of principle, perhaps even against their own self-interest, as opposed to those who view their votes as more-or-less transactional on an economic or financial level?

But there's something else. Rural and working class people do want things like cheaper health care and better schools, but they don't trust the government to provide them. They don't want to send their hard-earned tax dollars to fund what they see as a corrupt system that pays people who don't want to work. Mensink understood these counterarguments, at least tacitly. For despite his exasperation with his conservative neighbors, he couldn't help but admire the ones who had voted for Trump because of his promise to nominate conservative judges to the US Supreme Court.

Earlier that day, Justice Anthony Kennedy had announced his retirement, giving Trump the chance to nudge the court to the right with a conservative replacement for the centrist justice. I asked Mensink for his reaction to the news. "I think a lot of Republicans kept their eyes on the prize (during the 2016 election)," he said. "The prize wasn't the presidency, the White House. It was the Supreme Court. And they did well on that, they really did. They didn't get too focused in on what (Trump) said. They focused on the thing that will be Trump's legacy long after he's gone."

Mensink couldn't think of a single positive thing Trump had done as president. "I think he's done more to harm this country and harm to democracy than any president we've ever had," he said. Still, Mensink didn't support impeaching Trump. "I might be one of the only massive lefties who does not want to see Trump impeached. (Vice President) Pence is a skilled politician. If he gets into the White House, the Republican agenda will move a lot, lot faster. And I don't want that. That scares me."

"If the economy stays where it's at, Trump has a very good chance of being reelected," Mensink continued. "Democrats—one of the biggest mistakes they make—they talk about how Trump won Iowa not because of the economy but because there was a lot of racist people that voted for him. They're still stuck on this identity politics."

For all of the division and tribalistic attitudes I encountered in Howard County, the problem of identity politics seemed like something people agreed on from all perspectives.

The next day, I headed back to Cresco and struck up a conversation with David and Maxine, a middle-aged couple working the Tri-County Right to Life booth at the fair. The booth was full of pro-life paraphernalia: anti-abortion leaflets, fetal development models, and graphic depictions of late-term abortions. David and Maxine told me they were devout Christians and the parents of seven children. "One mother," David said. "These days you have to specify that."

Todd Mensink outside the Lime Springs Municipal Swimming Pool in 2018. (Daniel Allott)

Maxine asked me if I was aware of "the truth about Planned Parenthood." I assured her that I knew the truth, prompting her to ask, "But you know who the capital T truth is, right?"

"Jesus, our Lord and savior," I replied, eliciting a satisfied grin from Maxine.

I learned that David and Maxine were also ardent Trump supporters, so I asked them whether as Christians they were troubled by Trump's lack of Christian virtue. David responded by simply pointing to a diagram of a late-term D&E abortion as if to say, "We're focused on saving babies, not the president's manners."

I understood David's logic—it's the same logic many of my pro-life friends have used to explain to me their votes for Trump.

"I wouldn't do that to an animal," an elderly dairy farmer named Allen said as he stood beside me, looking at the picture.

"That's what ticks you off about these Democrats," David said. "They complain about treatment of kids coming across (the border) illegally and yet have no trouble killing kids (through abortion)."

Still, I wanted to see whether they could allow for any nuance in assessing Trump's performance. The answer quickly became clear as Maxine began telling me what she likes most about Trump. "He doesn't have a big ego—unlike Obama and Clinton," she said. "He doesn't talk about himself all the time at his rallies. It's all about the people. It's never about him."

David then began to expound on the high abortion rate among black women. The abortion rate for black women is nearly five times higher than that of white women.[4] "People don't like it when we compare abortion to slavery, but you see it right there in that statistic—abortion's worse for blacks," David said.

I often asked interviewees to describe race relations in their community. In rural places, that question was sometimes met with bland assurances that things are fine. Other times it was met with a quizzical look or a chuckle. Or, as one perplexed rural resident of a nearly all-white county put it, "What race relations?"

Liberals are wrong when they claim that whites who live in racially isolated places are, as a consequence of their isolation, necessarily racist. That said, racial isolation makes people less aware of the experiences of people of other races. It can lead to a certain callousness that sometimes edges into or is at least interpreted as racism.

When I suggested to David that perhaps Russian meddling had played a role in Trump's victory, he insisted that President Obama was behind the Russian interference but that "they'll never admit it because he's black." Then the following bizarre exchange took place.

DA: "Do you think race played a role in Donald Trump's election?"

David: "No, I voted for the black boy in the primaries."

DA: "Black boy? You mean black *man?*"

David: Silence.

DA: "Ben Carson?"

David: "In the '90s"

DA: "Alan Keyes?"

David: "Yeah."

David's casual use of the words "black boy" to describe a sixty-eight-year-old Harvard PhD really should not have shocked me, but it did. I felt like I knew David, or at least his type. I've spent a good part of the last twenty years involved in the pro-life cause, even manning pro-life booths like this one from time to time. I've known dozens of older, white Midwestern couples just like David and Maxine—decent, hardworking, community-minded, and unfailingly nice. But I had to wonder: How could someone who is clearly capable of deep compassion for one historically aggrieved group of people simultaneously demonstrate so little compassion for another?

There was a time in my life when I would have shrugged off David's comment as little more than a poor choice of words. But now I suspected that David felt that his vote for Keyes insulated him from having to defend himself against charges of racism. It was as if David was saying, "Hey, I voted for a black guy for president, for crying out loud. So clearly I'm not a racist. Now let me say something racist."

David had not voted for Obama, of course. But perhaps there was something similar going on with Obama-Trump voters like Carla Johnson, who felt that their vote for Obama gave them license to embrace racist conspiracy theories about him. Then again, perhaps I was just overthinking it.

A few minutes later, I asked Maxine to assess Trump's performance. She gave him an eight out of ten. "I don't know how he gets the strength to do what he does," she said.

Of Obama, Maxine said, "I didn't like his look. And he was always stuttering." Perhaps recognizing the possible racial overtones of her comment, Maxine quickly added, "Have you interviewed Diamond and Silk?"

David and Maxine at the Tri-County Right to Life booth at the Howard County Fair in Cresco in 2018. (Daniel Allott)

I told her I had not interviewed those two black female pro-Trump social media personalities.

"Oh you have to!" Maxine said, her face brightening.

After all that talk of child murder and racism, I headed over to the beer garden in search of a beer.

With a $2 Budweiser in hand, I sat down at one of the Garden's benches and was introduced to Jackson, a young intern at a local plant business. Jackson told me he was from Haiti, where he was due to return two days later. A few months earlier, President Trump had committed a diplomatic *faux pas* by referring to Haiti and several other poor nations as "shithole countries." I asked Jackson whether he was bothered by what President Trump had said. Most Haitians were not offended, Jackson said. Instead, many saw Trump's comment as an indication of "the work we must do to change the view of our country."

Later, I walked by one of the concession stands at the fair. It contained an assortment of t-shirts, hats, trinkets, and flags. Several items were emblazoned with the Confederate flag. Remember—this was in

Iowa, solidly union country. I asked the concession worker how the Confederate flag items were selling. She said they were doing pretty well, but that they had been in really high demand about five years earlier, when a controversy over the flag was raging.

"We used to sell the flags for about $10. Then it shot up to $35," she said. "Now it's $20 for a flag. A couple of years ago we sold an entire semi-truck full of (Confederate Flag) bed sheets." She added that people in Minnesota and Iowa, where she sold most of her products, have no idea about the flag's true meaning.

"Would it matter?" I asked.

"Maybe not."

* * *

The rural Upper Midwest is a region of small towns and large vehicles. It's a place where people like their religion strong and their coffee weak, a place where housing prices and crime rates are low and many people leave their front doors unlocked and their truck keys in the ignition. Spend any time in rural America, and you realize just how culturally conservative a place it is. Church and family are still the cornerstones of rural life. Ask anyone in rural America to explain the local values and sooner or later (probably sooner) they'll mention guns and hunting. To many rural Americans, guns aren't so much a hobby as a way of life. Guns are a symbol of freedom, but they're also a tool, used for sport, self-defense, and food. And almost everybody—regardless of political affiliation—owns a gun and doesn't want the government or city dwellers telling them they cannot. I lost count of how many times I heard rural Democrats tell me they wished the party would just leave the issue alone. It's one thing to hear Ernie Martin, an elderly conservative white man, say that Hillary Clinton lost the 2016 election because she wanted to "take away all the guns."

It's another thing to hear Narren Brown say it. Brown doesn't fit the image of a gun-toting country boy. For one thing, he's a progressive college professor with a PhD. He's also black—one of the only black residents in Howard County, which is more than 99 percent white.

"Everyone here owns guns—like, everyone," Narren Brown told me when we meet at The Pub, a bar in Cresco, a couple of days after the county fair in 2018. "At that fair, there were more pistols in pockets than you would even think," Brown informed me. "There was a pistol in my pocket. There's a pistol in my pocket right now. It's legal to carry it. And as long as (the police) don't see it, I'm not breaking any laws."

Brown moved to Cresco from Oakland twenty-five years ago for the cheap housing and slower pace of life. He's a Bernie Sanders supporter who says he'd kneel every time he heard the National Anthem if he didn't think his two sons, who play high school sports, would get punished for it. But he's still very conservative on guns. "I actually think liberals would do themselves a favor if they got off the gun control," he said.

It's a sentiment I heard again and again in rural places: Vote Democratic and you'll lose your guns. I found the same sentiment among residents of Trempealeau County, Wisconsin, ninety miles north of Cresco. In the summer of 2017, I spoke with Kathy Vinehout, a Democrat who represented parts of Western Wisconsin in the state senate for a decade. "Hunting is just a huge part of my world," Vinehout, a former dairy farmer, told me when I met her at her office in the Wisconsin state capitol. She believed guns played a crucial role in Trump's strength in rural Wisconsin. She said:

> I heard over and over again from the election judges that if Hillary won, people would not be able to fill their freezer. This is really important in a rural area because people do hunt for food, and they have for generations. It's not just Republicans …That's the way people live, so I think that's an important part of the culture.

Then there was Erin Camp, the managing editor of the Grant County Press in Grant County, West Virginia. Erin described herself to me as "far more liberal than most people in the area" and supported Bernie Sanders in 2016. When I interviewed Erin in 2019, we had a lengthy chat about the appeal of rural life and the charms and challenges of small town journalism. Then, as I got up to leave, Erin stopped me—she had one more thing to say.

"I'll tell you," she said, "you want to lose an election in Grant County, take an anti-Second Amendment stance—Republican or Democratic."

"Anyone tried it?" I asked.

"No, not local politicians"

"So all local people are pro-gun?"

"All the ones I know are. Myself included," she said. "I don't think people from New York City know enough to be pro- or anti-gun. It's a lack of education."

She said that most city folks only hear about guns when they're used in inner-city gang violence or mass shootings in the suburbs. But that's not how they're used in the country. She said:

> My father got me my first gun at the age of six. So I've had guns, been around guns, my whole life. And they're not something that's scary to me. That's the difference. When we talk about guns, we're talking about rifles and shotguns used to go kill a squirrel. We're not talking about handguns, most of the time. I think there's this weird disconnect between rural America and metropolitan America on an understanding of the way guns are used and the role they play in your life. Guns play a different role in people's life here.... Guns play a really important role in rural America. People here get really defensive of that.

To Erin, this was more evidence of the disconnect between rural and urban America "My problems in Petersburg, West Virginia, are different than your problems in Washington, DC," she said. "That doesn't mean mine are more important or yours are more important. But they're different."

***

One day in summer 2018, I visited a Casey's General Store on the outskirts of Lime Springs. While there, I chatted with a group of Howard County farmers who gather there early each morning. In the weeks leading up to this visit, the Trump administration had announced a series of import tariffs on goods from China, Mexico, and other countries. In retaliation, those countries imposed or threatened to impose tariffs on goods coming from the US, including on some of the Midwest's most important exports—pork, dairy, soybeans, corn, and other agricultural commodities. With each new round of tariffs and counter-tariffs, media outlets deployed reporters to tell the story of how the White House's protectionist policies could prompt a backlash among voters in these pivotal Trump states.

"Trump's tariff war threatens to erode support of farmers," blared a Reuters headline.[5] "As Trump visits Iowa, farmers warn 'patience is wearing thin' on tariff fight," an ABC News headline reported.[6] But that's not what I found talking to farmers in Lime Springs. In fact, I couldn't detect any erosion of support for Trump. These farmers were preaching patience, not losing it. None of the farmers I spoke with at Casey's wished to be quoted by name, but all were happy to share their political opinions. They said they were nervous about the tariffs and had already seen significant drops in crop and livestock prices. When I asked if they were worried about how the tariffs would affect their prices, one farmer said, "It already is affecting us—in a big way."

"Crop prices, grain, livestock prices. It's had a tremendous effect," another farmer said. "We've lost a dollar-and-a-half on the beans and seen a drop on the corn in the last month. It's really affecting people that have to have that cash flow. For them, it's traumatic."

But I didn't sense any anger at Trump or hear anything to suggest he'd lost their support. To the contrary, they all said they appreciated that a president was finally pushing back against other countries' unfair trade practices.

"I think we've been giving our wealth away for way too many years," said one farmer. "We've made terrible deals," another said. "Terrible."

I asked the group whether an ongoing trade war would affect their vote in 2020. "Last time there wasn't much of a choice," one elderly farmer said. "Depends on who's running. If it's a socialist, no."

Another man chimed in, "You'd never vote for a Democrat, I know that." To which the first guy replied with a chuckle, "I'd have to take my NRA hat off!"

"We were hoping with GW," someone said, referring to George W. Bush. "And then along comes this young, good looking, charismatic black guy. Figured we'd give him a chance. Didn't turn out to be like what he was."

"I think he turned out exactly what he was," another countered. "He was good friends with Bill Ayers, someone who hated this country from the first day."

"We did have eight pretty good years under Obama. But we doubled the debt."

All of the farmers saw the Democrats as devoid of ideas and viable presidential candidates. "I don't think the Democrats have anything to run on," one said. "Who's going to beat (Trump)? *Pocahontas?*"

"For years we were told that 2 percent growth was the new normal," someone said. "Now we're at 4 percent. We have more jobs than workers. Everyone's got a (help wanted) sign out."

I asked the group whether they had been Trump supporters from the beginning.

"Not really," one said. "A lot of arrogance. But once he started running and we saw the alternatives, I thought he was a breath of fresh air."

Here are some of the other things this group of farmers said about Trump during our forty-five-minute discussion:

"Kind of a maverick."

"Not afraid to speak his mind."

"The only way I can see him losing is if the economy goes clear to shit."

"He's done so many things already that don't get reported."

"His tweets kind of let you know he's still not a politician."

"He's not polished. But he's doing what he said he would do."

"I don't think he's lost his base at all."

"No, the base is gaining."

"The Democrats are all hard left, you know?"

Then the group started talking about immigration. A few mentioned their support for a wall along America's border with Mexico. I asked them whether immigration affects them much locally.

"I know that the dairy industry would be in deep trouble, the packing industry would be in deep trouble, the vegetable, wine industry, the services would be in deep trouble without immigration," one of the men said. "We need these people; we just don't need bad ones. Isn't that what Trump says too? He's not against immigration. But we can't just let anyone in here without checking them first. I just don't know why Democrats don't understand that."

I'd come to talk about tariffs, but each time I tried to return to that topic, we'd end up on something else—guns or immigration or the media's mistreatment of Trump.

When I asked the group whether there was something specific Trump could do for Howard County, their unanimous answer was ... welfare reform. "I wouldn't mind having welfare reform for the whole country," one farmer said.

Another said, "My sister has had polio from the waist down since she was five years old, and she's always held a job, raised a family. She didn't get any welfare."

"Do you know anyone who isn't working but could be?" I asked.

"No, they're not in my social circles," one said. "They're losers as far as I'm concerned. Like the little gal who comes in here every morning. She works two jobs to take care of her deadbeat boyfriend."

"You can't have open borders and have our welfare system," another offered.

In context, this conversation was really quite remarkable. As I noted earlier, it strikes at the heart of what people think when they discuss self-interest as a political motivator. As journalists reported on the devastating economic impact of Trump's trade war and speculated that it could cost him the farm vote in 2020, these farmers wanted to talk about *welfare reform.* Their own ability to earn a living was at risk, but they were more perturbed by the idea that somebody was unfairly gaming the system and getting something for free.

I tried once more to steer the conversation back to the tariffs, but all of my efforts were to no avail. "We sure would like to see our prices improve," one farmer said, "but we want better trade deals so we're not giving away the store all the time."

"We're all hopeful, I guess," another said, having the last word. "Hopeful that we're going to get a wall built, that we're going to get good fair trade deals, and we're hopeful that we're going to get welfare reform."

My findings in Howard County contradicted what other journalists were reporting at the time. A May 2018 *Washington Post* piece reported finding "unease" among Trump voters in the Upper Midwest who were "increasingly concerned and conflicted" about their support for the president.[7] Perhaps some of the Trump voters were conflicted, but I didn't meet any of them. Among the scores of Trump voters I talked to in Howard County and throughout the Upper Midwest in 2018, his support hadn't diminished at all. Or, at least, any unease, concern, or conflict felt by Trump's voters was more than offset by the goodwill he had earned with them.

Reports predicting a Midwestern backlash to Trump's policies reminded me of what happened throughout the 2016 campaign, when every Trump misstep or perceived scandal was predicted to trigger a fatal backlash to his candidacy. He had called illegal immigrants "rapists"; he had disparaged John McCain's war service; he had disparaged the judge in his Trump University case as "Mexican" and therefore incapable of being fair; he had savaged Megyn Kelly for her period; he had raged on Twitter over all sorts of inappropriate things; he had proudly discussed his promiscuity in a loathsome taped conversation with Billy Bush. And that's just scratching the surface. Yet as many times as it happened, the backlash never came. And it wasn't happening in that part of Iowa in the summer of 2018, either.

* * *

If you look at county-level electoral maps of the United States from the early 1990s through 2012, you'll notice a large blue spot in the Upper Midwest—a group of counties located along the Upper Mississippi River and its tributaries in northwest Illinois, northeast Iowa, southeast Minnesota, and southwest Wisconsin. Democrats' dominance in this cluster of 100 or so rural, religious, overwhelmingly white counties became known as the Upper Mississippi River Valley Anomaly.

Carla Johnson outside the Howard County Courthouse in Cresco in 2018. (Daniel Allott)

But look at a map from the 2016 election, and the blue spot virtually disappears. Donald Trump turned scores of blue Obama counties red on his way to winning Iowa and Wisconsin (and nearly taking Minnesota as well). By the summer of 2018, support for Trump seemed so strong in this region that I wondered how in the world Obama had ever managed to win so convincingly in the first place. I wasn't the only one who was perplexed. Most people I encountered weren't clear either. "I have no idea," was the response from Todd Mensink, the Sanders-supporting professor.

In a week of reporting in Howard County, I failed to find a single Trump voter who regretted voting for him. What's more, as I asked around, I couldn't find anyone who *knew of* any Trump voters who regretted their decision. "I've never heard anyone who voted for him tell me they wish they hadn't," Carla Johnson said.

Some Trump supporters said he could do himself a favor by spending less time on Twitter. But many had nothing negative to say about the man. And all of them gave an upbeat overall assessment.

Almost everyone I talked to, including most Democrats, predicted that Trump would meet or surpass his 20-point win in Howard County in 2020. Mensink told me he thought Trump will win by "25 points or more" in 2020.

Laura Hubka attributes her community's political transformation in part to Democrats losing touch with rural voters. As chairwoman of the Howard County Democratic Party, Hubka got a front row seat to the Democrats' 2016 debacle. She subsequently resigned her post out of frustration with her party's neglect of rural voters. "We stopped talking to them and instead assumed they were 'ours' because, well, you know 'people that vote Republican are deplorable,'" she complained in an open letter to her party in 2017.[8] When I met up with Laura in 2018, she insisted Democrats wouldn't win those voters back solely by resisting President Trump. "We need to come away from 'We are not them' and come forward with big, bold ideas," she said.

At the time, the Iowa Democratic Party seemed to be in disarray. "Not many people walk around saying they are proud to be Democrats," she said. "Not many." Hubka believed Trump was on track to win reelection. Despite low approval ratings, Trump still had the strong backing of rural Americans, she said. "Trump is the perpetual underdog. People in rural areas still say the 'n-word' and 'Pocahontas,' and they don't want to be made to feel bad about it. They identify with 'deplorables.'"

***

On subsequent trips to Howard County—I visited seven times over three years—people's perceptions of President Trump and politics generally didn't budge very much. The trade war, Supreme Court confirmation battles, the Mueller investigation, the Ukraine scandal, impeachment, and even the coronavirus pandemic—none of it had much of an effect on how people I spoke with perceived Trump. During each visit, I would stop in to see Joe Wacha and discover that he still supported Trump and remained frustrated by the Democrats' unyielding opposition to him. I would meet up with Todd Mensink, who'd struggle to name anything redeeming about Trump while conceding that he would handily win the county again. I'd visit Laura Hubka, who in 2019 returned to her position as Democratic Party chairwoman but said she still didn't believe the county would be competitive for Democrats in 2020. And I'd talk to Narren Brown, who maintained that Trump was a sure bet to win reelection. When I asked him in late 2019 whether he thought Trump would win nationally, he said, "Oh yeah—this tribalism is cold, man."

Laura Hubka on her back porch in Riceville in 2017. (Daniel Allott)

I would talk to as many farmers as I could find. Most, while still concerned about what the trade war was doing to their commodity prices, were sticking with Trump, especially given what they viewed as a dearth of alternatives on the Democratic side.

The county's economy stayed quite strong throughout most of Trump's first term. Every time I visited, I would see "Now Hiring" and "Help Wanted" signs on the premises of local businesses, with some offering generous signing bonuses to new hires. Howard County's challenge isn't available jobs—it's finding enough people to fill them. The plant business of Mike and Rachel Gooder, who hosted me during my visits, seemed to undergo one long expansion over the three years of my study. By the end of 2019, they were in the middle of a multi-million-dollar expansion that they were able to undertake in part because of tax cuts and easing of regulations ushered in by Trump.

I was always on the lookout for switchers—people who had voted one way in 2016 but planned to vote another in 2020. I'd ask around, and there would usually be someone who'd say something like, "I think my friend's cousin's neighbor might be starting to change her mind." Then I'd check it out and discover that no, the person's friend's cousin's neighbor still felt pretty much the same way she did in 2016. An example came during a trip to Howard County in November 2019. One day I found myself sitting in the banker's seat of a corn combine harvester, talking to Dave Neubauer, a farmer in his early sixties.

I had been told that Dave, a Trump voter, was complaining loudly about some agriculture policy that the Trump administration had implemented and that it sure sounded as if Dave had changed his mind about the president. Neubauer owns nearly 2,000 acres of land on which he farms corn, soybeans, and some cattle. "Times are tough, real tough," he said of the overall financial environment for farmers.

A lifelong Democrat who twice voted for Obama before turning to Trump in 2016, Dave was upset with the president for allowing the Environmental Protection Agency to undermine a recently announced ethanol proposal by changing the formula for determining how many gallons of ethanol refineries would be required to blend into their fuels. But he was still sticking with the president. "I can't find a Democrat to vote for," he said, his voice barely audible over the sound of corn being threshed. "And that's what happened last time. I mean, if they don't have anybody to vote for, what do you do?"

Dave said he doesn't like the way Trump "handles social media," but he appreciates that he went after China on trade and thinks Trump understands rural America better than any other recent president. He also likes that Trump is visible to the public. "He's the most visible president we've ever had in the history of the country. He's not hiding anything; he's in the news every day. He's not easily pushed around."

I asked Dave if he thinks Trump will win Howard County again. "I think he will," Dave said. "I think he will. Who are the Democrats going to come up with?"

2

TREMPEALEAU COUNTY, WISCONSIN

WHEN BARACK OBAMA WON the 2008 presidential election, exit polls showed that he had captured 95 percent of black voters amid record-high black turnout.[1] And whereas the number of white voters remained roughly unchanged from 2004, black turnout grew by two million votes.[2] Obama was America's first black presidential nominee, so it wasn't surprising that he should have attracted such overwhelming and enthusiastic support from black voters. Many of them surely hadn't expected to see a black man reach such heights only a few decades removed from the Jim Crow era.

Obama's first term produced mixed results for black Americans. For instance, black unemployment rose by nearly two points, from 11.5 percent on the day Obama was elected to 13.3 percent on the day of his reelection.[3] Some prominent African Americans also complained that Obama was downplaying his race and reacting too cautiously to racist attacks. They included in this his calm handling of the birther conspiracy theory, which posited that Obama had not been born in the United States and was thus ineligible to become president. Obama often dismissed these attacks as having as much to do with ideological differences as racial animus, frustrating some black supporters.

As the 2012 election approached, professor and activist Cornell West and broadcaster Tavis Smiley emerged as prominent black critics of Obama, whom they saw as too willing to compromise on matters of racial justice. West and Smiley embarked on an eighteen-city tour to draw attention to issues surrounding race and poverty and Obama's unwillingness to address them.[4]

But when election day arrived, Obama's support among black voters dipped only slightly, to 93 percent. And turnout among black voters actually rose above 2008 levels, to a record 66 percent, eclipsing the share of whites who voted for the first time in history.[5] That worked out to an additional 1.7 million black voters, whose overwhelming support for Obama proved critical in swing states such as Ohio, Wisconsin, and Florida—states Hillary Clinton would lose four years later, due in part to low turnout among black voters.

Working on the assumption that black turnout would not match the levels of Obama's historic first election, the campaign of Obama's opponent, Republican Mitt Romney, was caught by surprise by Obama's continued ability to energize black voters. "The surprise was some of the turnout...especially in urban areas, which gave President Obama the big margin to win this race," Romney running mate Paul Ryan said a few days after the election.[6]

When the 2008 presidential campaign began, African American voters didn't immediately embrace Obama, a mixed-race intellectual and son of an African father, whose ancestors had not been slaves. He sometimes seemed a stranger to black American struggles. An October 2007 poll showed then Sen. Hillary Clinton with a twenty-four-point lead over Obama among black Democrats.[7] But Obama gradually forged a bond with black voters that would not be broken. His win in Iowa convinced them that he was for real—he could also win white voters, and he was clearly a strong bet to win the election. With his victory, Obama achieved something monumental for all black Americans. His election, the culmination of centuries of struggle, gave all black Americans a sense of dignity, pride in their race, and hope for the future.

Yes, African Americans might have grumbled about some of Obama's policies or actions. But generally, there was no chance they wouldn't show up for him on election day, much less vote for a different candidate. The bond of identity and solidarity was too strong. *This* president had their backs for once, and the viciousness of some of the Right's attacks on Obama only added to their resolve.

A similar dynamic is at play with Donald Trump and the support he receives from many rural and working-class white voters. A constant feature of the media's coverage of the Trump presidency has been the question of whether and under what circumstances these voters would abandon him. With each new development in Trump's trade war with China, with each new impeachment-related story, and with every errant tweet demonstrating Trump's flawed character, reporters have been deployed to Middle America to predict an erosion of support for Trump. But for the most part, it hasn't happened, and I don't think it ever will. After dozens of visits and many months in the rural and industrial heartland, I have come to believe that those who think Trump will lose his supporters here over volatile commodity prices, a dubious impeachment narrative, or a few (or a few hundred) offensive tweets simply fail to understand the nature of Trump's support base.

Many of these voters were not immediately drawn to Trump and voted for other candidates in the 2016 primaries. But over the course of the 2016 campaign, Trump forged a durable bond with millions of people that has only strengthened over the course of his first term in office. And as with Obama, the persistent and nasty attacks against Trump (this time coming from the Left) have only added to their resolve to support him. That bond has been portrayed as being rooted in racial resentment, cultural victimhood, and economic grievance. But it is also rooted in something more edifying: a reclaiming of dignity.

Nearly 70 percent of farmers voted for Donald Trump in 2016.[8] This baffled many journalists, who wondered how a billionaire with soft hands and New York values could win over Heartland voters. After the election, the media consensus seemed to be that farmers and other rural people would renounce their support for the president once they figured out that he was a fraud. But I had my doubts, so I sought out farmers, ranchers, and others working in agriculture whenever I could. Almost without exception, those who voted for him in 2016 are sticking with Trump because they believe he has their backs.

Black voters didn't abandon Obama in 2012 because their unemployment rate ticked up a couple of points or because they thought he'd been a little timid on racial matters. In the same way, these white, conservative farmers weren't going to abandon Trump because his tariff battle with China was temporarily hurting their crop prices. For one thing, declining commodity prices had preceded Trump and his tariffs. Still, the many farmers I met were unhappy with how the tariffs were affecting their bottom lines, yet they didn't mind. They still appreciated that Trump was taking on China and other countries. Some even seemed to regard the damage from the tariffs as something of a patriotic sacrifice. They reasoned that for decades, US presidents refused to stand up to China as it stole American intellectual property, manipulated its currency, protected its home market by placing tariffs on US imports, and dismissed environmental, health, and safety standards by which most other countries abide.

Farmers I talked to saw the tariffs as a way to hold accountable an adversary who had exploited the system. As one of the farmers in Lime Springs had told me, "I think we've been giving our wealth away for way too many years." I heard something similar in August 2019 when I visited Henry and Noel Filla at their family farm in Osseo, Wisconsin. Osseo is located in the northeast corner of Trempealeau County (pronounced *TREM-pa-loh*), which sits at the confluence of the Mississippi and Trempealeau Rivers in west-central Wisconsin.

The Fillas grow crops and own a herd of buffalo and a dairy farm that they rent out to another farmer. When I asked them about the effect the more than year-old trade war was having, their first reaction was to talk not about commodity prices or their own finances, but rather about their belief that America was getting cheated. "Well we're getting cheated by all these countries," Henry said. "Sending money to all these countries anyway. Why don't we cut the money out and make it right? That's what I think about the trade thing anyway. It's going to hurt us for a little while, but hopefully in the long run, it's going to all straighten out."

"Have you been hurt by tariffs?" I asked.

"The grain prices had gone down," Henry said. "Also milk, but that predated Trump. That's been going on since there is so much overproduction worldwide, because the dairies keep getting bigger and bigger. It's gonna hurt, but it's going to be a tough time in the short term, but the end result will be good, I think. This problem (of China's unfair trade practices) needed to be dealt with a long time ago, so we can't just keep kicking the can down the road because then how are our kids going to survive? So maybe if the can would have been picked up thirty years ago, maybe we'd have more rural farmers. Right? Because we'd have a real price."

I heard this same assessment again and again from farmers I met, including from Democrats who otherwise had nothing nice to say about the president.

Bernie Killian in his kitchen in Trempealeau County, Wisconsin. (Daniel Allott)

A few days after speaking with Henry Filla, I met a chicken and soybean farmer named Bernie Killian. As he waited for a delivery of more than 150,000 chickens, Bernie invited me into his kitchen for a chat.

Anticipating my arrival, he had jotted down some notes on a piece of paper, and occasionally glanced at them during our interview. A lifelong Democrat, Bernie had nothing positive to say about Trump—except when it came to China.

I asked: "Do you think Trump was right to challenge China with the tariffs?"

"Oh, yes," Bernie replied. "That's the thing he took on that every president should have at least addressed. It was long overdue."

"The trade practices that were unfair, the stealing of intellectual property, currency manipulation, and all that?"

"Oh, that's terrible!"

Bear in mind: Farmers are the American constituency most committed to free trade and its greatest beneficiaries. By the summer of 2019, Trump's trade war with China was in its second year, causing massive problems for farmers wanting to export their products. And yet Trump's standing with farmers hadn't worsened; if anything, it had improved. A *Farm Journal* poll of nearly 1,000 farmers in the summer of 2018 found that 62 percent supported Trump. A year later, a similar poll found that 71 percent approved of Trump's job performance.[9] In August 2018, a poll of 1,000 farmers conducted by *Farm Futures* magazine found that 60 percent said they would vote for Trump; a year later, that share had risen to 67 percent.[10] Again—and this bears repeating—this surge in support came just as Trump was taking specific actions that farmers understood to undermine their livelihood.

Yet polling found that most farmers supported Trump not despite his trade policies, but *because of them.* An August 2019 Iowa State University survey of more than 700 Midwest farmers found that 56 percent were still "somewhat or strongly supportive" of Trump's trade dispute with China.[11] It would be easy to say that these farmers were acting against their self-interest. And that's often the way it's reported in the media. As a *Politico* sub-headline put it: "There's a disconnect between the negative effects of Trump's policies in farm country and their unwavering support for him."[12] But the real disconnect was happening between a blinkered media and a part of America where most reporters rarely deign to set foot for more than a few hours at a time.

Most farmers were giving Trump the benefit of the doubt because they trusted him and agreed with his underlying strategy. They also believed he had their backs.

"He acknowledged that we're here," Henry Filla said. "Trump said, 'We love our farmers.' He understands that farms are businesses. And that's why farmers voted for him. He thinks a little bit like we do."

Henry's wife, Noel, added, "I definitely feel like (Trump) made the rural people feel that they were being listened to and that they are important. That made us trust him."

As a token of the bond of trust between Trump and farmers, in 2018 and 2019 the Trump administration paid out more than $28 billion in trade-related aid to farmers.[13] The $16 billion in subsidies in 2019 was the highest amount in fourteen years, all of it paid without any action by Congress. And Trump wasn't above bragging about the largesse he'd provided to farmers, mentioning it in tweets and at campaign rallies. In April 2020, as the coronavirus pandemic entered its second month, President Trump announced a $19 billion economic rescue package for farmers and ranchers.[14] The aid, in the form of cash payments as well as the purchasing and redistribution of farm products to food banks, was a response to the sudden shift in the ways consumers were buying food as a result of the near shutdown of schools and restaurants. Again, Trump touted the decision, tweeting that he had ordered his agriculture secretary to "use all of the funds and authorities at his disposal ... to expedite help to our farmers, especially to the smaller farmers who are hurting right now."[15]

* * *

Trempealeau County is home to quiet towns and quaint villages nestled among rolling hills in the rugged Upper Mississippi River Valley. Most of the county's 30,000 residents are white, churchgoing, employed, and fond of outdoor activities such as hunting, fishing, snowmobiling, camping, and canoeing. Despite its conservative makeup, Trempealeau has historically voted for Democratic candidates for president. Barack Obama won the county twice by double digits.[16, 17]

A view of the Mississippi River from Main Street in Trempealeau, Wisconsin. (Jordan Allott)

In 2016, Hillary Clinton was expected to win there too. As election day approached, almost every poll had her ahead comfortably, and pundits mocked the Trump campaign for the attention it was giving the region. "If the Trump campaign believes flipping southwestern Wisconsin could happen this year," wrote *Daily Beast* columnist and Wisconsin native Erin Gloria Ryan, "I'd like a slice of whatever cheese it is they're eating."[18]

The Clinton campaign took a similarly cavalier approach to Wisconsin. Hillary Clinton never visited the state during the 102-day period between the Democratic convention and the election. This "was something that got people angry," Andrew Dannehy, managing editor of the *Trempealeau County Times*, told me when I visited him at his office in 2017. "That ticked people off, like she didn't care about Wisconsin." Meanwhile, Trump appeared in the state five times during the general election campaign.

Trump won Trempealeau County by thirteen points. He swung twenty-two Wisconsin counties that had voted for Obama in 2012, including eleven in the rural western part of the state. This helped him become the first Republican to win Wisconsin in thirty-two years.[19] Here was the odd part: Trump received about the same number of votes in the state as the 2012 Republican nominee, Mitt Romney. But whereas Romney had done well in the suburbs, Trump thrived in rural places like Trempealeau.

Trump's uncouthness may have actually helped him there, according to University of Wisconsin-La Crosse political scientist Joe Heim. "Rural people are not terribly sophisticated in a general way," he told me. "You hear people criticize him for his lack of vocabulary. That didn't bother rural people. They understood him and knew what he was trying to get at. He gets down to very basic things and that's exactly what they want to hear."

* * *

Geography, more than race or class, has become the crucial dividing line in politics today. That's partly because rural and urban Americans embrace different values and increasingly live lives that are wholly removed from one another. Rural people tend to value tradition, familiarity, and having deep community ties. They will often forgo more lucrative job opportunities in cities to be closer to family. There's a welcoming spirit to rural places that's mostly lacking in cities. As Bryan Ward, sheriff of Hardy County on West Virginia's Eastern Panhandle, put it about the charms of rural life compared the city in which he grew up:

> When you can go into a restaurant anywhere in the county and know and be able to call by name 50 percent of the people that are seated, that's just hometown. I went to the barber and sat down, and 10 people came into the barber shop while I was seated, and I could call nine of them by name. Striking up a conversation was effortless. Folks were anonymous in the city. You could be a strange creature and people two doors down in Baltimore city might not know who you are.

If your car breaks down and you need help fixing it; if you're feeling a little lonely and wish someone would take a few unhurried minutes to chat with you; if you like greeting your neighbors with a friendly "hello" and having them reply instead of looking down at their phones as they walk past you, you want to be in rural America. I know this because that's what I experienced at various times during my travels. In the media's portrayal, rural America is backward, boring, and unpleasant—a place where you live only if you have no other options, a place you want to escape from if at all possible. The countryside has its challenges. It can be hard to get a decent cell phone signal, a good cup of coffee, or much variety in terms of cuisine or culture. And, as I'll chronicle in the chapter from Grant County, West Virginia, the opioid crisis has had a particularly devastating impact on rural America. But there's a reason why just 15 percent of Americans live in rural areas, but nearly twice as many would prefer to live there.[20] People tend to be happier there.

Why don't they move? It's mainly because there are fewer opportunities in rural America. Good health care and schools are harder to come by, which makes it difficult to attract new residents. The result is that there is a huge gap between rural and urban America, with each side hardly recognizing the other. I was reminded of this while visiting the dairy farm of Ken Jereczek and his son, Paul, in Dodge, Wisconsin, in 2018.

As Paul showed me around their barn and explained some of their farm's innovations—the Fitbit-like sensory devices that signal when the cows are in heat; the water beds that keep the cows comfortable while lying down; and the mechanical brushes that allow the cows to groom themselves—it struck me how unfamiliar I was with farming life. I'm not alone. Two hundred years ago, farmers made up nearly three-quarters of America's workforce. One hundred years later, the share had dropped to under a third.[21] Today, less than 2 percent of Americans live on farms.[22] The average age of a farmer is fifty-eight.[23] Ken told me there were forty-five dairy farms in his township thirty-five years ago. Theirs is the only one left today.

Ken and Paul Jereczek on their farm in 2018. (Daniel Allott)

"There's a reason why people are selling off," said Paul. "This isn't an easy lifestyle." Paul's days begin shortly after 3 a.m. and end after 8 p.m. Dairy farming is a seven-days-a-week job, and the cows must be milked twice a day.

When you add in the decline in dairy consumption and the trade war, it's not hard to understand why 600 Wisconsin dairy farms shuttered in 2018, the biggest decline since records started in 2004.[24] In 2018 and 2019, Wisconsin led the nation in family-farm bankruptcies.[25] Henry and Noel Filla told a similar story. "We do a little of everything," Henry said. "We're trying to do as much as we can to survive."

Like the Jereczeks, the Fillas are their town's sole surviving farmers. Henry told me there were six working farms in Osseo when he and Noel moved to the area twenty-five years ago. Their farm is the only one left today.

"In rural areas, there are no kids left who know how to work or understand the farm," Henry said. "Not that kids in town don't know how to work, but it's a different mindset."

Today, ambitious kids in rural areas often leave home for schools located in another part of the state or region, where they're enticed by more lucrative and less physically demanding careers and frequently also inculcated with liberal values. They rarely return. One of the Filla's daughters is studying environmental engineering at the University of Wisconsin at Madison, one of the most progressive cities in America. Henry lamented that she'd been "brainwashed quite a bit about 'equal and fair.'"

"She voted for (Democratic Governor Tony) Evers, and I was so upset," Noel added.

Mike Gooder of Howard County, Iowa, talked about how difficult it can be to attract new talent. Gooder owns an international plant business with more than 100 employees. "One of the greatest challenges running a small business in rural areas is finding people," he once told me.

> When recruiting for our leadership roles, getting college graduates and young professionals excited about opportunities with our company is the easy part. Convincing them to move to and integrate into a rural community is often the conversation killer. We recruit heavily from Iowa State University and area community colleges, but even though a majority of the students come from rural communities, they see college as the opportunity to move to an urban lifestyle, whereas those that come from larger communities just can't imagine living in a town of 4,000 people.

When young people leave the countryside, it deepens the divide between rural and urban America. So does the perception that the cities ignore the countryside.

"Look at the roads," Ken Jereczek said of the disparity in resources available to address infrastructure in urban and rural Wisconsin. "If you go to Green Bay, Madison, or Milwaukee, you see all these overpasses and all that, and their roads are getting fixed and ours are just patched. But our milk truck has to get down the road." Trempealeau County roads are some of the worst in the state. They are bruised and cracked from decades of farm equipment and tractor trailers rolling over them without repaving. According to one estimate, the county needs $60 million to $80 million worth of road repairs. The county also has the worst bridges in the state, with the highest share having a D safety rating.[26]

Ken Jerezcek was echoing the sentiment that Katherine Cramer found was common throughout rural Wisconsin while researching her 2016 book *The Politics of Resentment*. "Ignored by government and by the news media," Cramer wrote about rural Wisconsinites, "these folks felt neglected by the powers that be."[27] Cramer continued: "They weren't getting their fair share. They felt nobody in the cities was listening to them. They didn't like that their money was going to prop up bad schools in Milwaukee."

As Cramer put it, "In their eyes, decisions about funding for schools mean that small communities are the victims of distributive injustice."[28] I'd often ask people in rural areas whether they resented people in the cities. Typically they'd respond with an emphatic "yes!" or a quick "Hell yeah I do." It's easy to see why rural Americans feel resentful. It often seems that people in the power centers don't appreciate the knowledge they have or the work that they do—whether it's the farmers who produce the food we eat, the manufacturers who make the products we buy, or the truckers who deliver those products to our doorsteps.

"You know what upsets me the most?" said Jeff Praxel, a milk hauler I met at the Jereczek's farm.

When I became a milk hauler, I never realized how much comes off this farm. It's not just the milk. It's all the byproducts—the creamery, the powdered milk, the candy bars, the syrups. (People who live in cities) just don't realize everything that comes off a dairy farm. Let alone every fricken' hamburger. Every fast food burger comes from places like this. Not a beef farm. From a dairy farm, because (dairy beef) is cheaper and leaner.

This sentiment was echoed by Dave Neubauer, the Iowa corn farmer from Chapter 1. When I asked him whether a divide exists between urban and rural America, he said "Absolutely. It pisses us off a lot that we feel people don't know where their food comes from."

"We feel we are villains—we are (seen as) villains in the big city," he said. "They think all we do is get welfare."

Later, during the coronavirus pandemic, there seemed to be a newfound appreciation for the farmers and truckers who represent the beginning of the food supply chain. But for the most part, rural Americans feel taken for granted. They feel like the knowledge they have and values they hold are mocked and disparaged by the urban elite, the opinion makers, the people who decide where resources are spent. They feel like they don't get their fair share of resources, respect, or power. They're making the things that make America work, but nobody listens or seems to care. They're witnessing more and more of their land being taken over by extractive, predatory corporations, and more and more of their jobs leaving. As people leave, the school funding dries up.

Rural folks also resent being labeled racists and ignorant for voting for Donald Trump and other Republicans, or simply for living in the countryside. In much of the media, rural America is seen as violently inhospitable to anyone who's nonwhite. Many racial minorities in cities might fear for their lives if they ventured into rural America.

Racism does exist, or course, and I encountered it in my travels. I heard it in the casual use of the "N-word" on several occasions by older white people. I saw it in rural West Virginia, where a man who gave me a ride in his Trump bumper sticker-clad truck answered my question about why he likes living in the area with, "Cuz there ain't no black people here."

But racism doesn't always take the form one expects. One evening in North Carolina in 2019, I met a young woman named Lilith for a dinner date. During our conversation, I mentioned that I had once been engaged to a black woman. This prompted Lilith to double over in mock revulsion. She then launched into the vilest and most racist rant I had ever heard. In essence, her argument was that whites were genetically and culturally superior to other races, and that blacks were at the bottom of the racial hierarchy. At the end of our hastily-eaten dinner, Lilith gave me some advice: Don't ever tell a white woman that I'd dated or been engaged to a black woman.

The interesting thing about Lilith wasn't her hatred of black people, or even the astonishing ignorance that formed the basis of her view. Rather, it was that Lilith is black.

Most of my conversations about race were much more edifying and nuanced. One of the most illuminating was with Narren Brown, the black pro-gun, progressive college professor I introduced in Chapter 1.

"Most folks I meet here, I might be the first black person they've ever met," he once told me. "Most of them are hardworking, decent folks, which boggles my mind that (Rep.) Steve King continues to get elected when I would assume that most of his (voters in the adjacent) district are hardworking, decent folks too." (When King, who has a history of making racist comments, lost a primary bid for reelection in 2020, Brown said he wasn't really surprised.)

Ask a white conservative in a rural area if they feel that they benefit from white privilege, the idea that societal privilege benefits white people over nonwhite people living under the same circumstances, and they're likely to say no. They may also suggest instead that people of color benefit more from racial privilege. Again, it can be difficult for whites living in almost exclusively white areas to understand the experiences of other races.

Narren had a more nuanced understanding. When I asked him about white privilege, he didn't just complain about the

Narren Brown outside The Pub in Cresco, Iowa, (Daniel Allott)

unfairness of the privilege he saw all around him. Instead, Brown acknowledged that white privilege was real and talked about incidents where he felt he had been singled out by law enforcement or been discriminated against because he's black. But he added some nuance, "I don't even mind the privilege so much," he said. "What I mind is when you don't acknowledge it." Then Brown spoke about how there's a certain level of black privilege that he has experienced as one of the only black people in a community that's more than 99 percent white. "I've gotten laid because I'm black," he confessed with a smile.

"I've always liked this bar," Narren said as we moved to the outdoor patio in back of The Pub. "It's the one where there's no problems, in the sense of no drama. There's definitely some political talk, and occasionally someone will use some off-color language. But this is the one place in town where it's rare to find."

Brown's family back in Oakland, California, sometimes asked him how he managed to live in such an overwhelmingly white place. Part of it, Brown would explain to them, was his "I don't give a fuck" approach to the looks he got when in public with his white wife and biracial children. Part of it was having close white friends he could count on to support him, even in a fight. "These parts, I have really good friends here, people I call family. I believe they'd have my back in a fight," he said.

Brown's insights are the result of his having to think deeply about race because it's something he encounters every day. In contrast, when I questioned pro-life Dave at the Howard County Fair about his use of the term "black boy" to describe Alan Keyes, he seemed shocked that I'd even object to his use of the term, responding with stunned silence.

It's not just policymakers who are removed from rural America. It's also the media. With the demise of local news, it's been left to national outlets to report for the entire country. But most people in the media work far away in coastal cities. According to one study, nine in ten internet publishing employees live in counties won by Hillary Clinton in the 2016 presidential election.[29] Very few of those counties are located in rural areas. The result is that people who have rarely if ever set foot on a farm are devising budgets and enacting rules and regulations that profoundly affect farmers, while journalists living in liberal urban enclaves are reporting on them. When people are so disconnected from the process of making the things they consume, they cannot fully appreciate the resources required to produce and maintain them.

As Neubauer put it, "Our biggest problem is we are not heard. We are not understood. Trump has brought some light to us. He talks about ag. He knows we are here." When I asked him whether Trump, a wealthy New York City developer, understands rural America better than previous presidents, he said, "I think so. I cannot think of anyone who's done a better job. Sure as hell wasn't Obama. It wasn't going to be Hillary Clinton."

In the 2016 election, urban counties voted for Clinton by 32 percentage points, while rural areas supported Trump by 26 points. Trump's margin was 10 points higher than Mitt Romney's in 2012.[30] The question for Democrats is whether their 2020 nominee, former Vice President Joe Biden, will do any better. An August 2019 Politico piece summed up the Democrats' predicament heading into 2020: "Dems fear another rural wipeout will reelect Trump."[31]

At the time, there were some twenty candidates vying for the Democratic nomination, and most had made overtures to rural voters. Many rolled out rural policy proposals. But as the article noted:

> Those individual pitches aren't yet translating into a primary-wide conversation. During the first two Democratic National Committee debates, only one question focused on farmers, and candidates made only passing mentions of rural voters. (The word "rural" has been uttered 10 times over more than 10 hours of debates so far.) Meanwhile, decriminalizing border crossings and gun control have lately dominated the primary conversation.

Jeff Link, an Iowa-based political consultant, put things bluntly, telling Politico that if candidates are "talking about who is using what bathroom, we're not going to get there with rural voters."

The piece quoted Democratic strategist and pollster Mark Mellman, who said, "Unless a candidate can build bridges across that gap on the basis of values, it's very difficult to make any policy proposal matter. Right now, no one is building those bridges."

*　*　*

Ramon Romero doesn't remember much about the first few years of his life, other than the carefree days he spent climbing mango trees outside his home in the village of Las Lajas, Honduras. His most vivid early memory is of the day he was told he would be leaving his birthplace.

When Ramon was seven years old, his grandmother told him that they would soon begin a journey to reunite with his mother in the United States—"El Norte," she called it. Ramon's mother and grandmother (he has never known his birth father) felt that only by moving to America would Ramon escape the lure of gang life and a likely early death.

Ramon and his grandmother set off on the perilous 2,500-mile trek to Texas with a group of about a dozen other migrants. "We walked a lot, jumped on and off trains," Ramon recounted when I met him in early February 2018. "There was the fear of someone hurting me, of getting killed. Rape. Anything can happen."

Then something did happen. Making their way through Guatemala, the group was kidnapped by a group of men posing as Guatemalan border patrol agents. Ramon later learned that their abductors were members of Mara Salvatrucha, better known as MS-13, who stole the captives' passports and other valuable documents. Ramon spent the next two days cleaning gang members' guns, handing out food, and fearing for his life. At one point, when Ramon refused to distribute food to the other hostages, a gang member pointed a gun at his grandmother's head and threatened to kill her. "I was the only one that never got tied up," Ramon said. "But I saw other people get hurt."

After two days, Ramon and his grandmother were let go—he thinks it was because he was too young and his grandmother too old to be of much use to their abductors. Frightened but undaunted, they resumed their trek north. After nearly three months of travel, Ramon and his grandmother finally crossed the border into Texas, where they were apprehended by Immigration and Customs Enforcement (ICE) agents. Ramon's grandmother was immediately deported, but Ramon spent ninety-two days with a host family in Texas before being reunited with his mother in Arcadia, the largest city in Trempealeau County.

When I met him early in 2018, Ramon was an energetic and smiling eighteen-year-old. On the brink of high school graduation and having recently been awarded academic and athletic scholarships to attend the University of Wisconsin-Parkside, Ramon had reason to smile—except that he lives in constant fear of being deported. Ramon is one of nearly 700,000 immigrants who were brought to the United States illegally as minors and subsequently granted temporary legal status under a program called Deferred Action for Childhood Arrivals, or DACA.

President Trump ended DACA in September 2017, calling it an "unfair system," and giving Congress until the following March to legislate a replacement. After that date, pending a court ruling, recipients—sometimes called "Dreamers"—could be subject to deportation, in many cases to countries they hardly know.[32]

"I'm feeling fear, but my mom always tells me, 'Have hope,'" Ramon said.

> But every day I feel like I'm running out of hope. The news makes me angry, because not all of us are bad, not all of us are rapists, like (Trump) said. I don't know Honduras. I have nothing there. I have nothing more than my birth there. I love this country. I feel like I'm between a country that doesn't want me and a country I don't know.

I met Ramon at the Arcadia Family Restaurant on a frigid Wisconsin Friday evening about a month before DACA was to be repealed. We were joined by Jon Schultz, Ramon's cross-country coach, and Ashley, who asked that her last name be withheld to protect her family. Ashley graduated with Ramon from the Arcadia High School that spring.

Ashley was born in the United States to Mexican parents who are living in the country illegally. Ashley suffered from depression, which she said has worsened by President Trump's harsh rhetoric. "I already don't want to exist, and I hate hearing people say things that strengthen that idea that I shouldn't exist," she said. Ashley and Ramon channeled their anxiety into their schoolwork and earned partial scholarships to attend college. Ramon became one of the state's top runners. As a senior, he finished fourth in the Division II cross-country state championships.

I asked Ramon and Ashley how other DACA recipients at school were handling the uncertainty about their status. "Everyone has fear," Ramon said.

Fear is the defining emotion of America's immigration debate. Both political parties stoke voters' fears about immigration for partisan gain. Republicans argue that undocumented immigrants are simultaneously stealing their jobs and bleeding the welfare system by refusing to work. During the 2016 presidential campaign, Donald Trump exploited conservatives' fear that gang-banging illegal aliens would rape their daughters and murder their families. In Arcadia, nearly every immigrant

Ramon Romero at Arcadia Family Restaurant in Arcadia, Wisconsin. (Daniel Allott)

I spoke with mentioned with anger and frustration Trump's contention that Mexican immigrants are criminals, drug dealers, and rapists.

Democrats, meanwhile, exploit the fear of many immigrants that ICE officers are roaming the streets waiting to deport any unauthorized immigrant they can get their hands on. And Democrats regularly talk about Republican immigration proposals in explicitly racial terms. House Minority Leader

Nancy Pelosi did just that when she said that Trump's immigration proposals were an effort to "make America white again."[33]

In the middle of this debate, immigrants and the communities they live in can sometimes feel like pawns in a high-stakes game of political brinksmanship. Arcadia has undergone one of the most rapid demographic transformations in the country. Two decades ago, according to Census Bureau data, less than 1 percent of Arcadia's residents were Hispanic or Latino. Today, more than 40 percent of them are.[34] Most came to work at Ashley Furniture, America's largest furniture manufacturer, or Gold'n Plump, a chicken processor, both based in Arcadia.

At Arcadia High School, Hispanics make up a majority of the roughly 300 enrolled students.[35] Once Hispanic students started to trickle in around 2007, Spanish teacher Olga Dedkova-Hasan began teaching English-language learner classes, the first time the school earnestly began teaching their Hispanic students. Soon, the school recruited more bilingual teachers and Hispanic administrators.

Dedkova-Hasan has overseen several mentoring and career readiness projects for Latino students, and launched a "parent college" to educate the parents of immigrants about the US school system and scholarship opportunities for their children.

Superintendent Louie Ferguson doesn't know how many of his kids are DACA recipients because the school doesn't ask about their legal status. "We have tried to assure (the immigrant students and their parents) that they are safe in school, and they don't have to worry about officials coming and taking them out of school," he told me. Dedkova-Hasan estimated that DACA recipients make up at least 10 percent of the high school class. Ferguson said the experience has made him more sensitive to the plight of the families and the legal and financial hurdles they must surmount to attain legal status. "The vast majority of these families just want to fit in, get a good job, and be contributing members of society," he said.

Some pundits depicted Trump's victory in Trempealeau County as a racist backlash to the influx of Hispanic immigrants. As a particularly egregious *Daily Beast* headline put it: "Trump is banking on Wisconsin being racist enough to go red for the first time since 1984."[36] But Hispanics have been settling in Arcadia for two decades, so it's reasonable to ask why the electoral backlash didn't occur much earlier—say, in 2012, when Republican presidential nominee Mitt Romney suggested unauthorized immigrants would "self-deport" under his presidency, or possibly even before that.[37] And Trempealeau County wasn't the only rural Wisconsin county that Trump won. In fact, he won more than a dozen rural Wisconsin counties that Obama had previously claimed. Most of them have not experienced such an inflow of immigrants.

Father Sebastian Kolodziejczyk, a Spanish-speaking Polish priest at Arcadia's Holy Family Catholic Church, said one of his main challenges as a pastor is bringing the native-born community and Hispanic immigrant community together. "In Holy Family Parish, the ratio of Spanish baptisms to English baptisms is more or less six-to-one, so you know what that means in the future," he said. "This is going to be a predominantly Hispanic community. The English-speaking community may feel a bit insecure because it happens so fast. And that's why the parish, I think, plays an important role, to bring them together and make them realize that this actually could be good. It is good."

Kolodziejczyk said it helps that although the two communities speak different languages, "We have the same common denominator, which is Christianity. We're all Christians."

Father Sebastian Kolodziejczyk preaches during Sunday Mass at Arcadia's Holy Family Catholic Church in 2017. (Jordan Allott)

Carmen, a Mexican immigrant whom Kolodziejczyk introduced to me at Holy Family, said she was immediately welcomed when she arrived here a decade ago. "When I come here, people was really open with me," she said. "I had really nice people. I had really nice friends. Everyone here is so friendly." Carmen said that many newcomers don't speak English. But the church and many businesses offer dual language and translation services, which is an immense help. "Our community, they are welcoming, so they open their arms for us, and this is why I am so happy to live in this place," she said.

This is not to say that Donald Trump's anti-immigrant rhetoric and pledge to "build a wall" on America's southern border didn't resonate with some people here. Nor is it to suggest that there haven't been some difficult moments. Carmen's daughter Rossellin recounted that during the 2016 presidential campaign, some students at her high school expressed anti-immigrant sentiment and "were very rude towards the other Latino kids at our school." When I asked residents for examples of anti-immigrant incidents, the same one kept popping up—a chant of "Build the wall!" at a football game several years ago. But that this was the only incident I kept hearing about spoke to the overall welcoming environment in Arcadia.

Granted, it's easy to see why some immigrants would be reluctant to talk to me about racist incidents, and even easier to see why long-time white residents would be careful not to reveal racist views to an out-of-town reporter. This is something Chris Danou reminded me of every time I spoke with him. Danou is a former cop and Democratic state representative from Trempealeau County. After losing his bid for reelection in 2016, he moved to a suburban community south of Madison, in part because his wife had pursued a new job opportunity there and in part because he no longer felt comfortable living in a county that voted for Trump.

Each time we spoke, Danou was adamant that I was missing the bigotry in plain sight. In an email exchange, he criticized my "refusal to honestly reckon with the xenophobia, resentment and racism that are very real, and is an important component of the reason Trump received a lot of his support" in the county. "The Arcadia area is full of a lot of very nice people," he said. "But it also contains a lot of people who are racists, or hold racist views. Period. I know. I spoke with them regularly and frequently. Some of them probably even voted for me."

By and large, however, immigrants I spoke with felt welcomed. Laura Torres, a Mexican immigrant who moved to the area with her husband in 2010, said she loved Arcadia's small town charm. Torres worked assembling furniture at Ashley, then as a teller at a local bank before opening her own tax preparation and insurance business on Main Street to cater to the Hispanic population. She said she was "really happy" that she had moved to Arcadia. There are certainly challenges, she said, "but I feel really comfortable and in a way safe because it's a small town."

"I don't know how long I'm going to be here," she continued, "but I know as long as I have a job, I don't have a reason to move out."

Jackie, who I met at a park as she waited for her daughter to leave a friend's *quinceañera,* said Arcadia is "perfect" for her family of five because the city's small size means they "won't get lost. I like the people, they welcome us, and I have never had a bad experience with anybody," she said. She also appreciates that Hispanic immigrants and the native-born residents are going out of their way to mingle. "A lot of people try to communicate with the Hispanic community," she said. "I know there's a lot of Hispanics who are going to English classes, and they're trying also to get better with English."

In the end, the fact that so many immigrants have settled here, and their alarm at the possibility of having to leave, is a strong indication of how welcoming Arcadia is. "I know a lot of people who have been here for years, so that's something," said Jackie. "I mean, if they didn't like it, I don't think they would be here."

At Arcadia's elementary school, Principal Paul Halverson was directing traffic amid the controlled chaos that is lunchtime on the day when I visited. Halverson praised Arcadia's newcomers. "With Latino families, they don't have the boats and the other nice things that better-off families have," he said. "They have family."

At a time when many rural towns are disappearing, Arcadia's immigrants are not only a welcome presence here, but also a necessary one. They are keeping the place alive. "Everybody knows that many area

Carmen and daughter Rossellin at Arcadia's Holy Family Catholic Church in 2017. (Jordan Allott)

businesses would not be able to exist the same way if it wasn't for them," Kolodziejczyk said of the immigrants.

"Without the influx (of Hispanic immigrants), we would be cutting programs and staff, just like other districts," Ferguson said. "Without them at our schools, we would be in a lot of trouble, cutting jobs left and right, so they're definitely a plus for us and our economy. We have job openings in the community already. I can't imagine what it'd be like without them here." Ferguson estimated that 80 percent of elementary school students are Hispanic immigrants. "Makes me think, what would those classrooms look like without them here?" he asked. Without its Hispanic residents, Arcadia's school district likely wouldn't have undergone a $16 million expansion. Its largest employer, Ashley Furniture, likely would not have broken ground on a $30 million expansion.

After speaking with Ferguson and Halverson, I met with Arcadia's mayor, Rob Reichwein, who gave me a tour of his city. As we drove down Main Street in Reichwein's Ford F-150, I saw just how integral Arcadia's Hispanic immigrants have become to the city. Hispanic-owned businesses line both sides of the road. There's Don Juan Mexican and La Tapatia restaurants, MM San Juan grocery store, Ramos Tax and Services, and Laura Torres Services.

"I think it's great," Reichwein said of all the Hispanic-owned businesses. "I grew up here and I've seen the (demographic) change. I don't think it's a bad thing. A lot of small cities in America are dying."

Reichwein is right. Rural towns across the country would be disappearing if not for inflows of immigrants. In Arcadia and places like it, immigrants have arrived in numbers substantial enough to offset the departure of many whites, extending the lives of towns that otherwise might have already vanished. According to the U.S. Census Bureau, Arcadia's population increased by about 25 percent between 2000 and 2018, from 2,412 people to 3,013. During that period, the number of whites living in Arcadia dropped by 25 percent, a net decrease of 564 people. But the Hispanic share of the population rose from 3 percent to 42 percent, a net increase of nearly 1,200 people.[38, 39]

Hispanic immigrants have also made Arcadia younger. The city's average age dropped from thirty-seven to thirty-one over that eighteen-year period.

Trempealeau County's unemployment rate has trended downward during the time that immigrants have arrived. By the end of 2019, its unemployment rate sat at 2.7 percent, nearly a point lower than the national average.[40] Reichwein said his biggest challenge is enticing people to move to Arcadia to fill vacant jobs. He said the *Trempealeau County Times* usually features two pages of "now hiring" ads. I saw several signs throughout town broadcasting the same message.

DACA had a particularly positive effect on unauthorized immigrants in rural towns like Arcadia. According to data compiled by the Joint Economic Committee, at the time 91 percent of DACA recipients living in rural areas were employed, and nearly two-thirds said DACA allowed them to pursue educational opportunities not previously open to them.[41] Throughout 2018 and 2019, DACA remained in legal limbo. The Supreme Court took up the case and heard arguments as 2019 ended. In June, 2020, the Supreme Court blocked the administration's plan to dismantle DACA, at least temporarily protecting recipients from deportation.

Ramon dreaded the moment during the university application process when he had to mention his uncertain legal status. No matter how American he might seem, his foreign nationality makes him ineligible for federal student aid. The University of Wisconsin-Parkside sidestepped the issue by designating Ramon as an international student and offering him academic and athletic scholarships. Ramon appreciates that Parkside accepted him for who he is. "I run fast, so they're like, 'We'll help you as much as we can,'" he said. "That was the big worry—not knowing if I can study, with what's been happening with DACA. But they accepted me with my status."

Ashley, who is a US citizen, planned to take a gap year to save money by working at McDonald's and improving her mental health. She wanted to use the year to establish Wisconsin residency as an adult so she could qualify for in-state tuition. Because her parents are unauthorized immigrants, she had not been able to qualify as a minor resident.

Ashley and Ramon would both be the first in their families to go to college. But America's failure to adequately address its immigration problem is making that journey much more precarious than it would be otherwise. "I felt like DACA gave me wings to go to school and get a Social Security number," Ramon said at the end of our meeting at the Arcadia Family Restaurant. "And now I feel like someone has come along to cut my wings."

* * *

I was struck as I traveled through America how often I heard men say that they saw part of themselves in Donald Trump, or vice versa. "Like me, Trump is …" they'd start, or "Trump is sorta like me in that …"

"I've met Donald Trump and talked to him for a good five minutes and came away with the conclusion that he was a street guy, just like me," Michigan State Sen. Jack Brandenburg, who owns an industrial supply business, once told me. "The only difference is about 18 billion dollars!"

"He's a worker. He never quits, like me," Clint Mongold, a forty-year-old chicken-farmer-turned-handyman who lives with his mother in Petersburg, West Virginia, told me. "Stubborn. Stubborn."

"Didn't it bother you that he went bankrupt?" I asked.

> Nope! He was the richest man who was bankrupt. He fell, just like everybody else. He's just a normal person. Makes him more like an everyday person to me. I mean, I fell. I feel like I fell. Growing chickens and stuff. But I didn't quit. That's what he taught me—not to quit. To me he's a teacher. To me.

Many men identify with Trump because they imagine a shared plain-spokenness and chip-on-the-shoulder, get-it-done approach to life. There was something aspirational about Trump and his life. It's almost like they felt that if a few things had gone a little differently in their lives, they could be in Trump's place.

The first time I met Noel and Henry Filla, in 2018, I asked them why they'd voted for Trump. "For me, it was illegal immigrants and it was health care," said Noel, who twice voted for Barack Obama before turning to Trump.

Then it was Henry's turn. "And I liked him because he's a little like me," he said. "I'm pretty straight forward. I say it like it is, and I like to do things. I don't like to talk about it. Oh, we should change the light bulb on the street corner, and then we talk about it for six weeks. On a farm, we just get it done and move on. In the political world, it wasn't getting done. They just talk and talk."

As a businessman, Trump was seen as coming from a world where results were all that mattered. He was seen as decisive. Or in Henry's words, Trump is "a doer." Henry used the word "doer" five times to describe Trump and his appeal.

"He's always *doing* stuff," he said. "He's up early, when most people are sleeping. He's doing the job of commander in chief … twenty-four hours a day."

Later, Henry and Noel's friend Jeff, an exotic farmer, dropped by and joined the conversation, letting his pet camel roam free in the yard as we chatted. Jeff said:

> My wife grew up in New York City, and Trump would say, 'I'm going to build this in Manhattan or do that in Atlantic City.' And people would say, 'You can't do that.' And goddamn it he'd do it. Of course, he went broke a few times, but he's a doer, and he's not afraid of it.

When I asked Henry if he thinks Trump will win Trempealeau again in 2020, he said, "I think so, because he's a doer and a lot of people in rural areas are doers."

Then we returned to the trade tariffs. "I can see Trump's plan to straighten things out," Henry said. "Well there are going to be some things along the way that make it difficult. People are gonna get mad, people are gonna jump ship. And the media are going to play it up to

Henry and Noel Filla, their son Noah and friend Jeff and his pet camel on the Filla's front porch in Osseo, Wisconsin. (Daniel Allott)

get people against it 'cause that seems to be a common thing they do. But the real die hard farmers … we're kind of in it for the long haul."

"Are you in for Trump for the long haul?" I asked.

"Yeah. That's what we do. At least the rest of the world knows where we stand now. Before, they could sort of do what they wanted with us. We're not going to just bend over for you. We're not going to give you money to solve this problem. You're going to have to earn it."

3

ORANGE COUNTY, CALIFORNIA

AS ELECTION DAY APPROACHED IN 2016, Eddie Lopez was mostly decided about how he would vote, but not quite. Eddie, who emigrated from Mexico to the United States thirty years ago, liked Hillary Clinton and was thrilled with the idea of casting his ballot for America's first woman president. But Eddie had also been drawn to the Republican Party since the days of Ronald Reagan—his favorite president. And he'd grown wary of the Democratic Party under Barack Obama, who had failed to deliver on his promise to repair America's broken immigration system. When election day arrived, Eddie couldn't bring himself to vote for Donald Trump. "He just offends us too deep," Eddie said, reflecting on how he and many of his fellow Latinos felt toward Trump.

Eddie is a builder and contractor who owns and manages several businesses in and around Orange County. His clients have included Hollywood entertainers such as Bradley Cooper and Jussie Smollett. I met Eddie on my first trip to Orange County in January 2018. I was staying at an Airbnb in Tustin, an upscale city that's about a ten-minute drive from Disneyland. It was my first experience home-sharing, but certainly not my last. This would become a convenient way to meet people and learn more about the places I was visiting.

Eddie Lopez in Tustin, California, in 2016. (Daniel Allott)

On my first night there, it happened that the house's water heater broke. Eddie and his team were the ones who showed up to fix it. On the evening the repair work was being done, I was talking politics in the kitchen with my Airbnb hostess and her friends. Eddie offered his opinion, and then accepted my request for an interview. Eddie told me he was exasperated by Trump's pledge to build a wall on America's southern border. But what offended him most of all was Trump's denigration of immigrants—particularly his campaign-launching claim about Mexican immigrants: "They're bringing drugs. They're bringing crime. They're rapists." It was little consolation to him that Trump had thrown in the obligatory, "And some, I assume, are good people."[1]

"I thought, 'My son is thirteen years old. I have to do a lot of explaining to him,'" Eddie said. "We are not all rapists and drug dealers. I have to explain to my young son not to be ashamed of who we are."

Eddie and his son cried during that conversation, and again on election night. "It was an emotional night," he recalled. Still, when Trump won, Eddie held out hope that he would take a page from Reagan by enacting an immigration amnesty. "It's too soon to hate him," Eddie said he counseled his fellow Latinos as Trump took office.

Eddie Lopez highlights the dilemma facing Republicans in Orange County and other parts of America's rapidly diversifying suburbs. Do they double down on Trumpism at the risk of alienating minority voters? Or do they try to steer clear of Trump while emphasizing the conservative values and policies that many of those voters support?

***

To appreciate the sudden political changes that have occurred in Orange County over the last two election cycles, one must first understand the gradual demographic changes that have occurred there over the last two generations.

On my second trip to Orange County early in 2019, I drove to Little Saigon in Westminster and adjacent Garden Grove, where nearly half the residents are Asian American. Strolling through the Asian Garden Mall one weekday evening, I didn't see even one non-Asian face, aside from a black security officer.

I then drove a few miles east, to Santa Ana, the county seat. More than 90 percent of residents there are nonwhite, and the street signs are written in both English and Spanish.[2] To walk down Calle Cuarto (Fourth Street) is to be transported to another part of the world. The street is lined with Latino jewelers and tax preparers, stands selling churritos, and more than a dozen bridal and *quinceañera* shops. Few of the people I tried to talk to spoke English. A storefront display featured a box set of "Ingles sin Barreras (English without Limits)" videos to help Spanish-speakers learn English. I asked the storeowner if the videos were selling well. He said they were not, which wasn't surprising. Learning English is not necessary in a place where the law requires city council meetings to be simultaneously translated into Spanish. Even the cop writing me a parking ticket as I returned to my rental car initially addressed me in Spanish.

Later, while driving down coastal Highway 5 from Irvine to San Clemente, I counted at least sixteen AM stations on my car radio dial that featured non-English programming. Some were Spanish-speaking stations, while others I didn't recognize—probably a mix of Vietnamese, Mandarin, Korean, and Tagalog, to cater to southern California's large and expanding Asian and Pacific Islander communities.

Orange County reminded me of other growing, vibrant, diverse places I'd been, like my home base in Northern Virginia and the suburbs of Houston, Atlanta, and Salt Lake City—places, not coincidentally, that have turned from red to purple to blue in recent elections. Today's Orange County is not the Orange County that birthed Richard Nixon or the one that was a bastion for the John Birch Society. It's not the Orange County which in 1979 named its airport after native son John Wayne, an icon of rugged American masculinity and an outspoken Republican. It is not the lily-white Orange County that twice gave Ronald Reagan 75 percent of its votes for president.[3] And it's not the bleach-blonde Orange County of television shows like *The Real Housewives of Orange County*, *The O.C.*, and *Laguna Beach: The Real Orange County.*

A view of the Pacific Ocean from San Clemente. (Daniel Allott)

Orange County's population has more than doubled in the last fifty years, from 1.4 million people to nearly 3.2 million people. It is now more populous than twenty-one of the fifty states.[4] In 1970, whites made up 86 percent of the county's population;[5] now they make up just 40 percent,[6] which means that over 90 percent of Orange County's population growth in the last half century has been nonwhite. That trend will continue: nonwhites comprise three of every four Orange County Public School students.[7] Orange County is also younger and more highly educated than it once was. Much of its middle class has been driven away by California's high cost of living. Many of the white Midwestern and Los Angeles transplants of a few decades ago have moved away to lower-tax, more business-friendly states such as Idaho, Colorado, Utah, and especially Texas.

In 2019, there was even a movement to rename the county airport after an old television interview resurfaced of John Wayne making racist remarks.[8]

There are still plenty of conservative corners of this thirty-four-city county—in moneyed places such as Newport Beach and San Clemente or in Yorba Linda, Nixon's birthplace, where American flags are abundant and nary a "Hate Has No Home Here" yard sign can be found.

And Republicans continue to win at the local level. In the spring of 2019, the older, whiter voters who turn out in special elections propelled Irvine mayor Don Wagner to victory for a seat on the Orange County Board of Supervisors.[9] "The Orange County comeback starts now," Fred Whitaker, the Republican Party's county chair, optimistically declared afterwards. But the trend is clear: Republican dominance has evaporated as Orange County has gotten more diverse. Donald Trump's election has accelerated that trend. In 2016, Trump became the first Republican presidential nominee in eighty years to lose Orange County.[10] In 2018, Gavin Newsom became the first Democratic gubernatorial candidate in forty years to win the county. That year, Democrats swept all seven US House seats in Orange County, including four that had been held by Republicans.[11]

If Republicans hope to regain control of the House in 2020, they'll probably have to win back at least one or two of these seats.

***

Orange County Democrats used to kid that they could hold local club meetings in a telephone booth. But such modesty is no longer necessary. In fact, the mood was self-congratulatory one evening at an Aliso Niguel Democratic Club meeting that I attended. It was held not in a phone booth, but inside something nearly as obsolete—a Presbyterian church. New clubs like this one have been popping up across the county for the past few years. Upon arriving at the meeting, I introduced myself as a reporter to the club president, who then introduced me to various club office holders. An Asian American woman—the outgoing club president, I believe—asked me for the name of the publication I was writing for.

"*The Washington Examiner*," I said.

"Oh, I'm so sorry," she replied.

"Why?" I asked.

"That it's not the *Washington Post*," she responded, laughing.

The meeting was soon called to order. These progressives didn't start their meeting with a prayer or the Pledge of Allegiance, as Republicans always do. Instead, a woman stood up and recited a very different sort of invocation. "We always want to focus ourselves before every meeting and remember why it is that we come together," she started.

"*It's for social justice, to protect those who are vulnerable, support economic opportunities for all, work to protect the environment and elect Democrats who support these goals.*"

"Amen?" I thought.

Then the church offering plates were deployed to collect party dues and some other club business was conducted. There were roughly fifty people in attendance—mostly an older and white crowd. I counted only four or five people of color and just a handful who looked under forty years old. This didn't stop the club's leaders from congratulating themselves on how diverse they thought they were. Inviting the club officers to assemble at the front of the room, they spent several minutes specifying the sex, race, ethnicity and sexual preferences of everyone standing.

After the meeting, I spoke with Ada Briceno, chairwoman of the Orange County Democratic Party.

"I'm sitting in churches with hundreds of people in them every night," she said.

Briceno said that Democratic voter registration in the county had grown 40 percent since 2016, bringing them nearly on par with Republican voter registration numbers.

After the meeting, I drove an hour up the coast to meet a friend at Shannon's Bayshore, a dive bar on Second street in Long Beach. The place was packed. As I waited for the bartender to fix my old fashioned, a middle-aged man whose name I didn't catch struck up a conversation with me. He said he worked for the Port of Entry and was looking forward to retiring in six years. He said he couldn't wait to leave California's high taxes and move to Colorado or Texas, or even to Spain.

We started talking politics, and, inevitably, about President Trump. "He's a son of a bitch," the guy said. "But he's getting the job done so far." Then he walked off.

* * *

Some Democratic voters I spoke with worried that their leaders were steering the party in a direction that will cost them seats in 2020. "I'm very concerned that ill-informed people will be easily influenced by articulate people like (Alexandria Ocasio-Cortez) and Bernie," said Bob Bruce, a retired engineer I met at a Laguna Beach Starbucks. "For me, there's progressive and there's socialist. I'm not a socialist."

Bruce felt that three or four Orange County seats that turned blue in 2018 could flip back to Republicans in 2020. He was particularly concerned about freshman Rep. Katie Porter, an Elizabeth Warren acolyte he liked and for whom he had volunteered. He worried that she was too liberal for her 45th congressional district, which had never previously been represented by a Democrat.

Orange County Republicans mostly blame their recent troubles on an unprecedented infusion of money into the 2018 races and the

Democrats' use of ballot harvesting. Ballot harvesting allows activists to collect sealed absentee or mail-in ballots on behalf of voters who failed to send them in time. In most states where ballot harvesting is legal, only family members or caregivers are permitted to harvest ballots, so as to prevent abuses. But California changed its rules ahead of the 2018 election to allow anyone to collect and submit ballots on behalf of others. Huge last-minute submissions of ballots delayed election results in several Orange County congressional races. All of them showed the Republican candidate ahead on election night, but the Democrat won once the ballots were all counted.[12]

Mission Viejo's Republican mayor, Greg Raths, doesn't believe ballot harvesting was much of a factor. "It's bullshit," he told me one evening at a Young Republicans mixer at a Del Frisco's restaurant in Irvine. "We lost. Suck it up. I don't like harvesting, but suck it up."

"We got a problem here in Orange County," said Raths, who subsequently declared his candidacy for Porter's seat. "Instead of bitching and crying (about ballot harvesting). Go do it yourself. It's legal."

* * *

A couple of days later, I found myself back at the Airbnb in Tustin. The proprietor, Michelle, is an immigrant from Iran who retains her Farsi accent. She's been very successful in real estate. In back of her palatial home, there's an enormous swimming pool, a fireplace, a wet bar, a basketball hoop, and several fountains and marble statues. Most nights, a Tesla and three Mercedes can be found parked in her driveway. When I arrived, I joined Michelle in the living room. She was talking with a girlfriend whose name I didn't catch. Soon, Michelle's brother, Cyrus, and friend Lois joined us for a chat.

When we first met in 2018, Michelle, Cyrus, and Lois all told me they had voted for Barack Obama before turning to Donald Trump in 2016. All regretted voting for Obama, who they believed had harmed race relations, weakened the economy, and proved too weak on foreign policy. Michelle and Cyrus felt that Obama had blown an opportunity to help Iranian protestors during their short-lived Green revolution in 2009. In contrast, they all were pleased with Trump's performance.

I was curious to see whether their views had changed after more than a year.

Anticipating my questions, Michelle volunteered that her support for Trump had gotten stronger over the last year, mainly due to the late 2017 tax cuts and the overall strength of the economy.

Michelle's friend was more ambivalent. She had voted for Trump but had become weary of his behavior—the unhinged tweeting and continuing revelations about his sordid past. At the time, Trump's longtime personal lawyer, Michael Cohen, had just admitted to paying off pornographic film actress Stormy Daniels to stay mum about an

affair she claimed to have had with Trump. The friend said she liked Trump's policies but was open to voting for another candidate, because she thought Trump was an embarrassment to the country.

Michelle, Cyrus, and Lois disagreed. All the vitriol targeted at Trump by the Left and the media, they said, had strengthened their support. "Honestly, they've put him through the wringer," Michelle said.

Lois Morales in Tustin, California. (Daniel Allott)

I mentioned that Trump has some character flaws, but Lois took issue with that. "Look at the Clintons," she said. "They got away with basically murder, and nobody is harassing them and showing such disrespect for the president. How does the world look at that?"

I asked Cyrus if he was happy with Trump.

"As far as the country, yes," he said. "His personal life doesn't matter to me because we didn't elect a saint. He's the president, and his personal life before is not relevant. Like this lady (Sen. Kamala) Harris. She had admitted she used marijuana and other things in college. It doesn't matter."

Cyrus said he believed Trump would "definitely" win reelection. He also predicted that Trump would engineer a peace deal between Iran and Israel, get the border wall built, and secure a peace deal with North Korea.

"I don't think he'll run again," Lois interjected. "He's already gotten done everything he set out to do."

∗ ∗ ∗

The waves of Asian immigrants who settled in California in the 1970s and '80s identified strongly with the Republican Party, in part because of its firm stance against communism. George H. W. Bush won an estimated 55 percent of Asian American voters in the 1992 presidential election.[13] But they have slowly been moving toward the Democratic Party in recent times.

"What we are seeing today is a generational divide," said Linda Trinh Vo, who teaches Asian American studies at the University of California-Irvine. "The younger generation is more supportive of the Democratic Party." The change has been quite pronounced. Depending on the survey, Trump won between 18 percent and 27 percent of the Asian American vote in 2016.[14]

More than 200,000 Vietnamese-Americans live in Orange County. Many have been angered by the Trump administration's order to deport 7,000 Vietnamese refugees who committed crimes after arriving in the US. "There are still some people in our community that no matter what will support the Republican Party," Vo said. "But (Trump) is alienating some Vietnamese Americans ... including the older generation."

Some California Republicans believe the party hasn't done enough to reach out to immigrants and minorities. "The local party has dropped the ball with immigrant communities," Tom Tait, a former two-term

Republican mayor of Anaheim, told a reporter after the 2018 elections.[15] Others pin the blame on Trump specifically. Republican Young Kim said she would have won her race for California's 39th congressional district seat if Trump had not engaged in "so much anti-immigrant rhetoric."[16]

In a possible sign that some California Republicans want to chart a subtle path away from Trump, delegates to the state convention in February 2019 elected Jessica Patterson to lead their party. The thirty-eight-year-old Latina was chosen over Travis Allen, a loud Trump-defender. But not everyone was pleased. Raths said he received blowback when he posted a congratulatory message to Patterson on his Facebook page. "Man, I got blasted," he said. "'She's part of the establishment! She's not the right person!' So people didn't appreciate her. A lot of the grass roots were Travis Allen fans."

* * *

With Trump as their standard-bearer, Republicans may be losing an opportunity to reach many immigrant voters. But as Democrats embrace increasingly socialistic policies that remind them of the regimes they fled, he could have an opportunity to gain at least some of their support. I met some of them one sunny Saturday afternoon in February 2019, when I wandered into a phone bank organized by Orange County Republicans for Don Wagner. Wagner was the mayor of Irvine who was running in a special election for Orange County supervisor. When I arrived, I noticed that several Asians seemed to have taken lead roles in organizing the phone bank. One who immediately approached me was Saga Zhou.

A few days later, I interviewed Zhou, who had moved to the United States from China in 2009. Upon arriving, Zhou steered clear of politics. The Communist Party rules supreme in China, so most Chinese immigrants bring a built-in aversion to political involvement. "Politics was a joke to me," she said. But Zhou's interest in politics increased as she began to see the American Left embracing policies that reminded her of those she'd fled in China. One such policy was the Left's support for late-term abortion. When she lived in China, Zhou, like many young Chinese, didn't consider abortion to be a big deal. Her view changed after moving to America, getting married, and bearing two children.

"After I became a mother, my understanding about life fundamentally changed," she said, becoming emotional. "Now I am totally a mother."

Zhou said her heart broke upon learning about a Virginia bill to loosen restrictions on late-term abortions. Appearing on a radio show as the bill was being debated, Democratic Governor Gary Northam pledged to sign the legislation, even suggesting that it would sanction infanticide.[17]

"Oh, when I saw the news, I cannot even open it (the article)," Zhou said through tears. "It was really hard. I just felt something really strong into my chest. And then I said, 'Let me adopt him, don't kill him.'" Hearing this story prompted Zhou and her husband to consider adoption. The proposed law hit especially close to home for Zhou, whose mother had become pregnant with her just as China's government began implementing its brutal One Child policy. The policy prohibited most couples from having more than one child. Women

who became pregnant with a second child were often forced to undergo sterilization; sometimes their babies were killed in the womb. Though she was her mother's second child, Zhou escaped death because the One Child policy was not yet being implemented in her city.

"Somebody has to understand the roots, where these policies come from," said Zhou,

Saga Zhou at a Panera Bread in Irvine. (Daniel Allott)

whose maternal grandparents were imprisoned during the

Cultural Revolution. "That's why I'm so pissed. I finally found a country that I think I can truly settle down to enjoy my ideals, to do my best to achieve the most. But now you are coming here to destroy it and force me to leave. Why the heck is that? So I was so mad. Damn socialism. Why are you chasing me?"

In 2018 and 2019, as Democrats began to embrace policies such as Medicare for All, "free" college, 70 percent tax rates, the Green New Deal, and late-term abortion, Republicans saw an opportunity to frame the 2020 election as a referendum on socialism. President Trump began including a riff on the dangers of socialism in most of his speeches. "Tonight, we renew our resolve that America will never be a socialist country," he told Congress and the nation in his 2019 State of the Union address.[18]

An internal memo from the Congressional Leadership Fund, a Republican super PAC, discussed its plan to win the suburbs and retake the House of Representatives by framing the 2020 election as a choice between socialism and economic opportunity.[19] The Republican Party's anti-communism has long attracted many Cubans, Vietnamese, Eastern Europeans, and other immigrants who fled communist countries during the Cold War.

Chinese immigrants have historically been an afterthought, but their numbers are rising. There are more than three million Chinese immigrants living in America today, up from fewer than half a million in 1980.[20] And as their numbers grow, Chinese Americans are becoming more active in politics. In 2014, a group of Chinese Americans in Orange County formed The Orange Club (TOC), a political action committee whose purpose was to prevent a ballot referendum, Senate Constitutional Amendment No. 5, to lift the ban on affirmative action in state university admissions. The club argued that the change would unfairly hurt their high-achieving children's chances of getting into California's top state-run universities. The measure ultimately failed, due in part to strong opposition from Asian American groups including The Orange Club, which remains active in local public policy debates and endorses candidates for office.

Zhou joined TOC in 2018, and ever since she has been attending meetings, signing online petitions, and protesting at public events—all things she couldn't have imagined doing in China.

In 2008 and 2012, many Chinese American voters cast their presidential ballots for Barack Obama, believing Obama's Democratic Party was more hospitable to immigrants. "On the first day when we land here, the media and Left reinforce the concept that minorities and immigrants are supposed to vote for Democrats and not supposed to be aligning with conservatives," said George Li, a Chinese immigrant I met at a Starbucks in Irvine. But many Chinese-Americans are repelled by the Democrats' more recent embrace of policies they consider to be socialistic. Socialism "is a great, great concern to (Chinese Americans), which is why I'm really motivated to stop that," Li said. "It's our duty."

As a college student in China in the late 1980s, Li was active in China's democracy movement and knew some of the students involved in the Tiananmen Square protests. Not long after, Li moved to the US, earning a master's degree in computer information systems and starting a family. Li became active in local politics through The Orange Club, which he led in 2018. Li believes the Republican Party is a natural fit for Chinese-Americans. Traditional Chinese culture is conservative, he said, emphasizing hard work, independence, education, and family values. He finds the Left's obsession with political correctness maddening because it intimidates people into silence. "This intimidation is so bad for freedom of speech," he said. "A lot of things I see in this country are very similar to what I saw in the Cultural Revolution era in China," He calls political correctness a "form of cultural Marxism."

Benjamin Yu, also of Irvine, saw the Democratic Party moving toward socialism long before some of its members began embracing the term. Yu immigrated to the US with his mother in the late 1990s. In the immediate aftermath of 9/11, Yu, then a US Green Card holder, felt a "surge of patriotism" for his new home, prompting him to join the US Army.

"When something happens so close to you, it doesn't matter if you are an American by legal status," he said. "You get a sense that that's your country. You feel part of the community."

Yu saw a nascent socialism developing under President Obama, for whom he voted twice before turning to Trump in 2016. He believes that more and more Chinese are voting Republican, although he thinks many are reluctant to say so for fear of being ostracized.

Zhou, Li, and Yu believe Republicans can win over Chinese American voters by emphasizing the Democrats' embrace of socialism and the GOP's staunch opposition to it.

"I just want America to be America," Li said, "not another Soviet Union, Cuba, or China."

**

Orange County Republicans may be able to attract some immigrant voters to their party by emphasizing the Democratic Party's leftward turn. The problem is that Trump's hardline immigration stance and combative rhetoric alienate many other immigrants who would otherwise be open to a Republican message. Trump is also alienating white voters who care about immigrants. In fact, the president seems to be turning some Republicans into Democrats. Two former Republicans— Harley Rouda and Gil Cisneros—beat incumbents to win congressional races in Orange County in 2018. They did so running as Democrats disillusioned by the direction of their former party under Trump.

Bob Bruce is a former Republican whose political views changed after he moved to Orange County and began to appreciate the diversity he didn't encounter growing up in segregated Chicago.

"What's interesting, my daughter is married to a Persian guy," Bruce said. "He's not a Muslim, but his parents are, and they're not jihadists, you know? So when someone starts dissing the Muslims, it kind of hits home a little bit. It's like, my granddaughter, who I love to death, her other grandparents are Muslims!"

Orange County has clearly changed Bruce, a well-educated white retiree who voted for both Reagan and George H. W. Bush for president. "On my block, there's an Indian family, an Asian, a guy from the

South, a couple of Jewish families. If you'd said twenty-five years ago that I was going to live here, I'd say you were crazy. And I love it. I love it. It's changed my own views, my politics. I've changed my outlook."

"It's the diversity and the vibrancy," he said of what he loves most about living in Orange County.

The vibrancy gap between Republican places and Democratic places is real, and it's widening. As suburban counties like those outside Washington, DC, Houston, Atlanta, and Los Angeles are becoming more diverse and more economically and culturally vibrant, they're trending Democratic. According to data from the Brookings Institution, in 2008 the real GDP per Republican House district was $33.3 billion.[21] In 2018, it fell slightly to $32.6 billion. In Democratic House districts, the average real GDP increased nearly 50 percent, from $35.7 billion to $49 billion. In that time, median household income per district has increased 17 percent in Democratic districts and fallen 3 percent in Republican districts. Similar trends are found in education and pro-ductivity patterns. This has happened as Democrats have become more powerful in cities and tech hubs, and Republicans have gained ground in rural areas heavy in agriculture, mining, and manufacturing.

Other Orange County residents I met echoed Bruce's sentiments on diversity.

At a Laguna Niguel coffee shop, Lacey, a thirty-five-year-old nurse, told me it was Orange County's mix of cultures that brought her back after living in Colorado for several years. "I love how diverse it is here," she said. "Even as a kid, everyone would always say how much of a melting pot SoCal is, and you don't understand that until you leave SoCal. When I went to Colorado, I was literally the kid of color."

Half-white and half-Hispanic, Lacey is the type of voter both parties desperately want, and she knows it. "I'm the educated female who is multi-national who refuses to be a Democrat or a Republican because both of them have their heads in their ass," she said. After twice voting for Barack Obama for president, Lacey voted for Trump in 2016 mainly because she couldn't stand the thought of Hillary Clinton becoming

America's first female president. "There's an exalted-ness to the title of the first female president," she explained. But she thinks that by framing immigration as a moral issue instead of an economic one, Trump has revealed himself to be "a racist bigot." Lacey voted for Trump as the lesser of two evils, knowing he'd likely be president for only one term. "How much can he literally fuck things up in four years?" she thought. "We need a change anyways."

"Trump being president, we knew exactly what would happen. Shit was going to hit the fan. We knew things were going to get shook up. That's what people wanted. … Sometimes you need a little anarchy to reset things.

"That's why I'm not looking for him to be a two-term president. … It's not bad to shake things up and wake people up and help people start paying attention. I told my parents, we've been through the thunderstorm, now maybe a light drizzle would be good."

Lacey said she will not be supporting Trump again in 2020. She will either vote for the Democratic nominee or not vote at all.

***

According to the Pew Research Center, Hispanics will become the largest group of minority voters in 2020.[22] How crucial will Hispanic voters be? If Trump can improve his performance with this voting bloc by 12 percentage points, he'll be poised to win swing states such as Florida, North Carolina, Georgia, and Arizona, be competitive in Colorado and Nevada, and be close to a sure thing for reelection.

Hispanic Democrats are more moderate than most Democrats. According to an analysis by FiveThirtyEight, Hispanics comprise 12 percent of self-described Democrats while making up 22 percent of Democrats who describe themselves as moderate or conservative. In other words, a significant portion of Hispanic Democrats are not woke socialists who support abortion-on-demand, open borders, and the Green New Deal. Many are like Eddie Lopez, a Reaganite Republican who just cannot bring himself to vote for Trump because he offends him too much.

Republicans seem to understand that they must reach out to these voters. They talk about it all the time. But they never seem to know how.

On a spring morning in 2019, a group of fifty or so mostly retired white Republican women gathered in Fullerton to listen to two millennial Latina guest speakers point the way. The event was held in a room at the back of a buffet restaurant. "I've been waiting all month for this," a woman said as she hustled past me looking for a chair in the packed room. One thing that struck me about the meeting was that the American flag was placed prominently in the front of the room, and a prayer and the Pledge of Allegiance were solemnly recited, a stark contrast to the Democratic meeting I'd attended a few days earlier. First up was Jazmina Saavedra. A handout with her biography touted her work history as a purveyor of anti-aging products, a solar-energy entrepreneur, and a 2018 US Senate candidate.

"Every time I get invited to a Republican club, I just see white people," Saavedra began. "I'm sorry."

That comment was met with silence in the room. But Saavedra recovered with lines like, "I never call this country my second country. This is my first country"; "Hispanics are Republicans, they just don't know it yet"; and "The wall is a message of love to the American people."

At this last line, I turned to an eighty-five-year-old woman sitting next to me, named Claudia, and asked for her thoughts on why the county had turned blue. "The Latinos," she said.

"Can they be won over?" I asked.

"I don't know."

"Is it worth trying?"

"I hope it is. I guess we'll see."

Claudia was in a talkative mood, and I was there to listen. She said she felt like a hypocrite because her church supports LGBT pride, which she cannot abide. She told me she wants a border wall and is *definitely* pro-life. "I just can't go with this late-term abortion," she said. She insisted that though she's been involved in Republican politics her entire life, she's not an extremist. She said she appreciates what Trump is doing for the country but that "his personality drives me up the wall."

"How do other women feel?" I asked.

"Oh yeah, we all hate his personality," she said. But she stressed that her friends are also focused on what he's doing for the country.

"Nobody's perfect," she said.

Next up at the podium was Elsa Adeguer of Latinos 4 Trump (not to be confused with "Latinos for Trump"), who delivered a testimonial about fleeing violence in Latin America to come to the US. She explained that she was drawn to Trump because, like her, he'd once supported abortion but is now pro-life.

Both women elicited the most applause when they assured their audience that they had done things "the right way" by entering the US legally.

A few days later, I drove to the City National Grove of Anaheim, where hundreds of people were standing in line, waiting to do things the right way.

Orange County Republicans had set up a registration tent outside the arena on a day when it was hosting a series of naturalization ceremonies. "Come with patriotism and enthusiasm as we welcome and register our new members at our Republican Booth," an online invitation said. But here in Anaheim, any welcoming would have to be done from afar, as the half-dozen or so Republican volunteers had been penned off in a "free speech zone." They were reduced to shouting "Thank you for registering!" And "You're doing the right thing!" to bemused passersby who, unfortunately for the activists, weren't their target audience. The new citizens were standing in a line on the opposite side of the arena.

One of the activists said she's often there all day and is lucky to register ten people. During my hour there, just one person registered. With the dearth of registrants, the activists were more than happy to chat with me, so long as I promised not to print their names. I asked them what Orange County Republicans needed to do to win over immigrants. "We need to convince people we don't have horns on our head," one woman said.

"We need to emphasize faith," said a second. "And no open borders."

"I would not take 2018 as gospel that everything has changed," the first added.

The two women blamed ballot harvesting for Democrats' success in 2018. They said they were certain Democratic volunteers simply filled out people's ballots for them. I asked them why Republicans don't harvest ballots too.

"We tried to harvest," one of the women said. "We got like ten." Republicans prefer to physically take in their ballots, she explained, not trusting them to some volunteer who comes by their home. "Republicans don't trust."

"It's like marrying a woman you've never met," added a male volunteer who was listening in.

I asked them whether President Trump makes their job harder.

"No! In fact, he emboldens me!" the second woman said.

"We all love Trump. We're glad he tweets. But some in the Republican Party think we should be more like Democrats," said the first. She mentioned Jessica Patterson, whose name elicited sighs and head shakes from several of the volunteers.

"We don't want to be politically correct," said the second. "We have to get people to look at policy instead of personality, facts instead of feelings."

* * *

But personality and feelings matter, too, for better and for worse. After all, it was Trump's no-holds-barred personality that originally attracted many Americans who felt forgotten by politically correct, establishment politicians. But that same personality drove away the likes of Eddie Lopez, Bob Bruce, and, eventually, Lacey—the types of voters Republicans will need to win consistently again in Orange County and places like it.

When I visited Lopez again in March 2019, I asked him to assess President Trump's performance at the mid-point of his first term. He gave Trump a 5 out of 10 on policy, mainly for presiding over a strong economy and enacting tax and health care reforms that have benefited Lopez's businesses and employees. He reiterated that he supports more of Trump's agenda than he opposes, and that he hopes Trump will set aside his obsession with the border wall and grant illegal immigrants a pathway to citizenship. "He's the only guy who can do it at this point," he said. "And he's crazy enough that it just might happen."

If it does happen, Lopez said, he thinks Republicans will begin to win majorities of Latinos, whose religiosity, social conservatism, and support for free enterprise are a natural fit for the party. Short of that unlikely scenario, Lopez will be voting for the Democratic nominee next November. He thought former Vice President Joe Biden was the only candidate who could defeat Trump. "Biden can get into a street fight with Trump and win," he said.

I asked Lopez whether he still thinks it's too soon to hate Trump.

"Yes, the only thing that gives us reason to hate him is what he said about my race," he said. Then Lopez paused, and added, "To *really* hate him, that would make me part of the extremism that he created."

* * *

On January 3, 2020, a US drone strike near the Baghdad International Airport killed Iranian General Qassem Soleimani. Soleimani had led Iran's Islamic Revolutionary Guards Corps and was commander of the Quds Force, which the United States considers a terrorist organization. Iran responded by launching a series of missile attacks on US bases in Iraq, which produced no casualties. The killing of Soleimani escalated tensions between the two countries, raising the specter of a new war in the Middle East. Donald Trump was at risk of becoming the wartime president he vowed never to be.

A few days later, I was back at the Airbnb in Tustin, speaking with three Iranian-Americans—Michelle, her brother Cyrus, and Cyrus's wife, Roya. All three approved of Trump's decision to take out Soleimani. They also repeated their disappointment that President Obama hadn't supported the Green movement protestors in Iran in

2009.[23] "He supported the government of Iran—it's his fault," Roya said of Obama and why the Green Revolution failed. Roya believes any Democratic president would back the repressive regime in Tehran over the pro-democracy opposition. "They scare us," she said of how Iranian-Americans feel about the Democratic candidates. All three were certain Trump would win reelection, and that he would do so with the help of Iranian-American voters.

"Why are you so sure?" I asked.

"He's kept his promises," Cyrus said. "It's that simple."

I asked the group whether they knew any Iranian-Americans who hadn't voted for Trump in 2016 but planned to in 2020.

"I didn't vote for him last time, but I will this year," Roya announced. "I've never voted before in twenty-five years, but I'm scared. I'm scared of what the Democrats would do in Iran."

***

Two developments in 2019 boosted Orange County Democrats' prospects heading into the 2020 elections. In February, the Orange County Board of Supervisors voted to eliminate traditional polling places, replacing them with hundreds of voting centers and drop-boxes located across the county, and automatically sending every registered voter a mail ballot. All voters will be able to drop off their ballots at any of the voting centers as early as ten days before election day.[24] A new state law also lets people both register to vote on election day and cast a ballot at any vote center. Earlier and easier access to voting is seen as an advantage for Democrats, who typically have a harder time getting their supporters to vote.

Then, in August 2019, the number of registered Democrats surpassed the number of registered Republicans in the county for the first time.[25] It was a moment that crystalized the long-term demographic shifts occurring in Orange County.

A third factor—President Donald J. Trump's presence at the top of the ballot—may prove crucial in determining whether Democrats retain the four House seats they flipped in 2018. Democrats seem convinced Trump will be an asset to them. I attended several local Democratic Party meetings during my January 2020 trip. I came away with the impression that Democratic activists believe Trump's unfitness for office has become so obvious that they don't need to talk very much about their own candidates or policies to succeed. But not every Democrat I talked to saw Trump as an obvious drag on down-ballot Republicans. When I met up with Bob Bruce again, he said he'd seen a difference in the way his neighbors were responding to Trump. In 2018, many of the voters in the upscale beach neighborhoods where he canvassed for Katie Porter responded positively to the anti-Trump message. But suddenly, things were different.

> Now when you go and you talk to the same people about anti-Trump, they're looking at their 401K, they're looking at the fact that their kid's got a job, they're looking at the fact that things are okay. The world didn't collapse, we're not at war. ... So now the people who were Republican who didn't support Trump before because they abhorred his actions are going to say, "You know what, I'm going to forget that. I can take four more years of this."

Bruce said even his own opposition to Trump had softened over the last year or so. "I never thought I would say this, but this guy could win again," Bruce said, looking somewhat surprised by what he was saying. "Our current president could win again in November. And that's saying a lot because when we spoke last year, I was convinced he wouldn't even run again." Bruce put the odds of a Trump victory at 55 percent.

Bruce arrived at that conclusion after seeing the ideological fracturing within the Democratic Party while attending two state party conventions in 2019. Bruce complained about the party's continuing leftward shift. "If it's Bernie, forget it, it's over. If it's Elizabeth (Warren), it's over," said Bruce, a former Republican. He added that if either of these candidates becomes the nominee, Trump would be able to tar

Bob Bruce in Laguna Beach, California in 2020.
(Daniel Allott)

them with the "socialist" label. He also said that if the nominee is Sanders or Warren, he himself might vote for a third-party candidate.

Lacey, the former Trump voter, said something similar when I met with her again. "If it's Warren or Bernie, I won't vote," she said. "I could do Biden or Buttigieg—Yang too."

I asked her if there was anything Trump could do to win back her support. She said there was not. "I happen to agree with some of the things he does," she said. "I also think he's a racist and a bastard." Lacey supported impeaching and removing Trump from office. But, interestingly, she said she still wouldn't change her 2016 vote if she could. That's because her vote for Trump was a vote against Hillary. Also, she said, "I think we needed the thunderstorm," applying the same metaphor she had shared with me a year earlier to describe Trump's election. "But with so much hate in the world right now, we could use a period of calmness."

Another factor that will help Democrats in 2020 is the increasing share of the electorate composed of racial minorities. Latinos now make up 21 percent of Orange County voters, up more than a third since 2016.[26]

Before leaving Orange County, I chatted with Eddie Lopez one last time. I met him at one of his businesses, in an industrial park in Paramount, just north of the Orange County border with Los Angeles County. A year earlier, Eddie was convinced Joe Biden was the only candidate who could beat Trump. "Biden can get into a street fight with Trump and win," he had said in 2019.

Now Eddie had significant doubts about Biden, who he said looked weak and past his prime in the debates and on the stump. "He used to be more faster and sharper and accurate," Eddie said. "I think right now, he's doing a lot of damage."

On the economy, Eddie thought Trump was "a fucking blessed motherfucker," benefiting from a strong economy he inherited from Obama. Eddie was convinced that the economy would tank, but not until 2021.

Eddie also said he was bothered by his suspicion that his two older sons, who are in their late 20s, voted for Trump in 2016 and still support the president. He attributes their admiration for Trump to their being born in the US and their inability to share their father's empathy for the immigrant struggle. Eddie was sure Trump would win reelection, and was concerned about what will happen when he does.

"Can America survive four more years of Donald Trump?" I asked.

"Maybe in the next ten years we will see all that this guy's (done) outside the country and inside the country with the economy and with the way there's so much anger," Eddie said. "Right now, we're inside the bubble, so we're not exposed to it. We can't see all of it yet. But one day, we will look back and understand all the damage this guy has done."

4

MACOMB COUNTY, MICHIGAN

ROBERT RASCH had never voted for president before 2016. Then Donald Trump came along. Finally, there was a candidate he could get excited about. Rasch admired Trump's business sense and political courage. "For somebody to stand up and run for president that has no political background, that's a set of brass," he told me when we met one day in 2019 at his Detroit-themed memorabilia store in New Baltimore, a forty-five-minute drive north of the Motor City. Rasch is one of millions of so-called "lost voters" whom Trump coaxed back to the voting booth in 2016. At the time of our interview, election day 2020 was still a year-and-a-half away, but Rasch had already decided that he'd be voting for Trump again, based largely on the president's stewardship of the economy.

"When you drive down Eight Mile, Nine Mile, Ten Mile (Roads), a lot of those small industrial shops were closed a few years ago," he said of the manufacturing-heavy southern part of Macomb County. "But now you see them being reconstructed to get new tenants in there."

Rasch and his wife Laurie's small business, LR Embroidered Creations, paid less in taxes in 2018 thanks to the Trump tax cuts. "We've felt the difference," he said.

"On a scale from 1 to 10, I think he's doing an 8," Rasch said of Trump's overall performance. "He's making a change for the good for everybody. I think he's growing on people here."

Rasch was seeing that growing support at the Anchor Bay Pit Stop Diner, where he and his friends talk politics on weekends. And he was seeing it among his store's customers.

"One gentleman came in and asked us to print that Trump hat," Rasch said, pointing to a display case featuring red ball caps with white lettering that said, "TRUMP: Elect That MF'er again! 2020."

"The hats sold like crazy," Rasch said. "And the guy's been in numerous times and re-ordered. It's been a big seller."

Asked whether he thinks President Trump will win Michigan in 2020, Rasch was ready with the same answer he gave a CNN camera crew that had stepped into his store a few months earlier: "If (Trump) was going to the optical store to get some new glasses, he'd have 20/20 vision."

A best-seller at Rob and Laurie Rasch's memorabilia stores in New Baltimore, Michigan. (Daniel Allott)

My interview with Rasch was one of more than two-dozen I conducted during a week in Macomb County in the summer of 2019. I had come to find out how residents of this famous swing county perceived Trump. Specifically, I wanted to know whether, two-and-a-half years into his term, Trump's support there was diminishing. It's an important question in a state Trump won by fewer than 11,000 votes, the slimmest margin of any state in the 2016 election.[1] Trump won Macomb County by 48,000 votes, making it the county that delivered Michigan to Trump, and one of three counties nationwide that could be said to have determined the presidency.[2] Macomb County voters are accustomed to determining elections. They have sided with the winner in all but three of the last twenty elections for governor and president.[3]

After speaking with Rasch, I swung by Bad Brads BBQ in another part of New Baltimore. There I met Doug, a clinical psychologist who eschews party labels. He voted for John McCain in 2008, Barack Obama in 2012, and Donald Trump in 2016.

"I'm not a party person," Doug said. "If Trump had run as a Democrat, I would have voted for him."

Doug said he thought "things are going great" under Trump. And he "definitely" planned to vote for him again in 2020. He was even toying with the idea of coming out of the political closet with his Trump support.

"I was thinking of putting a Trump sign out in my yard in '16, but I thought, nah," Doug said, explaining that as an Airbnb host, he doesn't want to alienate guests.

"I think I would do it more this time than last time because he's president now, so there's nothing the Trump-haters can really do. And if people asked me about it, I'd say I voted for him."

I asked Doug some other questions, including whether he thinks Donald Trump is a racist. He gave the same answer almost every Trump supporter gave: of course not. Doug even seemed a little bothered by the question, and I suspected I knew why. I had gotten to know Doug during a trip to Macomb County the previous year, when I'd spent more than a month living in his basement as an Airbnb guest.

One day stands out in my memory. It was Labor Day, and I had just returned to Doug's home after a weekend trip to Canada. Shortly after I got back, Doug walked downstairs to chat. But something seemed different—Doug looked distraught. He told me that while I had been away, he'd had a guest in one of the upper rooms that he rents out.

The guest, a young woman, had booked four nights, then cancelled her reservation before booking again. The woman had informed Doug that she would arrive in the afternoon, so Doug and his girlfriend waited for her. But the woman didn't show up until after 10 p.m. When she finally arrived, she walked into the bedroom she'd booked, laid down on the bed and abruptly announced that she no longer wanted to stay in Doug's home. The bed was too small.

Airbnb has several cancellation policies for hosts to choose from.[4] But none of them allows a guest to arrive late and receive a full refund for a stay that's already begun. Doug said he told the woman that Airbnb would return her money in the standard timeframe, three to five days. According to Doug, the woman became belligerent and insisted she get reimbursed immediately. She said she wouldn't leave until the transaction had processed. After some wrangling, she eventually left and got her money back. Doug awoke the next morning to discover that the woman had left a nasty review on his Airbnb page.

To promote trust and transparency, Airbnb doesn't allow reviews to be deleted. They remain on the host's page for all future prospective guests to see. But it wasn't the negative review that exasperated Doug; it was that the woman, who is black, had accused Doug, who is white, of racism.

I had come to know Doug as a conscientious, somewhat highly-strung, and exceedingly nice man. Before I ever interviewed him about politics, we had spent hours chatting about his experiences as a psychologist, the revitalization of Detroit, and our shared affinity for ping-pong. I had never gotten the slightest indication that Doug harbored racist views.

When we spoke that night, Doug was in the middle of haggling with Airbnb to remove the review (which the company did). Doug seemed distraught because the review was visible not only to prospective Airbnb guests but also potentially to his clinical patients, many of whom were people of color. Doug's experience highlights how potent the charge of racism has become. There is no more pernicious insult in America today. As the linguist John McWhorter has written about the label in its modern usage:

To be a racist is considered not just a matter of bland categorization but of evil, a charge only somewhat less damning than being called a pedophile, as chilling a prospect in modern American life as being tarred as a communist was in the late 1940s and early 1950s.[5]

I can't say for sure what happened that night at Doug's place. I wasn't there. But I know that many Americans have grown wary of how promiscuously the term is applied.

In politics, President Trump has been persistently accused of being a racist. And so have his supporters. Polls show that half of Democrats believe people are racist merely for the fact that they voted for Trump.[6] The accusation deeply offends most Trump voters—including the estimated 7–9 million who, like Doug, also voted for America's first black president.[7] And it invites an important question: Do Democrats believe they can win back these voters by echoing Hillary Clinton's accusation that they are "deplorable and irredeemable"?

The ostensible point of calling people racists is to shame them. But it rarely has that effect, especially on Trump supporters. To people like Doug, such an accusation has the opposite effect. It angers, it frustrates, and it saddens—but it doesn't shame. It doesn't prompt them to rethink their support for Trump. Rather, it hardens and deepens their support for him. Research shows that "telling voters that some people oppose Trump because he supports racism" makes many voters much more supportive of Trump.[8]

When I mentioned the Airbnb incident to Doug a year later at Bad Brads, he still remembered it like it was yesterday. And he still seemed bothered by it. As he recounted the story, it occurred to me that the incident might have played a role in Doug's more overt support for Trump. It made me think that there was no way Doug would not be putting a Trump sign on his lawn in 2020—negative Airbnb reviews be damned.

***

In 2016 Donald Trump became the first Republican to win Michigan in nearly thirty years. But Michigan Republicans took a step backward in 2018. Democrats swept races for governor, US Senate and attorney general, and they gained two US House seats. Michigan Democrats also prevailed in several ballot initiatives, including a referendum on recreational marijuana and a constitutional amendment to streamline the voting process.[9] Even so, Republicans argued that 2018 shouldn't be seen as a harbinger for 2020. By their calculation, 50,000 Trump voters hadn't shown up to vote in 2018. That number includes voters such as Rasch and Doug.[10]

Later I met up with Catherine Bolder, another Obama-voter-turned-Trump-supporter who hadn't voted in the midterms. We met at a restaurant just outside Macomb County. Bolder had been in cancer treatment a year earlier, the first time I had met her. This time, I barely recognized her when I walked in. That's because she had successfully completed chemotherapy. Her hair had grown back, and she looked much healthier. Catherine is a self-described liberal who supported Bernie Sanders in the 2016 Democratic primary. The first time we met, she had described Trump as the lesser of two evils compared to Hillary Clinton. This time, she had much more fulsome praise for Trump.

"Honestly, I'm beginning to think he's a genius," she said. "The way he trolls Democrats and gets under their skin and makes them say stupid shit."

Like Rasch and Doug, Bolder had already decided to vote for Trump in 2020, and she was confident he'd win Michigan again. "He's making people money," she said. "Why change if it's not broke?"

"Michigan men are manly men, and Macomb I think is still Blue Collar" she continued. "People here like Trump because he's a strong alpha male. Nobody's going to vote for Beto O'Rourke. Come on, you pussy."

"So you're a convert?" I asked.

"Yeah. Yeah. I'll vote for Trump in 2020, but I don't know what I'll do after that."

I asked Bolder what prompted her unlikely journey from Obama to Bernie to Trump in just a few years.

"The biggest thing that changed me is what the Democrats did to Bernie," she explained, referring to how Hillary Clinton's 2016 presidential campaign conspired with the Democratic National Committee to ensure that the outsider Sanders would not win the nomination.

"And now they're shutting down any kind of debate, using the race and victim card. I don't want to hear it anymore," Catherine continued. "You can only use it so much. They've used it too much. People are tired of it. I mean, are you going to call me a racist for voting for Trump? I was married to a black man and have a biracial son."

Bolder also sees the party as having moved too far leftward on many issues, citing abortion as a prime example. "I was always pro-choice," she said. "I still am. But with New York and Virginia approving them to abort babies after they've been born—look, if you carry a child for nine months and only then decide you don't want it ..." she said, trailing off then shaking her head in exasperation.

"Would you now consider yourself pro-life?" I asked.

"I'm conflicted. I don't think you should kill a human being after it's born. (The Democrats) have become radical on a lot of issues."

As Bolder and I were speaking, she turned to a middle-aged couple sitting beside us at the bar and took on the role of interviewer. "Hey, folks, if the election were held tomorrow, who would you vote for?" she asked.

The man, an off-duty police officer and security guard whose name I didn't catch, seemed ambivalent at first. "I think they're both full of shit," he said of the Republicans and Democrats.

But eventually he said, "It'll probably be Trump. The more I hear negative about him, the more I like him. Because I know if you're pissing them off, you must be doing something right."

I asked who the "them" was. He said the media, the Democrats, and "everyone in Washington."

"He's a liar, he's a bully. He's a womanizer," the cop continued of

Trump. "But he's the first president I've seen who actually had a prayer meeting in the Oval Office."

The cop also said he'd become concerned about the growing Muslim community.

"Once I landed at Minneapolis airport, and I looked out the window," he said. "Everybody working on the runway was Muslim. And everybody inside too—they're all Somali. I'm afraid."

"I think they're out to destroy this country," Catherine interjected of Muslim immigrants.

The cop said that when he retires, he plans to move up to Michigan's Upper Peninsula, stock up on food and ammunition, and live a solitary life.

Neither Bolder nor the cop could think of any Trump voters they knew who had turned against the president. I wasn't surprised. Among the two dozen people I interviewed in and around Macomb County on this visit, not a single one could think of a Trump voter who no longer supported him. That included some Democrats I met, too.

That night, I attended a meeting of the Warren Democratic Club, which was held at the Warren area Elks Lodge. Many local candidates were in attendance. I was struck that this meeting of Democratic activists began not with the recitation of some progressive manifesto, as the Orange County Democrats had done, but with the Pledge of Allegiance and with an American flag displayed prominently at the front of the room. Like most Democratic meetings these days, a significant portion of the meeting was spent discussing ways to make it easier to vote and to expand voting rights to new communities.

Afterwards, I met a young woman named Shelby Nicole, a member of Macomb County Young Democrats. Nicole told me she had knocked on thousands of doors across the county canvassing for the Democratic Party.

"A lot of people will look you in the eye and say, 'I voted Dem all my life until Trump came along. And I'm not voting Dem ever again,'" she said. "Or they'd say, 'I stopped voting a long time ago, then voted for Trump and am not going back.'"

I asked Nicole whether she thinks Trump will win Macomb County in 2020. "No doubt in my mind," she responded before I could even finish my question. She added that many Trump voters took 2018 off but will be back to vote for him in 2020.

Nicole also talked about Joe Biden, whom she was certain the party would ultimately nominate. I mentioned that Biden had been doing a lot of apologizing of late, giving a speech in Germany in which he apologized for America under Trump.[11]

"Excuse my language but I don't want to hear that shit," Nicole said. "And blue collar voters don't either."

***

Macomb County is composed of twenty-seven cities, villages, and townships. It stretches from the industrial wasteland of Eight Mile road on its southern border with Detroit to the small towns and open fields of the northern part of the county. Politically, Macomb County gained prominence in the 1980s as the birthplace of the Reagan Democrats—socially conservative, pro-labor union, blue-collar white voters who backed Ronald Reagan but still considered themselves Democrats. The county lost more than half of its manufacturing jobs between 2000 and 2010.[12] Trump visited the county several times during the 2016 campaign, portraying its residents as victims of international trade. His promise to renegotiate NAFTA, which he referred to as the worst trade deal ever made, resonated with these voters.[13] His criticism of Ford's decision to expand auto production in Mexico appealed to the county's many autoworkers.[14] Trump seemed to understand that manufacturing creates wealth, and that America would not become great again by relying solely on a combination of high-tech jobs and low-wage service work.

Macomb County is a markedly different place from Wayne County to the south, which is dominated by sprawling Detroit. Much has been made of that divide, and the Eight Mile Road that separates the counties. But Macomb is also noticeably different from adjoining Oakland County to the west. I discovered that Macomb County doesn't have a very good reputation in southeast Michigan. Whenever I informed new acquaintances in Oakland County that I was reporting on and staying in Macomb, it was often met with a derogatory comment or a sympathetic remark. A college friend of mine who lived in Oakland County texted, "Land of the Deplorables, lol."

A physician friend who lives in Oakland but works at a hospital in Macomb told me she was appalled by the habits of some of the nurses she worked with. "Just give me one nurse who doesn't smoke and has all her teeth," she said.

One day I drove along the border between Oakland and Macomb Counties. On the Oakland side, I saw art supply shops, boutique cafés, and diners. In Rochester, I saw upscale beauty salons, a bike shop, and several juice bars. The liquor stores advertised fine wine, spirits, and cigars. However, as I drove east over the county line on 12 Mile Road, I was greeted by the sprawling General Motors technical center. I also noticed that Michigan's famously poor roads seemed to go from bad to terrible when crossing over from Oakland to Macomb. Then I drove north on highway 53 and noticed that on the Macomb side there were several tanning and tattoo parlors, numerous dollar stores, pawnshops, and fireworks stores. There were at least two gun and ammo stores, a psychic, and several tobacco shops. The liquor stores didn't mention fine wine and spirits—only discount "liquor and lotto." There was even a large Family Video store.

All you really need to know about the difference between Macomb and Oakland Counties is that Kid Rock, famous for displaying enormous Confederate flags and middle finger sculptures at his concerts, was born and grew up in Romeo, a village in Macomb County; meanwhile, Madonna, a frequent Trump critic, grew up a few miles away in Rochester Hills, in Oakland County.

Statistically Oakland is far more prosperous and vibrant than Macomb. Oakland's median family income is nearly $95,000, putting it at the top of the state's eighty-three counties and nearly $28,000 higher than Macomb.[15]

Nearly half of Oakland's residents over the age of twenty-five have a bachelor's degree, whereas less than one-quarter of Macomb's residents do.[16][17] In 2016, Trump won the support of white voters without a college degree, 66 percent to 29 percent.[18] Given these numbers, it's no surprise that Trump won Macomb County, and Clinton won Oakland County.

During the 2016 presidential campaign, Trump pledged to revitalize Michigan's manufacturing base. "We will make Michigan into the manufacturing hub of the world once again," Trump promised at a huge rally in Sterling Heights a few days before the election.[19] At the time of my 2019 visit, nearly three years after that, many manufacturers were nervous about rising tariffs and the status of the North American Free Trade Agreement, which was in the process of being considered by Congress. Meanwhile, Michigan's crumbling infrastructure still hadn't been addressed. Infrastructure Week had become an internet meme and a symbol of Washington's inept attempts to discuss serious policy.[20]

Even so, jobs were abundant and wages were up in the region. In February of that year, the U.S. Bureau of Labor Statistics reported that Macomb County had added 9,118 manufacturing jobs between the fourth quarter of 2016 and the second quarter of 2018, the largest increase of any county in the nation.[21] Fiat Chrysler had recently announced plans for more than $1.5 billion in investment in two Macomb County auto plants that were predicted to create over 1,400 well-paying jobs.

* * *

Later in my 2019 visit, I caught up with George Martin, whom I had met with his friend Darryl Howard two years before. Black men in their late twenties, George and Darryl defy easy political stereotypes. George is a former sailor who voted for Obama in 2012 before turning to Trump, primarily because of his promise to clean up the Department of Veterans Affairs, whose medical facilities he frequented.

Darryl, a married real estate agent with two children, had voted for Mitt Romney in 2012. In 2016, he initially supported Bernie Sanders before "reluctantly" turning to Hillary Clinton, in part because his wife threatened to divorce him if he didn't vote for the Democrat. I couldn't tell if he was kidding about that.

Over the next two years, I had many conversations with George and Darryl. Neither had budged much from their initial assessments of Trump.

Darryl Howard and George Martin in Macomb Township in 2017. (Jordan Allott)

George gave the president credit for the "night-and-day difference" between his experiences at the VA, his efforts to reform the criminal justice system by signing the First Step Act, and the economy, which was humming along. "No matter where you stand on Trump, he's gotten a lot done," George told me in 2019. Like Rasch, Bolder, and Doug, George didn't vote in the 2018 midterms, but he told me he planned to vote for Trump again in 2020.

George is represented in Congress by Rashida Tlaib, one of the president's loudest critics. She came to national prominence by shouting at a party on the night of her swearing in, "We're going to impeach this motherfucker!" in reference to Trump.[22]

Interestingly, George, a Trump supporter, had nice things to say about Tlaib because she's fighting to drop Michigan's highest-in-the-nation auto insurance rates. "When it comes to actual governing, I think she's doing a phenomenal job," he said.

These Michigan voters highlight a trend. Many pundits said that the 2018 midterm elections in which Democrats made significant gains in places Trump won in 2016 presaged success in battleground states for Democrats in 2020. But that's probably not true. A November 2019 poll by *The New York Times's* Upshot newsletter and Siena College found that nearly two-thirds of voters in six battleground states—including Michigan—who had voted for Trump in 2016 and for Democratic congressional candidates in 2018 planned to return to Trump in 2020.[23]

George told me he planned to vote for Trump again. When asked whether he thought Trump would win Macomb County again, he said, "Anywhere that he won before I think he'll win again. I don't think anybody who voted for him wouldn't vote for him again." But George added a note of caution. "I don't think he's picked up any voters either."

I heard something similar from former State Sen. Jack Brandenburg when I met with him at the Crews Inn in Harrison Township on

Lake Saint Clair. A Republican, Brandenburg had spent six years in the Michigan state house and eight in the state senate. When I asked him how he thought Trump was doing, he said, "He's rockin' and rollin,' man. They love him here. Love him here."

Brandenburg explained the thing that matters most to Macomb County voters but, like George Martin, included a note of caution:

Michigan State Sen. Jack Brandenburg in his office in 2017, (Jordan Allott)

I myself think the guy's doing great. The things that I've always deemed important—GDP, unemployment, trade, people vote with their pocket books. I have seen no slippage of his support, but I haven't picked up on people coming over. And I think that's very, very important. You've got to continue to grow your base.

As the week wore on, I was desperate to find at least one regretful Trump voter. So as a last-ditch effort, I wrote an ad on the politics page of Craigslist Macomb County, asking people to respond if they had switched their vote. I got just one reply, but it was illuminating.

"I was a lifelong Democrat until this last election," wrote Don Soulliere in an email to me. "And to be honest everyone I know feels that way too! Every person I have talked to said the same thing: the Democrats have gone off the rails. They have lost a lot of their base."

I asked Soulliere whether any of the former Clinton voters he knows plan to vote for Trump in 2020?

"Everyone I know!" he responded.

* * *

Donald Trump won white women voters in 2016, despite a long history of sexism and despite running against the first female major-party nominee in US history. An important question going into 2020 is whether Trump can replicate or even improve upon that success with this important group of voters. The question is whether the weight of Trump's conservative policies, erratic governing style, and character flaws will alienate white women, and specifically well-educated suburban white women.

But breaking down voters' policy preferences by sex is rarely illuminating. The surprising truth—surprising even though polls bear it out so consistently—is that women generally want the same things men do, even when it comes to so-called women's issues. Consider abortion. When Democrats and journalists talk about the issue, it's usually with the assumption that women support fewer restrictions on it. But according to decades of Gallup polling, women are as likely to think abortion should be "legal under any" circumstances as they are to think it should be "illegal in all" circumstances. And compared to men, women are actually *more likely* to support a blanket ban on abortion and less likely to support its legality "under any" circumstance.[24] In my interviews, women were more likely than men to raise the Democrats' embrace of late-term abortion as a barrier to their voting for Democratic candidates. In spring 2019, as Democratic lawmakers in New York and Virginia were considering laws to loosen restrictions on late-term abortions, at least half a dozen women raised the issue with me.

Consider the controversy over Brett Kavanaugh, who in 2018 became President Trump's pick to replace retiring Justice Anthony Kennedy on the Supreme Court. As Kavanaugh's nomination was being considered, several women accused him of sexual misconduct decades before. Many pundits predicted that women across the country would be sympathetic to the accusers and demand that Kavanaugh's nomination be withdrawn or voted down in the Senate. But most women came down the same way men did—along party lines. I asked more than a dozen Trump-supporting women to respond to the accusations. I wasn't surprised to learn that every one of them vehemently defended Kavanaugh. It never seemed to occur to the pundits that women have fathers, brothers, husbands, and sons, and that they would fear a world where the men they love could have their personal and professional lives destroyed by an unproven, uncorroborated accusation.

During my 2019 trip, I attended a local business awards dinner called the Eddy's in Port Huron, a small city just north of Macomb County near the Canadian border. A middle-aged woman named Crystal Mosher rushed over to me when she heard that I was a journalist researching Trump voters. Perhaps I'd found my regretful Trump voter, I thought. But it wasn't to be. Mosher told me that even though she had been taunted on Facebook for supporting Trump in 2016, she was excited to vote for him again in 2020.

On this trip, I talked to several women who had not voted for Trump but who said their opposition to him had softened. One woman, an immigrant from the Dominican Republic in her mid-thirties, said her opposition to Trump had diminished from "12 out of 10" to "8 out of 10" on the strength of his policies. She said she'd never vote for a Democrat, though she didn't elaborate on why. Still, she wasn't ready to consider voting for Trump.

Later I spoke on the phone with a woman named Kate, a friend of a friend who lives in Macomb County. Kate grew up in Upstate New York, and moved to Michigan more than a dozen years ago. Kate and her husband, who works for General Motors, have two grown children. Kate told me she had initially supported John Kasich in the 2016 primaries, before ultimately turning to Trump. "My vote was for Trump but it was also anything but Hillary," she said.

"He's a savvy businessman," she said. "And I believe if he can manage all of his assets and companies and be as successful as he was, he certainly can help the country. I believe in taking care of vets before people that are here illegally. If I share that with a Democrat, I'm evil. Well, so be it. I guess I'm evil."

I asked Kate whether there was anything Democrats could do to win her vote.

"No, I'll be honest. No," she said. "And I'm not a far-right Republican. I just feel like a lot of Democratic policies are leaning toward socialist policies, and I'm not going down that road. I'd venture to guess that I'm not alone."

That's not to say some women I met weren't reconsidering their support for Trump. An example was a woman named Megan, whom I met in 2017. A middle school principal and teacher in her late thirties, Megan had voted for Trump in 2016. But during our initial meeting in July 2017, Megan was already starting to have second thoughts. She was nervous that Trump was trading grade-school taunts over Twitter with North Korean dictator Kim Jong Un.

The following year, Megan invited me to a chocolate fondue party at her parents' home near Grosse Pointe, just south of Macomb County along the shores of Lake St. Clair. Roughly a dozen family members were present—mostly aunts, uncles, and cousins. Megan and I were the youngest in the group, and the mood was somewhat somber because Megan's mother had recently died. Megan's family is Catholic, and the walls of her parents' home were adorned with religious icons—crucifixes, angels, saints, and the like. A prayer was said before the meal, and then each family member took his or her turn sharing a memory of Megan's mom. Chatting with Megan's family after dinner, I sensed that most were Trump voters.

One uncle said he worked for the city government in Dearborn, where more than a third of residents are Arab American, the largest proportion of any city in the US. He told a series of stories of Middle East immigrants gaming America's welfare system, shaking his head as he relayed each story of fraud and abuse.

Megan reiterated her anxiety about Trump, as did her father, also a Trump voter. They had become weary of Trump's unhinged behavior. "He's an embarrassment," Megan's father said of the president. "I feel like I don't want to leave the country 'til he's gone." Megan said she wished Trump would carry himself more like JFK. I suggested that President Kennedy was as much a philanderer as Trump. Megan agreed but said she didn't care about the sexual stuff. At least Kennedy acted like a statesman, she said.

* * *

Donald Trump won Macomb County on the strength of his support from white working-class voters, to whom he had promised to restrict immigration and bring back jobs. But he also won by attracting the support of Chaldeans and other Middle Eastern Christians, who came out in strong numbers to vote for Trump. Tens of thousands of Iraqi Christians have resettled in the United States in recent decades, first to flee the chaos of the Iran-Iraq War of the 1980s, and more recently to escape the genocidal intentions of the Islamic State and other jihadist Islamic groups. About 120,000 Chaldeans live in southeast Michigan—the largest concentration of Chaldeans anywhere in the US.[25]

Chaldeans practice Eastern rite Catholicism. They have erected churches, started businesses, and become pillars of their communities. Chaldeans have also become reliable supporters of Republican political candidates, including Donald Trump in 2016. But shortly after Trump's term started, some Chaldeans were regretting their vote for Trump. On my first visit to Macomb County, I corresponded with a Chaldean woman. She texted:

> You are not allowed to use my name, but I can tell you that Trump won Michigan bc he lied to the Chaldeans saying he would protect Iraqi Christians. The churches asked everyone to vote for him. Chaldeans from east side went out in droves to vote. My mom has lived here for over 40 years and never voted. She went out that day and voted for him (angry emoji). That's where your story is. He won by like 100k votes here right? ... 80% (of Chaldeans) voted for him ... All for the promise that he would protect Christians in the Middle East. Then made a deal with Iraq to deport Christians home. Not home but back to the county they were born in.

On the 2016 campaign trail, Trump regularly lamented the deaths of Middle Eastern Christians at the hands of Islamic jihadists, and promised that if he became president, he would protect them. In between talk of a Muslim ban and building a wall along the Mexico border, Trump assured besieged Christian minorities that his commitment was ironclad. But on June 11, 2017, Immigration and Customs Enforcement agents arrested and detained 114 Detroit-area Chaldeans in immigration raids. Another 85 Iraqis from other parts of the country were also incarcerated.[26] Most of the men (and a couple of women) had come to the US legally and acquired green cards, which were revoked after they were convicted of crimes. But these men and women had not been deported because Iraq refused to take them.

That changed soon after Trump became president. The Iraqi government agreed to accept the immigrants in exchange for being dropped from the list of countries on Trump's travel ban. The immigrants were taken to a detention center in Youngstown, Ohio, where they awaited deportation for two years. Some of the detained immigrants had committed serious crimes, including murder and rape. But most had committed lesser, nonviolent crimes, paid their debt to society, formed families, and begun contributing to their communities.

Hadeel Khalasawi falls into the latter category. I learned of Hadeel's story when I visited his family at Kabob and More, their restaurant in Hazel Park, just outside Macomb County. Hadeel had immigrated to the US as a child. When he was seventeen years old, he committed a nonviolent gun crime and spent the next nine years in prison. With his criminal conviction, Hadeel lost his permanent resident status. Still, he was never forced to leave the country, and over the next couple of decades he married, had two children, and became a stepfather to his wife Sumar's daughter, Marcella.

Sumar, Marcella, and Hadeel's two sons, Mariano and Malano, are US citizens. Sumar doesn't protest the US government's right to deport criminal immigrants who have lost their permanent resident status. But she says that it's wrong that the government waited so long to do so. "They should have deported them from day one after they committed their crimes," she said. "If they didn't want them in this country, they should have sent them back, not let them go and after twenty or thirty years, come and snatch them away from us and break our hearts…. My husband did make mistakes. He paid for his crimes. They let him out. He started a family. And now they just came after we built this life together."

What's more, Sumar and other Chaldeans said, their loved ones would face near-certain death in Iraq.

"Eventually he's going to get killed," Sumar said of Hadeel if he is forced to return to Iraq. "My husband has tattoos of Christianity. He's a target there after he goes there…. This is my home, this is his home," she said of the US. "He came here when he was four. He doesn't know nothing about Iraq."

Sumar blamed the Trump administration for her family's

Sumar Khalasawi and her daughter, Marcella, and sons, Mariano and Malano. (Jordan Allott)

predicament. "Mr. Trump promised he would help the Chaldean community, he said this is his number one priority, to help them. We voted for Trump. All the Christian people, the Chaldean people, voted for him, that was the first thing he said, that he was going to help them. But he did the opposite."

Hadeel's stepdaughter, Marcella, said it "felt like a really big piece of me was stripped away" when her father was taken away in June. "He took a piece of all of us with him. He was the one to wake me up in the morning, take me out to eat…. We did everything together. He is my father, not biologically, but he earned the privilege to be my father."

"I blame Trump," Marcella added. "(Hadeel) has a family. All of them have families … and he took away the one thing that built the family, the father."

Sumar added, "We respect this country; we love it. We pay our taxes. We voted for Trump because of the things he said, and he lied to us. I'm so embarrassed to say this, but our president lied to us."

Later that day, I spoke with Hadeel, who called in from the deten-tion center. Hadeel said he hoped Trump "could find it in his heart to look over this, and give us a second chance."

The Trump campaign also repeatedly called for the creation of safe zones for persecuted people across the Middle East.[27] Many Chaldeans and other Christians have been calling for a safe haven for Christians in the Nineveh Plain, the establishment of which many Iraqi Christians see as their only chance of survival there. During the Obama administra-tion, Congress and the US State Department declared that a genocide is taking place against Christians and other religious minorities in parts of Syria and Iraq.[28]

Nahren Anweya, an Assyrian Christian activist in Macomb County, believes the Obama administration didn't do enough to help persecuted Christians. She became an outspoken supporter of Trump. Anweya's activism included speaking at several Trump campaign rallies in Michigan and appearing as a surrogate on national media outlets. Many Iraqi Christians voted for Trump with the expectation that he would champion the creation of a safe haven for their loved ones in Iraq, she said, "and I really hope he does not let us down."

"We are still waiting," she said when I met her at her home in Sterling Heights in 2017. "We hope that we are not let down. It's a life-and-death situation for us. We still have hope for him, and we're praying every day that he will follow through."

* * *

On October 13, 2017, President Trump delivered a speech to several thousand people at the Regency Ballroom of the Omni Shoreham Hotel in Washington, DC.[29] The occasion was the Values Voters Summit, an annual gathering of conservative Christian activists from around the country. During his speech, Trump made a minor gaffe, referring to the governor of the Virgin Islands as the president of the Virgin Islands. That slip became the headline of many media outlets' coverage of the speech, reinforcing the notion that Trump is not just ignorant but also that he doesn't much care for brown people who live in US territories, such as the Virgin Islands or Puerto Rico.

"Trump says he met with the president of the Virgin Islands. But that's him," a *Time* magazine headline mocked.[30]

But the media characteristically missed the real significance of Trump's speech. For the thousands of attending Christian conservatives, the speech was a full-throated defense of their view of America's Christian founding, "In America, we don't worship government; we worship God," Trump said to wild applause. "We know that it's the family and the church—not government officials—who know best how to create strong and loving communities," Trump said.

Trump repeatedly used terms like "Judeo-Christian values" and "radical Islamic terrorism." He talked about respect for the flag and saying, "Merry Christmas."

The speech was everything these activists could have wanted and more. More important was Trump's presence at the event. Trump was the first sitting president to address that annual gathering of Christian conservatives.

President George W. Bush was a born-again Christian and conservative Republican. But he never attended the Values Voter Summit even once during his eight years in office, instead sending Vice President Dick Cheney or another surrogate. Like Hillary Clinton's absence in the Rust Belt during the 2016 campaign, Bush probably felt he didn't need to show up because these voters would support him regardless. But Trump didn't take their support for granted. He showed up and told them everything they wanted to hear. They roared their appreciation. Trump attended the summit again in 2019, garnering a similar response.

According to exit polls, Trump won a record 81 percent of white evangelical voters in 2016.[31] This baffled many experts, who couldn't understand how a man who hadn't darkened the door of a church in years and who seemed to personify many of the seven deadly sins could attract such robust support. But for most Christians, the calculus was simple and strategic. With Hillary Clinton, they knew their policy priorities—the appointment of conservative federal judges, the enact-ment of pro-life laws and executive orders, support for Israel, and the like—would be ignored. At least with Trump there was a good chance they'd get some of what they wanted.

And here's the thing: They now feel Trump has come through. He's delivered on the issues Christian voters care about most: two conservative, pro-life Supreme Court justices, hundreds of conserva-tive lower-court judges, a slew of pro-life laws and executive orders, religious conscience protections, unbending support for Israel to the point that the US embassy is moving to Jerusalem, and more. Trump has also delivered rhetorically. He has shown up and made speeches at events, like the Values Voters Summit and the March for Life, and given unprecedented access to pastors and Christian leaders to the White House to pray with him. Many of these same Christian activists had been frozen out of the Bush White House. But Trump regularly invites them to events at the White House, including into the Oval Office.

This is why Trump's character flaws ultimately do not matter that much to evangelical voters. Trump is delivering on policy in a way no other Republican president has done, and he's coming through symboli-cally too. As the cop Catherine Bolder I met at the bar put it, "He's a liar; he's a bully. He's a womanizer. But he's the first president I've seen who actually had a prayer meeting in the Oval Office."

This perspective was explained to me by Gayle, a woman I met at a Tim Horton's in Macomb Township one rainy Saturday morning in 2018. Gayle, a church-going Catholic in her early thirties, had spent most of her life in and around Macomb County. Gayle impressed me as thoughtful and self-assured in her faith. When I asked whether she had voted for Trump because of his personality or policy, she was quick to answer. "I didn't vote for Trump because of a(n emotional) connec-tion," she said. "It was policy." Gayle frequents conservative Christian websites such as LifeSitenews.com and Catholic News Agency, where Trump's speech at the Values Voter summit was covered in a much different way than at CNN or Time.

Trump's verbal slip about the Virgin Islands wasn't mentioned at all. But the content of Trump's speech was. LifeSite News's headline read: "President Trump: Our 'religious heritage' will be cherished, protected, and defended."[32]

When I asked Gayle which of Trump's policies she liked, she said, "I am very pleased with his Supreme Court nominations. Very pleased. So that's the reason I supported him, and he's coming through." Gayle added that she was very likely to vote for Trump again in 2020.

5

GRANT COUNTY, WEST VIRGINIA

WHEN BRENDA SAMS was released from prison in April 2016, she feared what would happen upon her return home. The Federal Correctional Institution in Hazleton, where she had served twenty-one months for conspiracy to distribute drugs, had become her "safe space" away from drugs and the culture surrounding it. Before her imprisonment, Brenda was shooting up two grams of heroin a day. Her addiction had such a hold on her that she would sometimes send ice water coursing through her veins just to experience the ritual of the needle. In prison Brenda had gotten clean, started going to church, and earned her GED. "I was scared," she said when I met her in October 2017 at the Petersburg Dairy Queen where she was a manager. "I didn't know how to do it on the outside. I prayed to God, and I asked God to surrender myself."

Brenda had reason to be fearful. One morning shortly after returning to Petersburg, she received a text from a local dealer named Larry, who said he had left her a surprise in her parents' mailbox. She walked out to the mailbox, opened it, and looked inside. She found an oxycodone pill, an implicit invitation to start using again. "I guess he thought I was going to pick up where I left off," Brenda said. But Brenda didn't pick up where she left off, at least not initially. In the year-and-a-half between her release and when I met her, Brenda had gotten a job, made new friends, and become certified in peer-recovery coaching and suicide prevention. Most importantly to Brenda, her parents had given her back their house keys—a remarkable gesture, given that they once feared she might kill them in her quest to get high.

Ray Blum, who owns the Dairy Queen store Brenda helped to manage, has hired several recovering addicts. He said it was a necessity, given the dearth of available workers in this city of 2,500 people.

Those who struggle with drug addiction often find it difficult to work, in part because their drug convictions scare off potential employers. A 2017 study suggested that one-fifth to one-quarter of the reduction in labor force participation in

Brenda Sams in 2017. (Jordan Allott)

recent years was due to opioid use.[1] When people talk about the opioid epidemic, they're generally referring to the increase in the use and abuse of prescription and nonprescription painkillers over the last two decades. These drugs include strong painkillers such as OxyContin as well as the ultra-strong Fentanyl, a synthetic opioid that's as much as 100 times as powerful as morphine and can kill in seconds. Fentanyl is so potent that first responders have been exposed to harmful or even lethal doses just by being in close proximity to the drug.[2] The use of heroin, which is also an opioid, and methamphetamines are also at crisis levels.

According to the US Drug Enforcement Administration, overdose deaths have reached epidemic proportions.[3] Drug overdose kills 192 people a day nationwide, making it the leading cause of accidental death in America and the leading cause of death of Americans under age fifty. To put the scale of the crisis into perspective, more than 67,000 Americans died from drug overdoses in 2018, exceeding the number of Americans who died in the Vietnam and Iraq wars combined.[4] Some public health experts estimate that the epidemic could kill nearly half a million people over the next decade.[5]

West Virginia is sometimes called Ground Zero for the opioid crisis. Its overdose death rate is nearly three times the national average and by far the highest of any state in the country.[6] In 2016, the state spent $1 million just on the transportation of corpses after overdoses.[7] Things have gotten so bad that some drug dealers are carrying NARCAN, a medication that blocks the effects of opioids in an overdose, to give or sell to customers who overdose. Dead customers, after all, are bad for business. Even worse, schools in some heavily afflicted areas are teaching young children how to recognize signs of overdose and administer NARCAN in the event that their parents need it.[8]

One of the main causes of the crisis was the over-prescription of opioid painkillers that started in the late 1990s. An investigation by the *Charleston Gazette-Mail* found that between 2007 and 2012, 780 million doses of the opioids hydrocodone and oxycodone were shipped to West Virginia—about 433 pain pills for every man, woman, and child in the state.[9] The investigation further found that the two drugs killed at least 1,700 West Virginians over that period. Judy's Drug Store, directly across the street from Dairy Queen in Petersburg, was sued in 2016 by West Virginia's attorney general for dispensing too many prescription painkillers. The complaint charged that over six years, nearly 2 million doses of hydrocodone and oxycodone were dispensed to a three-county region of just 34,000 residents.[10]

I asked Brenda's friend Adam Kesner, another Dairy Queen employee with a long history of addiction, what kinds of drugs can be found in Petersburg. "Anything and everything, my man," he said.

On October 26, 2017, President Trump declared America's addiction crisis to be a public health emergency. Trump pledged to expand access to telemedicine services, spend "lots of money" to push "very hard the concept of non-addictive painkillers," and launch "really tough, really big, really great advertising so we get to people before they start."[11]

On the day of Trump's declaration, I talked to nearly a dozen former addicts, parents and relatives of addicts, and recovery coaches at Welton Park, on the outskirts of Petersburg. Several themes ran through the stories I heard: early drug experimentation leading to spiraling addiction, which, aided by abusive spouses and doctors ever-willing to prescribe pain pills, left a trail of unemployment, suicide attempts, broken relationships, and fractured families.

Brenda Sams and Adam Kesner in 2017. (Daniel Allott)

August Parker explained how drugs became a cornerstone of her life after she began experimenting with them in her early teens. Even her wedding to a drug addict when she was eighteen revolved around her addiction. "We got married on 4-20. We made sure the wedding was at five o'clock, so that everybody could get high," she said. A few years later, she and her husband were arrested for manufacturing methamphetamines, an episode that sparked a turnaround in their lives.

Roger Dodd got hooked early too, pilfering Percocet pain pills from his grandmother when he was just nine. "She'd get out of bed, and she could barely walk," he recalled. "About fifteen minutes after taking that magic little pill, she was hopping and dancing and singing, and so I wanted to try it." That experimentation initiated decades of drug and alcohol abuse.

"I just destroyed a lot of lives along the way," Dodd said. "I just left behind this like, like a wake, like a boat does, except mine was broken hearts and shattered marriages, three of them. I let my addiction take its hold on everyone else."

Brandi Braithwaite knows what that hold feels like. She experienced addiction through her then-husband and her brother, who died from an overdose. She sees a lot of addicts in her job as a nurse at a local jail. Jails have become America's primary centers of opioid detox, a role they are not nearly prepared to assume. But even in jail and prison, illegal drugs "are available to anyone who wants them bad enough," Braithwaite said. "It's like nothing, like a walk in the park—if you got money."

Recovering addicts place a lot of emphasis on peer-recovery coaching, mentoring from someone who has struggled with addiction. "Addicts want to know that you've been where they've been," Bob Borror, a sixty-eight-year-old recovering alcoholic, explained later. "It's easy to say, 'Buck up.' But if you're an addict, you're more honest with them, and they're more honest with you."

All of the people I met at Welton Park dismissed the effect that a punitive approach to the drug crisis would have. "We can't arrest our way out of this problem," was the phrase I heard over and over. "Making felons out of people who have a disease is not the way to get out of it," said Dodd. "If you arrested people who had cancer, is that going to cure them? No, it's not. You offer them treatment."

Many of the people I spoke with lamented the dearth of treatment options available to recovering addicts in the area. "As many times as I went in front of a judge and went to jail, I was never offered rehab," Brenda said. "Not one time. I've never been to rehab. I've never gotten anything like that. I've done all of this with support from my family."

I asked if anyone had a message they'd like to give to President Trump. Dodd spoke up. "You consider yourself the people's president," he said, continuing:

You keep saying you're not (about) politics as usual, that you're for the people. Well, bring yourself down here and talk to these people. Take your tie off, get all your cabinet members, take your suits and your ties off, come down here, sit down and listen. Don't tell us what to do. Listen to us. Then maybe you'll know the right way to spend the money.

Former addicts and their families speak with Daniel Allott about the drug crisis. (Jordan Allott)

A couple of weeks later, I met with Cindy Corbin, who was then the executive director of Hampshire County Pathways, a recovery center for people with substance abuse and mental health problems. After showing me around her facility, which includes a drug recovery home for women, Corbin said there had been a huge increase in demand for recovery services since the organization opened in 2012. "It used to be we would help place someone in treatment every other month," she said. "Now we get twelve or thirteen a month and that doesn't include people who call in." At the time, advocates were waiting to see whether Congress would devote additional funds to address the crisis. President Trump's public health emergency declaration did not unlock new federal funds. But federal agencies were directed to devote more of their budgets to the problem, and many had already been spending more.

In 2017, the Department of Health and Human Services committed $144 million in additional grants to address opioid abuse, including funding for first responders and for pregnant and postpartum women.[12] The same month, the Centers for Disease Control and Prevention awarded more than $28 million in additional funding and the Justice Department nearly $59 million.[13, 14] But those numbers pale in comparison to the costs of the crisis. The White House Council of Economic Advisers estimated that the true cost in 2018 was $696 billion—six times higher than previous estimates.[15]

Corbin stressed how desperately her organization and others like it needed funding. She constantly worried about losing recovery coaches to Sheetz because the gas station chain can afford to pay them more and offers health insurance. Corbin said President Trump and other politicians talked a lot about combatting the drug crisis but hadn't devoted much money to it. "I want to see the money. Show me the money," she said. "Show me where you're going to put the money in helping the United States with this horrible epidemic. Let's get it into treatment; let's get it into recovery services."

Later I met with Bryan Ward, sheriff of adjacent Hardy County, where the overdose crisis is just as bad. Ward estimated that 95 percent of property crimes in his county are drug-related. Ward too said he doesn't know a family in his county of 14,000 people that hasn't been directly affected by the overdose epidemic. He said the root of the problem is a decaying culture in which faith is in decline and drug addiction no longer carries the stigma it once did. "The best chance of recovery is for people to lean on God," he said. "Almost all the people who have pulled themselves through have done so because of faith. We are never going to be able to arrest our way out of the problem because there's a never-ending supply of possible users."

Later, driving around Petersburg, Brenda showed me some of her old haunts—the house where she tried heroin for the first time and the place where she caught her federal charge. She pointed out Larry's house, saying that he still deals. "People try to call the cops but they don't do anything about it," she said. Back at her apartment behind Dairy Queen, Brenda and her parents told me their story. She started taking pain pills when she was twenty-four because they made her feel comfortable in her own skin for the first time in her life. "I could even look in the mirror and smile once in a while," she said about the effect the pills had. Heroin took the high to another level. "Heroin, the love of my life, my best friend … the people that loved me, they couldn't compare to the heroin, and I didn't know what to do about it."

In recovery, Brenda said she knew what she had to do to stay clean, including steering clear of old friends and staying close to her parents. Brenda's mother, Dianna Alt, said she had seen her daughter transform for the better in the last couple of years. "Before she was clean, you never knew what she was going to do. You didn't know if she was going to kill ya," Dianna said. "One time, she was standing there flipping a knife. And we got to thinking, 'Oh Lord, is she going to try to stab one of us because we don't have the money to give her? … But we never ever gave up on her," Dianna said through tears. "And we can't tell her enough that we love her and that we are so, so proud of her and so glad to have her home."

"Just to have them back and have the house key again and make them proud of me is worth sobriety to me," Brenda added. Something else Brenda said really stuck with me, reinforcing just how much she had invested in her recovery. "If I ever lost my clean date—August 29, 2014—I don't think I would try going through this all again," she said. "I would go to heroin overdose and end it."

* * *

Grant County is a rural county of roughly 12,000 people on West Virginia's Eastern Panhandle. It includes mountains, forests, wilderness, and fertile valleys along the south branch of the Potomac River and its tributaries. Geographically, it lies only 140 miles from Washington DC; culturally, it's a world apart. There is a striking dichotomy to the county. It's rich in natural resources and beautiful topography but poor in healthy food, transportation, and good jobs.

Grant County, West Virginia. (Jordan Allott)

Unlike much of the state, which has only recently turned Republican, Grant County has always voted overwhelmingly for the party of its presidential namesake. In fact, the county has never given a Democratic presidential candidate so much as 40 percent of its vote since its creation after the Civil War. That included 2016, when Hillary Clinton earned less than half that.[16] Grant County is the Trumpiest county in one of America's Trumpiest states. Eighty-eight percent of its voters backed Trump in 2016, the highest share of any of West Virginia's fifty-five counties. West Virginia was the second most pro-Trump state; 68 percent of Mountain State voters supported Trump, only 0.3 points behind Wyoming.

I included Grant County in my study as a way to keep my finger on the pulse of Trump's most ardent backers. But I soon discovered that Donald Trump was only tangential to Grant County's story. The real story was the public health crisis that had touched the life of nearly every resident there. Often, I would be interviewing someone about politics when I'd mention the drug crisis, and my interview subject would reveal that somebody close to them had died from an overdose. That's what happened when I spoke with Charlie Combs. He invited me over to his home in Cabins, just outside Petersburg. We talked about politics for nearly two hours.

Charlie explained that much of the overwhelming local support Trump received had to do with people's aversion to Hillary Clinton. "They did this," he said, holding his nose to suggest that many people here thought of Trump as the more acceptable of two undesirable options. "The Republicans are stupid," Combs said, "but the Democrats are godless."

Combs is a retired forest ranger and water resource inspector. He railed against America's $25 trillion national debt and complained that Trump would do little to reduce it. Lowering the debt and balancing the budget are moral issues to Combs. "I'm not smart, but I'm not clear stupid, either. If I'm that much in debt, I think my first order of business is to get that in order before taking on something like healthcare reform."

I asked Combs how he thought Trump was performing. "Alright," he answered, but "I wish they'd let him do his job." The "they," he explained, was everyone else in politics—Democrats, Republicans, and especially the media. Combs said he wished Trump would just shut up sometimes, though he conceded that "the rednecks, for lack of a better term," ate up Trump's name-calling, in particular his labeling of NFL players who kneel to protest the American flag as "SOBs."

"I'm not sure about Mr. Trump," he said after a short pause. "The things he's said are definitely not a Christian attitude. He scares me a bit. But I pray for him. Sometimes it's hard to."

Then my conversation with Combs, as with most of my conversations in Petersburg, turned to drugs and the devastating toll they've taken on this community. On the table beside me sat a Bible, and on the wall in front of me hung pictures of Combs's family, including his two sons, Brent and Ryan. I mentioned that I thought an artist's rendering of Brent, looking stolid and wearing a cowboy hat in a portrait hanging on the wall, looked very well done. "Yeah, but they didn't get the eyes quite right," Combs said.

"My son died of a drug overdose a year ago," Combs then said of Brent.

Combs said Brent had been struggling with an addiction that may have been precipitated by his parents' divorce. "Here was a young man, athletically and intellectually gifted," Combs said. "He fell in with the wrong people, just about the time of the divorce. We didn't know it. I'm as dumb as a hog (when it comes to) drugs. Most of this stuff had to be explained to me." At the time, Combs didn't understand that opioids activate the reward regions of the brain, causing intense pleasure and "that nothing else in life was giving (Brent) this pleasure." Combs said that his son thought he wouldn't allow the drugs to get the better of him. "My son was smart, an IQ in the 130s. (Brent and his friends) felt they were smarter, had more information." Brent became addicted, got clean, then relapsed. Eventually he was arrested for trying to buy drugs in Baltimore. He went to prison, was released, then relapsed again.

"Fentanyl killed my son," Combs said. "It's here in Petersburg. It's everywhere."

The overdose crisis in Petersburg was the subject of a 2019 documentary film, *Overdosed*, that chronicles how drugs took hold in this city of 2,500 people. The film features Breanne McUlty, who grew up around drugs, began using them, and became one of the town's leading dealers as a teenager.[17] McUlty sold it all—morphine, pain pills, meth, black tar heroin. The drugs were everywhere. Her father, boyfriend, and friends were all using, and many were also selling. "It was like passing out candy on Halloween," she told me in 2017. "I can't say there isn't one person I know who hasn't been strung out."

McUlty was eventually caught and served several years in prison. She

Charlie Combs of Cabins, West Virginia, standing next to a portrait of his son Brent in 2017. (Daniel Allott)

dreaded her release because she feared the environment that awaited her upon her return. She had reason to be scared. "I met my son's father, also a recovering addict," she said of what happened after her release. "I got pregnant really quickly and moved in really quickly. More drugs in the house, and I was losing my mind. I was so mad at everybody." In 2017 McUlty moved to Georgia after the overdose death of a dear friend. "I wanted to change this fucked-up situation," she said about what finally prompted her to leave.

Just about everyone I encountered in West Virginia seemed to have at least one close friend or family member who used or died from drugs. In Mia VanSant's case, she doesn't know a family member who *hasn't* been an addict. "I'm the only person in my family right now who hasn't had an active addiction," she told me when I visited her at the offices of Burlington United Methodist Family Services in Burlington, a few miles north of Petersburg. VanSant connects the children of addicts with foster families. "Right now in West Virginia, we're at a crisis point," she said. She estimated that 85 percent of her cases are the result of substance abuse.

I also spoke with Carrie Fradiska, who runs a recovery home for women. I asked VanSant and Fradiska how easy it is to obtain drugs in the area. VanSant laughed. "You can walk down the street," she said. "There were a couple of McDonald's where you could go through the drive-through and get it in your happy meal," Fradiska added.

VanSant said that from her office in Martinsburg (further east on West Virginia's Eastern Panhandle), "I can look out the window of my office and see people do drug deals."

Later I met with Allen Evans and Bill Hamilton, who served in the West Virginia House of Delegates. Again, I was there to talk politics, but again, the real story soon emerged, with all the familiar themes. "I don't think there is a family that's not touched by the disease of addiction," said Hamilton. "And addiction *is* a disease," he said, adding that he has a son with a substance abuse problem.

Evans said that employers are unable to fill vacancies because of drug-testing requirements. "Companies are interviewing fifty people and only ten qualify," Hamilton said.

I visited Erin Camp, managing editor of the *Grant County Press*. She said that the opioid problem is in the news just about every day. I asked her what issues were most important to people. I offered immigration reform and the border wall as examples. "A lot of people support the wall," she said. "But I'll tell you what people really want—they want an answer to the drug problem."

Back in Cabins, Charlie Combs told me he doubted that the government was up to the task of addressing the drug crisis. "I don't think the country has the morals and values to take an issue like this head on and deal with it," he said. What bothered him most was that the big pharmaceutical companies were still irresponsibly producing the drugs and seemed not to have been held to account. Then Combs sat back in his chair a little and glanced up at the portrait of his son. "It's been a year on April 28," he said, his eyes filling with tears, "and it's still surreal."

* * *

I saw Combs again a year after our initial interview. I had just walked through the back door of Main Street United Methodist Church in Petersburg when I spotted him. I approached, hoping to get his most recent thoughts on politics. But Combs politely said he wasn't interested in being interviewed. He had grown tired of the political discussion. He felt that it failed to get to the heart of what's ailing America. The thing that was really hurting America was much deeper than the political debates of the day. It was all a distraction, he said.

Charlie repeated that while he doesn't like Trump's behavior he didn't think the Democrats behaved any better. And he believed that Trump should be seen more as a symptom of the problem that ails America, not its cause. The real cause was that the nation had turned its back on its Judeo-Christian values. He mentioned abortion and gay marriage as fundamental issues that were tearing the country apart. "When we can't even agree on the truth," he said, pointing at a Bible next to him, "then how in the world would we agree on politics?"

After speaking with Charlie, I walked into the church and sat down in a pew near the back. The church was populated mostly by older men and women. Of the twenty-five or so congregants, only three or four appeared to be under forty years old, and only a couple more under fifty. The only person of color was a young black man sitting on the opposite side. Most of the service was spent praying for absent congregants and for the health of sick family members. At one point, most of the congregation got up and performed a laying on of hands to alleviate the stress the pastor was going through. A touching video was screened, featuring a boy with a physical disability whose father took him along with him on marathons and triathlons. It struck me that the church was a meeting place and social hub in a town that doesn't have many of either. But it's also a place of healing in an area that's in desperate need of it.

After the service, a lunch was held for the congregation. I grabbed a pulled pork sandwich and a bowl of chicken and rice soup and sat down next to the black man I'd spotted in church earlier. He told me his name was Dmitri. He was a medical student from Cameroon and was attending an osteopathic medical school in Maryland. He was about to enter his final year of medical school and was doing his medical training in Petersburg. Dmitri had been living in Petersburg for five months and said he'd been welcomed with open arms, both by the church and the broader community.

"There's not much to do here, but this is a nice community," he said. He confessed that he was a little surprised by how gracious people were. "I wasn't expecting to feel comfortable here."

"What were you expecting?" I asked.

"I was expecting people to be like, 'What are *you* doing here? Get out of here!" he said, laughing.

* * *

Brenda Sams and I stayed in touch over the next few months, occasionally sending messages over text or Facebook messenger. But one day she wrote to say she had broken the terms of her probation, relapsed, and was headed back to prison, where she wouldn't have access to her phone or the internet. My thoughts immediately jumped to what Brenda had said she might do if she ever lost her clean date—"go to heroin overdose and end it." I told her I'd pray for her and later wrote a letter of support to the judge presiding over her case.

About a year later, I saw on Facebook that Brenda had been released from prison and moved back to Petersburg. I contacted her, and she agreed to meet with me when I returned. But on the day we were supposed to meet, she canceled and then stopped responding to my messages. Later on her Facebook page, she described relapsing after three years of recovery as "the worst feeling that I had ever had in my entire life":

> Losing my clean date, hurting the people that love me, going back to prison for a year, and starting all over once again. So, if you are thinking of using, don't do it!! It's not worth it!! Relapse is not a part of recovery, it's a lack of it so pay very close attention to your thoughts and ask for help before making that choice. It will have consequences, I promise.

I contacted some of the other recovering drug addicts I had spoken with in 2017, but most didn't respond. Then one day, I saw Roger Dodd at a health care clinic at a furniture factory in Moorefield, a few miles from Petersburg. Dodd was volunteering at an informational table for the Russ Hedrick Recovery Resource Center in Petersburg. We exchanged greetings, and I asked him about Brenda. He said he had talked to her that day but wasn't surprised she didn't want to meet. Dodd said articles I had written about the drug problem in Petersburg had created something of a backlash—apparently some people didn't appreciate their dirty laundry being aired in public. Several people told me that the *Overdose* documentary film had split the town "down the middle."

There were people in Petersburg who weren't interested in talking about the overdose crisis. One person who seemed to want to ignore the problem was Petersburg Mayor Gary Michael. When I raised the issue to him, he downplayed the extent of the problem. "My opinion is, I don't think we have a bad drug problem," he told me. One person who would speak with me candidly was Cindi Corbin, the executive director of Hampshire County Pathways. She explained that shame is the dominant emotion among people who relapse.

"When they're doing well and then they fall off that pedestal, it's very difficult," she said. "That's especially true in small towns, where everyone knows everyone and knows each other's business.... When people with substance abuse disorders relapse, they relapse in their head well before they do anything," Corbin explained. "They stop doing the things they do every day that keeps them sober. Every addict who relapses says the

Chekpa Wilkinson and Devin Corbin in 2019. (Daniel Allott)

same thing: I stopped doing the things I know kept me sober."

Corbin said that Hampshire Pathways was caring for more patients than it could handle. It had added a recovery coach specifically to work with people who had overdosed and another to work with those reentering the community after imprisonment.

Corbin has had a difficult and colorful life. She was adopted as a heroin baby and started having kids early in life—three by the time she was in her early twenties. Before her work in health care, she owned a strip club for many years. Cindi was very open with me about her own serious mental health challenges. "Just like they struggle with cravings with drugs, I struggle with my mental health," she once told me over lunch in Romney, north of Petersburg. "Part of my depression and anxiety is when it gets bad, I go right to being suicidal, on an at least monthly basis, sometimes weekly…. Yesterday was a really bad day," she told me. "For probably an hour, I struggled with those thoughts. So, yeah it is a monster. It is the same monster as addiction. I struggled just like they do, and it really is a struggle."

"What do you do when that happens?" I asked.

I use some breathing techniques. I make myself utilize my wellness tools—take a walk, play with my dog. Read. Distract myself. I am very aware of what is happening. When the thoughts are there, I can usually pull myself out of it. But when the thoughts are there and then I start googling poisons or methods of suicide, I know that I am starting on that spiral. But I am aware of it and aware what that means.

Corbin's first husband was a drug addict, and her son Devin is a recovering addict. Devin and his girlfriend, Chekpa, are "travelers," or drifters. They don't work and roam the country full time, spending nights under bridges and at bus stops. I asked Corbin whether she's afraid Devin will relapse.

"Every day," she said.

He says that he won't use heroin again. My fear is he is so specific about heroin and opiates. I fear he is using other things. Other than marijuana … I know about that. But when I take the executive director hat off and put on the mom hat, I'll take that every day of the week over him putting needles in his arms.

Corbin said she thought more people were getting help but that just as many people were using drugs. She still felt insufficient money was being spent to address the problem. I asked for her thoughts on President Trump's commitment to tackling the problem. "Do I think he's doing a bad job?" she said. "No—it's just status quo."

Later I met up with Sheriff Bryan Ward at El Rancho Mexican Restaurant in Moorefield. "The opioid crisis, you could throw all the resources in the world at it," he told me after he had said a prayer over our food. "But until you get at the root of it, and have people aspire to do something other than become addicts, law enforcement is never going to be the cure." Born and raised in Maryland, Ward moved to West Virginia when he was eighteen. "It was Mayberry," he said of the sense of community and lack of crime before drugs moved in. "They gave me the keys to the cruiser before I had any training. I've had a neat career—storybook, really. I love the people here."

Then we talked politics. Ward said he had been elected sheriff twice as a Democrat. "I've been a Democrat since I moved up here. And about a year ago, I decided I just couldn't stand to be recognized as a Democrat anymore because they lost their way. They've been hijacked by socialists. I put a piece on my Facebook page, and I'll probably never get elected to anything because of that. I went ahead and wrote #Walk Away." He wrote on his Facebook page that he saw the national Democratic platform as "nothing short of a betrayal to the values of every God fearing, hardworking American." He said that he decided to switch parties after he could no longer explain to his daughter why he was a Democrat. "If you're a Democrat, what do you believe in?" he said. "No God. Punish those who succeed. Kill babies."

Then we talked about race. I asked him whether as a white man he feels he has privileges that others don't enjoy. "No. No. And I take great offense to that," he replied. "I have had the privilege of growing up around some of the hardest-working black people, Hispanics et cetera. They succeeded because of character and hard work." He continued: "If I'm on patrol, if I see a vehicle swerving, I turn on my blue lights. As I walk up to the car, the first thing I hear is that I must've pulled them over because I'm a racist. It infuriates me. I didn't know they were black when I pulled them over. It was dark out."

"You've heard that?" I asked.

"Oh, many times," Ward responded, becoming slightly agitated as he recounted some of the incidents.

"Are there racists?" he asked. "Of course, but there are probably just as many black racists as there are white racists."

A few days later, over a spaghetti dinner at his home, Ward explained that he doesn't recognize the party that he'd been a member of for most of his adult life. "I was always a Blue Dog Democrat. My positions haven't evolved. I've been a hopeless conservative my whole life."

He said he "absolutely loves" Trump's policies, on the economy, abortion, immigration as well as the priority he's given to tackling the opioid crisis. "Trump is the only time in my lifetime a politician has done exactly what he promised," he said.

* * *

As a presidential candidate, Donald Trump promised to fight the overdose epidemic by providing more aggressive interdiction of drugs at the US-Mexico border and more funding for treatment. "We will give people struggling with addiction access to the help they need," he said on the 2016 campaign trail.[18] Now, as he runs for re-election, President Trump has been touting his record in delivering on those promises. "With unyielding commitment, we are curbing the opioid epidemic," he stated in his 2020 State of the Union address.[19]

Most public health advocates say that the Trump administration has made some modest progress in alleviating the crisis, especially compared to the Obama administration's anemic response. In the year after Trump declared a public health emergency, his administration raised $6 billion in new funding to address the epidemic.[20] Trump signed two major pieces of legislation addressing both the public health and law enforcement aspects of the problem.[21]

Hardy County Sheriff Bryan Ward in 2017. (Jordan Allott)

Opioid prescriptions are down dramatically from their peak in 2012, and the last couple of years have also seen large increases in the amount of cocaine, meth, and Fentanyl seized at the southern border.[22, 23]

Overdose deaths from prescription drugs and heroin are slowing. In 2018, for the first time in twenty-eight years, there was a decline in the number of people who died from overdose, according to the Centers for Disease Control and Prevention.[24] Fifteen states saw declines in overdose fatalities, including West Virginia. The same year, for the first time in four years, life expectancy rose in the US.

I was aware of these statistics when I visited Grant County for the final time in February 2020. I expected to hear that the situation was beginning to improve, that people were finally getting the help they needed, and that residents were cautiously optimistic about Petersburg's future. But it quickly became clear that whatever progress was being made in combating the overdose crisis, it wasn't being made in Petersburg.

I spoke with more than a dozen rehab specialists, medical professionals, peer recovery coaches, volunteers, former addicts, police officers, local journalists, and others. The consensus among them was that the situation had actually gotten worse. "There's been more overdoses," Brandi Braithwaite said when she and her husband Kurtis met me for lunch at a Petersburg restaurant. "There was just one yesterday—a mother who has four young kids."

Kurtis added that a man he'd gone to school with had also recently died from an overdose.

"Anyone who thinks things are getting better needs to come here," Brandi said.

In addition to the good news of the drop in overdose deaths and increase in life expectancy, the CDC reported some bad news: overdoses from cocaine, synthetic opioids like fentanyl, and stimulants such as methamphetamines were on the rise.[25] That certainly seemed to be the case in Petersburg. "The meth and heroin has gotten really out of control," Brandi said. "We're losing a lot of people, a lot of young lives to it."

The resurgence of these drugs prompted the federal government in January to begin allowing states to use federal money earmarked for the opioid epidemic to assist people struggling with meth and cocaine.[26] As prescription opioids have become less available, addicts have been turning to drugs they can manufacture themselves. A police officer told Brandi that he'd recently raided a home whose occupants were shooting up Drano for want of anything else.

Kurtis said krokodil—a homemade heroin substitute whose poisonous ingredients quickly turn the skin gray and scaly like a crocodile's as it rots the user from the inside out—had been "going around" in nearby Cumberland, Maryland.

Some residents I spoke with said they were grateful that more treatment options were becoming available and that there seemed to be a greater awareness of the addiction problem in Petersburg. But others said that those most in need of help still weren't getting it. Brandi's fifteen-year-old nephew had recently been sent to a juvenile jail for drug use instead of being offered treatment. "Throwing addicts in jail is probably about the most pointless, useless thing you're ever going to do," she said. "You need to put them in a rehab facility."

All over the Petersburg area, I saw signs that the crisis had not abated. I saw it in the boisterous couple sitting at a nearby booth in a Mexican restaurant in Moorefield, euphorically high on something other than margaritas; in the woman who appeared to be passed out in her car in the Dollar General parking lot; and in the young man loitering outside the Petersburg McDonald's in the rainy darkness, waiting, perhaps, for a buyer to appear.

Both of the Braithwaites' ex-spouses are addicts, and Kurtis used to be one too. "I don't like to talk about it a lot, but I went down that path for a long time," he confessed. Kurtis's story sounded like so many others I had heard. He started out on prescription opioids after a bad accident in 2010. Then drugs took over his entire life, eventually costing him a marriage, his friends, and everything he owned. Meeting and marrying Brandi, and moving to a new city, put him on a new path. "I fought it for, shit, probably five years or better before I stopped," he said. "But it's been three years (of recovery) now."

I asked the couple to forecast what the drug climate in Petersburg would look like in ten years.

"I feel like it's probably going to be worse," Brandi said.

I feel like all you have is a bunch of children who are raising themselves, who their only coping skills are drugs, drinking, that kind of lifestyle. … I feel like that's kind of where it goes. And so when these children get older, you usually become what you are raised around. You're in a house where (the adults) are strung out on drugs or drunk, or never there. So the kids are raising themselves.

There's so many people in their twenties who look like they're in their fifties. …One thing that my children's generation is going to have in common in this area is there's going to be a group of kids who all lost their parents to drugs. That's going to be (what they have in) common.

It is often said that addiction doesn't discriminate, that it doesn't care how much money you have, what you look like, how old you are, or where you live; it's said that addiction is an equal-opportunity destroyer. That message is meant to democratize addiction, to lessen its stigma, and to encourage us to be less judgmental and more compassionate in our responses. But addiction *does* discriminate. In the same way that a viral infection strikes when our immune system is weak, the effects of addiction are most devastating in places where communities are weak—where good jobs are scarce, health is poor, families are fragile, and civil society has receded. Places like Petersburg.

A lot of attention has been given to the link between drug abuse and declining economic opportunities, particularly manufacturing job loss. But much less attention has been given to the link between broken families and substance abuse and addiction. Academic studies have found strong correlations between childhood abuse, parental substance abuse, family dysfunction, and subsequent drug abuse.[27]

Grant County's teen birth rate is more than three times higher than the national average.[28] And its share of children born to unwed mothers—an astounding 87 percent—is more than twice the national average.[29] According to a study by the Annie E. Casey Foundation, between 2000 and 2017, the number of children in foster care declined by 19 percent nationally.[30] But it rose by 96 percent in West Virginia. And as Mia VanSant of Burlington United Methodist Family Services told me, most of those cases—85 percent by her estimation—are the result of substance abuse.

The story of addiction and overdose cannot be told without also telling the story of fractured families. Almost every story I heard included a broken family as either a cause or consequence of addiction, and often both. Charlie Combs said he suspected his son's addiction had been triggered by his parents' divorce. Roger Dodd said his addiction left a destructive wake that included three failed marriages. A former addict named Charles told me that the "source" of his addiction was a broken home. "My dad did the best he could," Charles said. "My mom wasn't there. He raised me the best he knew how, which was chaos. That's what we grew up in."

Meanwhile, almost every story of recovery involved a family's patient and unconditional love. "I've done all of this with support from my family," Brenda Sams had said about her parents' abiding love through the ups and downs of her recovery.

Talking to the Braithwaites, it was clear to me that the presence of a smart, strong, and determined woman was keeping Kurtis focused on his family instead of drugs. "Everybody chases the adrenaline rush," Brandi said. "Everybody likes to feel good. But you have to find something that's healthy. Like now, he's got our family. And he makes long to-do lists of things that he'll have to do. I mean, those are things that he does to occupy his time and himself now. We make an effort to do things together. If we're not at work, we're doing family things."

* * *

My final stop in Petersburg was Vickie Smith's trailer on the north side of town. "This is the ghetto," Vickie announced with a laugh when I arrived. "Actually, they call it the field, the drug field. You got fields all around you, but on these two streets—drug houses."

Vickie's daughter Jenny and Jenny's husband, Kevin, both recovering addicts in their early thirties, joined us. Jenny estimated that every other house on the block deals drugs. "I know this because I've done them around here, and that's just where they are," she said. The police had raided a neighbor's home a few nights earlier, Vickie said, and the "guy who lives across the street, Otis, found crystal meth in his yard the other day that someone had dropped."

When Jenny and Kevin were addicted, they lost everything—their home, cars, and their two children. Kevin also spent some time in jail. "We had everything, we lost it all," Kevin said. Jenny said her newborn is with a foster family and toddler with her ex-husband, who she suspects is using drugs.

Kevin works at Pilgrim's Pride, a chicken processor, and says drugs are rampant there too. He and Jenny have been clean for about a year.

Vickie railed against the hypocrisy and holier-than-thou attitude of some people in Petersburg. "This community don't care," Vickie said. "They honestly do not care. If you are high up in this community, nothing will be posted about your drug addiction or your child's drug addiction or arrest. If you're a poor person, it's going all over Facebook and in the newspaper because this community flat-out don't care."

Then Vickie and Jenny discussed some of the "higher-ups" who had recently been exposed: The county commissioner's daughter, dead from an overdose the Friday before; the courthouse clerk from an adjacent county, arrested for running a meth lab; and so on. Vickie said Brenda Sams, who is a friend of hers, had stopped replying to her Facebook and text messages too. She suspects Brenda has gone back to prison because someone else was responding to messages she was sending to Brenda.

Vickie has another daughter, Jackie, who hasn't seen her kids in many years. They're living with Jackie's ex, who, according to Vickie, is "on his fifth wife who's in prison for drugs." Jackie lives in people's garages and basements, or in the woods on the outskirts of town. She is one of Petersburg's increasing number of homeless residents.

"Yeah, right now she's staying in a house with no electricity," Jenny said. "She burns her clothes for heat. It's crazy."

"She's only thirty-four, but she looks 60," Vickie said.

> Jackie doesn't come to see me much. She'll come when she's hungry, needs a shower, whatever, a few dollars here and there. And I don't give her money because I'm a recovering enabler. But you can come eat, and you can come get a shower and leave. You're not allowed to stay here because you are a drug addict, and I can't have that in my house. But that's still my child.

Vickie said there are people in the community who would "leave (addicts) in the streets and laugh at them" and identified her husband as among those people. "He's got a 'go to work, do your job, or go away,'" mentality, she said.

I tell my husband every day, these are my kids. I won't give up on them. We put seven kids together. Four are mine, three are his, and he disagrees with me every day. And I say, 'You know what, these are my kids, and I'm not giving up.' These are my kids. I love them regardless. They'll find their way. Tough love, yes, but I don't turn my back, unlike this community. These are my kids.

I asked Jenny and Kevin whether Vickie's tough love approach had aided them in their recoveries.

"Knowing somebody was there for me, yeah, it definitely helped for sure," Jenny said. "Thank God for my family, or I'd be on the street."

"I have to say, with the tough love—I got a lot of that," Kevin said. "I learned the hard way because I didn't really have any family except for this family," referring to Jenny and Vickie. "I've been with them for almost twenty years. I've been with Jenny for almost twenty years. Most of the family, everybody except for them, turned their back on me."

I heard again and again that the addiction crisis had split Petersburg in two—between those who would rather ignore the problem and hope that it goes away, and those who want to address it head-on, even if it brings them some negative attention; between those who rush to help their hurting neighbors and those who will laugh at them in the street or on Facebook; between those who will applaud addicts when they are in recovery and those who will put them down when they relapse.

And Vickie predicts it will ultimately have the same effect on her marriage.

"That'll divide us in the end, I guarantee it," she said of her and her husband's disagreement about how to handle her children's addiction. "I love him, but it'll be our undoing.... People need to remember, these are the next generation coming up," she said. "These are our kids."

After leaving Vickie's, I walked a few blocks to Maple Hill Cemetery, located on a hill overlooking the city. Alongside graves of Confederate soldiers who served in the 18th Virginia Cavalry, I found graves with dates that began in the 1970s and '80s, including several so fresh that their headstones had not yet been installed. From the cemetery, I could see the steeples of some of the area churches that few young people attend, the golden arches of the McDonald's where addicts purchase heroin and cocaine along with Big Macs, and the sign for Judy's Pharmacy, where two million pain pills were illegally dispensed. The cemetery is located just a few steps from Petersburg High School, where it casts an ominous shadow over the next generation of potential addicts.

6

ROBESON COUNTY, NORTH CAROLINA

MARK LOCKLEAR DOESN'T FIT THE PROFILE of a Trump voter. A Native American and a registered Democrat who twice voted for Barack Obama for president, Locklear still has a deep admiration for Obama. He even keeps a framed photograph of the Obama family on a mantle in his home office. But what really makes Locklear defy the stereotype of a Trump voter—and most other kinds of voters too—is his ambivalence toward Trump, a president who has otherwise divided the nation into two distinct and seemingly irreconcilable factions. When Locklear talks about his feelings toward Trump, he often uses the metaphor of a pendulum. "There are days I sway in a positive direction, then he tweets stupidity, and my thought changes to negativity," he once told me.

I first met Locklear at his home in Prospect, a "census designated place" located in the coastal plains region of southeastern North Carolina. A CDP is a statistical term the Census Bureau uses to describe small, unincorporated communities in rural areas, often places with more churches

Mark Locklear outside his home in Prospect, North Carolina, in 2017. (Jordan Allott)

than traffic lights. Donald Trump performed very well in CDPs in 2016.

My first visit to Robeson County came a few weeks after Inauguration Day. A Bible-Belt county whose economy has been hollowed out by NAFTA and other free trade agreements, Robeson has one of the state's highest poverty rates and a murder rate four times the national average.[1, 2] It's also America's most racially diverse rural county: roughly 38 percent Native American, 33 percent white, and 25 percent black.[3] It is also historically Democratic—very Democratic. Until recently, registered Democrats outnumbered registered Republicans 7 to 1.[4]

Like Mark Locklear, Robeson County as a whole voted for Donald Trump in 2016 after twice going for Obama.[5, 6] Native Americans from the Lumbee Tribe of North Carolina proved to be the difference makers.

Mark had invited me out to his house in Prospect, where more than 90 percent of residents are Lumbee and 73 percent of voters cast their ballots for Trump.[7, 8]

Locklear met me in his driveway. The first thing I noticed about Mark was his broad shoulders, thick graying mustache, and imposing presence. The second thing I noticed was his deliberate manner and the thoughtfulness with which he answered my questions. Locklear, 54, has lived in Prospect his entire life. As we stood in his front yard, he pointed out the place where he had attended grade school and where he goes to church, along the unpaved Missouri Road, named after his great-grandmother.

Locklear has been in law enforcement his entire life. He started as a jailer in the sheriff's department before working his way up to major chief general of detectives. Now he's a criminal defense investigator. Locklear wore an orange long-sleeved shirt with the image of an American Indian in headdress and the words, "Lumbee Native Blood" inscribed in large black letters. Despite Mark's tribal affiliation, he rejects the tribalism that defines modern politics. Mark is a Democratic precinct captain who once ran for county sheriff as a Democrat. But he had recently worked to elect a conservative Republican to the state senate. Then there was his swing from Obama to Trump.

Locklear was taken with Obama's charisma and his promise to fight for the middle class. Mark was a big Michelle Obama fan, too, and felt that the Obamas were ideal representatives of the country. But Locklear's confidence in Obama's governance waned somewhat, first when Obama withdrew US troops from Iraq, and then when Obamacare caused his health insurance premiums to skyrocket, along with those of millions of other Americans. So in 2016, Locklear joined his county, his state, and his country in turning from Obama to Trump.

Locklear liked that Trump was not a politician, that he promised to "drain the swamp" in Washington, DC, and that he pledged to repeal and replace Obama's signature health care law. But during my first meeting with Mark, it was clear he wasn't fully sold on the new president. "Has Donald Trump earned the people's respect yet?" he asked. "I don't think so. He hasn't earned mine." As he spoke, sitting on a couch in his home office, the Obama family portrait was on the mantle just over his shoulder.

"But with that being said, I am willing to give him a chance."

***

Robeson County is a hard place to figure out socially and culturally. It's a rural county that has a lot of the problems endemic to inner cities, with a toxic brew of poverty, racial segregation, drugs, and violent crime. Politically, it's even harder to understand. Phillip Stephens, who heads the county's Republican Party, emailed me before my visit, suggesting that the racial complexity and political shifts made the place a complicated case study. "I was once told that if you wanted an undergrad degree in politics, go to Yale," he wrote. "For a prestigious graduate degree in politics, Harvard would be best. But to get a PhD in political science, you have to come to Robeson. Good luck figuring it out."

Local connector Bo Biggs helped me set up interviews with people across the county. On my second evening there, I huddled with Biggs, Stephens, and a group of other local Republicans at Candy-Sue's Café in Lumberton, the county seat. Biggs said that during the 2016 campaign, the first indication that Trump would do well in the county was the overwhelming number of people who requested Trump campaign yard signs. So many people asked for them that the local Republican Party ran out, prompting people to take matters into their own hands.

It is not uncommon for people to steal campaign signs from other people's lawns in the heat of an election campaign. But normally people confiscate the signs of candidates they *oppose*. In Robeson County, Biggs said, as Trump gained traction, "people were stealing (Trump) signs to put them in their own yard."

Trump won North Carolina and its 15 electoral votes by carrying seven rural counties that had voted for Barack Obama in 2012, including Robeson.[9] An easy explanation of Robeson County's transition from blue to red focuses on economic stagnation and cultural despair. But from a slightly different vantage point, Trump's 5-point victory had more to do with his ability to tap into the same desire for hope and change as Obama had shown in his 18-point victory four years earlier. At the time of Trump's victory, registered Democrats outnumbered registered Republicans in Robeson two to one. Until 2016, the county hadn't voted for a Republican for president since 1972, or for a Republican state senator since Reconstruction. Both of those things changed in 2016.[10]

But the first thing I noticed upon entering Robeson County wasn't its racial diversity or its changing politics, but rather its pervasive poverty. It was there in the abandoned manufacturing plants I saw along Interstate 95 as I approached Lumberton. And it was also there in the trash-lined streets and abandoned homes of south Lumberton—remnants of Hurricane Matthew, which had laid waste to the city six months earlier.

Robeson County's median household income of $33,000 is half the national average.[11] A quarter of residents live below the poverty line, and two-thirds are classified as low-income, making it one of the most impoverished counties in the nation. Ask anyone in Robeson County about the causes of this poverty and sooner or later—probably sooner—they'll start talking about the North American Free Trade Agreement, any mention of which is usually accompanied by some form of the verb *devastate*.

"When NAFTA came about in the 1990s it devastated the local economy," said Stephens. "All the textile plants moved to other countries. You're talking about one of the poorest counties in the nation that was devastated. You can't find anybody here that doesn't know someone who lost their job from NAFTA."

Remnants of Hurricane Matthew were still apparent six months after it struck Lumberton. (Jordan Allott)

"It is a very economically deprived area. They've really been hit," said Robert Pittinger, who represented Robeson County in the US Congress at the time. "The loss of textiles, the loss of manufacturing. It already was a poor county, but (NAFTA) really devastated it."

Signed into law in 1994, NAFTA toppled trade barriers between Mexico, Canada, and the United States. Subsequent trade deals did the same between the US and other countries. Thirty-two Robeson County industrial plants closed over the following decade, displacing thousands of workers, many in the textile industry. First, Sara Lee Knit Products closed three plants and fired 1,275 workers. Alamac Knit Fabrics laid off 750 people. Then came the big one: Converse, the iconic shoemaker. Once the county's largest private employer with 2,400 employees, it shuttered operations in 2001.[12] One researcher estimated that Robeson County lost as many as 10,000 jobs due to NAFTA—more than any other rural county in America. That's out of a total population of just 134,000.[13]

Tech, industrial, and other professional jobs are scarce now. More residents find work in the hotel, food, and retail industries that serve travelers on Interstate 95, which bisects the county, than in manufacturing. "If it weren't for the interstate, we might not be sitting where we are today," said Stephens.

But Interstate 95 is also a strategic hub of opportunity for criminals and drug and human traffickers, making their way along the Atlantic coast between Miami and Boston. They often stop off in Lumberton, partly explaining the county's worst-in-the-state crime rate.

Against this backdrop, it is easy to understand how Trump's abject hostility toward NAFTA made him such an attractive candidate. When Trump pledged to create jobs, protect workers, and renegotiate NAFTA, which he assailed as one of "the worst trade deals" in history, many free-trade conservatives rolled their eyes.[14] But in Robeson County, it won him an enthusiastic following.

"When Donald Trump made this statement, it was very profound," Stephens said at my meeting with local Republican officials. "He says, 'You guys passed NAFTA, and that's supposed to be free trade, but it's

Phillip Stephens speaks at a meeting with Republican leaders in Lumberton, North Carolina, in 2017. (Jordan Allott)

not free trade if it's only free one-way.' That one statement resonated with citizens here regardless of their ideology, regardless of their party affiliation, because that transcended ideology. This was economy, which was even more important."

With his willingness to shatter what had been a bipartisan consensus on trade, Trump inspired hope among Robeson County residents not unlike what Obama had inspired in 2008. Obama, it should be remembered, actually pledged in 2008 to renegotiate NAFTA. He never did keep this promise, and as his advisors reassured Canadian officials at the time, he never really intended to.[15] But this was just a minor issue in his campaign—a day's worth of messaging, quickly forgotten.

In places like Robeson, what made Obama attractive was his promise to bring about an era of post-partisan politics and a post-racial society. But Trump, who seemed incapable of shutting up regarding NAFTA, emphasized something more meaningful for Robeson's residents— economic renewal.

"You mostly hear the word 'hope' associated with President Obama's campaign—I mean, it was a central tenet in his message," said Emily Neff-Sharum, who heads the political science department at the University of North Carolina at Pembroke in the western part of the county. She added:

> But when you think about the Trump slogan of "Make America Great Again," I think that really resonated with this area, (which) has really struggled since the closing of factories after NAFTA went into effect. For a lot of the country, most people don't really think about NAFTA. But those free-trade agreements, when they started becoming a centerpiece of debate, absolutely hit really close to home in this area.

It may seem counterintuitive, but *hope* and *change* were words I heard over and over again in 2017 while traveling through Robeson County and other Obama-Trump counties across the country. When you look at places that supported both Obama and Trump, you start to realize that Obama and Trump had a lot in common.

I asked everyone I interviewed in counties Trump won to try to sum up in just one word why they believed he won. There were many offerings, but hope and change were the two words I heard most often. And I heard those words from Trump supporters and critics alike.

The media covered Trump as a figure who went about sowing fear and pessimism. After all, he had published a campaign book called *Crippled America.*[16] He warned that violent criminals were crossing the borders and that complete idiots had negotiated America's trade deals. But to many of his voters, Trump the pessimist had paradoxically cultivated a sense of hope. This was in part because he seemed like a lone voice of reason, questioning a status quo to which everyone else was inexplicably and constantly paying homage.

Imagine for a moment that everyone in Washington had been praising cancer—the disease—for decades. They all said it was a godsend, the best thing ever. Then, after millions had died of it over the decades, one politician finally came along promising to fight cancer! In

Robeson County, where NAFTA is held up as the explanation for so much devastation, this is exactly how Trump came across. He openly disparaged the trade deals that everyone believed had devastated areas like Robeson—rural areas with large manufacturing bases.

By rupturing the bipartisan consensus on free trade, Trump demonstrated that he wasn't listening to the Washington politicians, K Street lobbyists, and think-tank ideologues who shape America's trade policy.

Trump's unorthodox thinking on trade was evidence that he was listening to those who had been most harmed by free trade agreements. It showed that he acknowledged their existence, their work, and their plight, and that he didn't much care what politicians had done before. He was going a new way—his own way.

***

The conventional wisdom during the 2016 presidential campaign held that Donald Trump's inflammatory rhetoric would alienate millions of minority voters. They would turn out in massive numbers on election day to deliver the presidency to Hillary Clinton. The thing about the conventional wisdom, though, is that it can be profoundly unwise sometimes. That's especially true with a candidate as unconventional as Trump.

Trump didn't perform very well overall with nonwhite voters. But he won a larger share of them than Mitt Romney had in 2012. And in some places, minority voters actually helped deliver victory to Trump.

The Lumbee Tribe of North Carolina is the largest Indian Tribe east of the Mississippi River. Robeson County's roughly 50,000 Lumbee Indians make up a plurality of its electorate.[17] Pembroke is the tribe's political and cultural center. It's home to the University of North Carolina-Pembroke, a historically Native American university. That's where I met up with Jarrod Lowery one rainy afternoon in March 2017.

"The reason Robeson County voted Republican is the Native American population voted Republican," Lowery, a representative on the Lumbee Tribal Council, said. He said that Lumbees started considering the Republican Party when Republican gubernatorial candidate James Holshouser championed the "Save Old Main" movement in the early 1970s. The Old Main, UNC-Pembroke's oldest and grandest building, was slated for destruction. After the building's destruction in a 1973 fire, the newly elected Holshouser had stood on the steps of the charred building and promised to rebuild it. It was restored in 1979.

"When Governor Holshouser said, 'We're going to rebuild Old Main,' there were a lot of elders at the time and people in the community who said it was the first time they considered voting for a Republican," Lowery said.

Lowery explained that Republicans' social conservatism and emphasis on law and order also resonate with the Lumbee, whose values focus on faith, family, and traditional mores. "Our people have always been fiscally conservative because we believe in working hard and saving our money. But social issues are what are really big." The Lumbee don't mind helping those in need, Lowery said, "but when the Democratic Party in America took that hard left on social issues, Lumbee people started backing up."

The media tend to focus on the economy as the main factor driving voting patterns, particularly in former industrial centers like Robeson County. But social issues play at least as big a role. This reality was hammered home for me repeatedly as I conducted my research in Robeson County. John McNeil, who led the Robeson County Democratic Party in 2016, also identified social issues as pivotal to Trump's success. McNeil said he was expecting Hillary Clinton to win the county with 60 percent or more of the vote. The reason she didn't, he later realized, was the level of involvement from Christian pastors during the campaign.

"The churches were very, very active in the election, and of course the big issue was abortion. That and gay marriage were the problems," McNeil said, pointing to the 86 percent of Robeson County voters had supported the state's 2012 constitutional amendment banning same-sex marriage in North Carolina, the highest share any of the state's 100 counties.[18]

On election day 2016, only 10 of Robeson County's 39 precincts voted for Clinton, and those that did were in heavily black areas. Sixty-six percent of voters in Maxton, for instance, in the western corner of the county, voted for Clinton, which is slightly higher than the 64 percent of its residents who are black.[19] Trump got about the same share of the vote in a neighboring precinct that's 67 percent Lumbee Indian. And Prospect, "the oldest Lumbee community, which is 96 percent Lumbee, voted 73 percent for Trump," Lowery said.

The most important issue for the Lumbee is official recognition by the federal government. This would require a federal law, and it would allow hundreds of millions of dollars to flow into the county. But the Lumbee are also looking for a more basic kind of recognition—one that comes from the human need to feel *listened to.* "A lot of time throughout the country, we are forgotten," Lowery said. "People go down the list of minorities, but nobody ever mentions Native Americans, Native Alaskans, or Native Hawaiians. So when you have a politician who points at you and takes an interest in you, you're like, 'Wow, somebody's finally paying attention to me.'" Lowery felt that Trump was one politician who might finally pay attention to them.

"Lumbees don't trust the government," he said. "And when you have a guy who comes in who looks like he's going to bust up the system, who admits there's corruption here and there's corruption there, we say, 'This guy's saying that same things I've been saying.'"

Lowery continued, "There (were) a lot of individuals I spoke to who would say, 'Well, this guy isn't liked by Democrats. He isn't liked by Republicans. Maybe this is the guy that is actually standing for me.'"

Later, over barbeque sandwiches at Papa Bill's restaurant outside Pembroke, Lowery continued on the importance of feeling listened to. "With us, what matters is that you listen to us," he said. "That people say, 'Those Lumbee, they're important, they're as important as people in Silicon Valley, as important as New York City; they're important.' That's all we want."

Another politician who listened was Danny Britt. In 2016, Britt became the first Republican since Reconstruction to win the state's 13th-district senate seat, earning 55 percent of the vote. He won in large part because of strong support from the Lumbee community.[20] "Senator Britt come to my home community of Prospect several times asking for our vote," Lowery said. "And when you have been told your whole life, 'You don't vote for Republicans,' and you have (a Republican) that comes to your door and says, 'Hey, can I have your vote?' That starts opening you up a little more."

Another thing that opens people up is being present for them in their time of need.

When Hurricane Matthew struck a month before the election in 2016, it laid waste to many communities along the Atlantic Coast. Robeson County, which is an hour's drive inland, was not spared. But

as residents hunkered down, Danny Britt stood up and got to work. "The whole town was thrown into absolute chaos real quick," Britt told me at his law office in Lumberton. "Roads were shut down, and there was no power. Bridges were out all over the place." In the ensuing deluge, which reached nearly twenty-three feet above flood stage on the Lumber River that runs through downtown Lumberton, Britt summoned his "go-fix-it" personality and

North Carolina State Sen. Danny Britt in his law office in 2017. (Jordan Allott)

the skills he'd acquired in relief efforts as a National Guardsman and did what he could to help.

"I'm a good ol' boy," he said. "So, when stuff like that happens—anything bad happens—I kind of jump to it." He started by helping a friend's aunt who had retreated to the roof of her house. He then hooked up a boat trailer to his truck, delivered food and supplies to those in distress, and helped rescue stranded neighbors.

Britt was in the middle of a closely contested race for the county's state senate seat. He didn't go out of his way to broadcast who he was during the storm. "He never wore a campaign shirt. He never did an interview," said Mark Locklear, who works with Britt as a criminal investigator. "He was just busting his ass to help people, and it was being noticed. People saw this. People began to talk about it—the passion that he had to help others."

When calamity strikes, people pay attention to who shows up to help and who doesn't. In this case, one of the people who showed up to help was a local attorney who happened to be the Republican state senate candidate. "He was going door-to-door helping everyone he could, you know, helping people get out of their houses, doing whatever he could," said Matt Walker, whom I met at Candy-Sue's. "He was rolling up his sleeves and getting dirty, and you just didn't really see that from the Democrats."

Another person who showed up—or at least whose campaign showed up—was Donald Trump. Matt Walker's mother, Susan, part-owner of Candy-Sue's, recalled how Trump's daughter-in-law Lara Trump delivered food and other provisions in a Trump campaign bus in the days after the flood.

"The thing about President Trump, when the hurricane came, there were people in the streets," Susan said. "There were homeless people everywhere."

> We had shelters. One day, I went down to the Bill Sap Center, and I was taking some food down there, and there was President Trump's big old bus, and they were delivering waters and stuff, and supplies. I think it was his daughter-in-law that was there. She actually came down. I think it had a big effect on a lot of people when they saw what he had sent to our county. He was trying to help us when we needed help.

"That swayed a lot of people," Tiffany Powers, a local attorney and Democratic precinct captain, said. "Hillary didn't come down here, and that's where she lost." When I asked Powers for one word on why Trump won Robeson County, she quickly offered two: "Hurricane Matthew."

Tiffany Powers and Daniel Allott in downtown Lumberton in 2017. (Jordan Allott)

* * *

Danny Earl Britt Jr. was born in Robeson County in 1979. After college at Appalachian State University, where he walked on to the football team, and law school at Oklahoma State, he worked at a law firm in another part of North Carolina. But he soon found his way back to Robeson County, working first as a prosecutor in the district attorney's office and then as a defense attorney. He also spent time as a military prosecutor in the Judge Advocate General Corps in Iraq. Britt's senate campaign focused on jobs and education, both of which were sorely lacking in the county. Britt said raising graduation rates is vital to attracting good jobs. One-quarter of adults in Robeson County have not finished high school, and only 13 percent of adults there have a college degree.[21]

In 2015, the Robeson County School District spent $525 per student, second to last among the state's 100 counties. In Chapel Hill-Carrboro, a district to the north, the per-student average is nearly eight times that.[22] Britt won his seat less because of the policy positions he took and more because of the commitment he showed to helping his community. He wants his children to have the option of living in Robeson County, so he thinks about its future. Britt is a big believer in the power of showing up and getting to know voters, including those who historically have not voted Republican.

Locklear said he initially had "a lot of concerns" about Britt's candidacy, specifically because he was running as a Republican. "We had never supported a Republican candidate, to my knowledge," he said of the Lumbee. Locklear drove Britt around Lumbee communities in his pickup and found that the simple act of introducing him was often enough to win votes. Britt also displayed energy. "Danny was a hustler," said Locklear. "As a Republican, I still thought we had an uphill battle, but he's a very likable and approachable person that has robust energy."

Britt visited every precinct in his district. "We had these little corner functions or went to the cafe, stopped at the station and went to the barbershop, or went and had a collard sandwich," Locklear said. "He got out and done these on a daily basis. That resonated with people."

In Lumbee-dominated Prospect, Locklear estimated that 80 percent of registered voters there are Democratic. Britt won them five-to-three.

During the storm, Britt recalled people saying, "'Man, this dude doesn't sleep.' You know. I didn't sleep much. Less now. But I think … a lot of folks just really like the idea of somebody that gets out and does rather than says."

***

Of all the interesting statistics to emerge from the 2016 election, one of the most compelling was this: Donald Trump won 76 percent of the

493 US counties with a Cracker Barrel Old Country Store; he won just 22 percent of the 184 counties with a Whole Foods Market.

That 54-percent gap is the largest ever recorded, according to the Cook Political Report.[23] It has widened in every election since 1992, when it was just 19 points. The gap was smaller even in the 2008 cycle, when Barack Obama cluelessly asked an Iowa audience, "Anybody gone into Whole Foods lately and see what they charge for arugula?"[24]

Trump's performance in these counties was a token of the increasing cultural divide between red counties and blue counties. But it's more than that, as I discovered during my trip to Robeson County. The county's only Cracker Barrel is just off Highway 95 in Lumberton. One evening I decided to stop in for dinner. The Lumberton Visitors' Bureau, the Greater Hope International Church, and the Lion's Den Adult Boutique are on the same road.

Cracker Barrel's 630 restaurants are located in forty-two states, but most are on the East Coast, in the Rust Belt, and in the South. It boasts meals that are "homestyle" and "made from scratch." I tried the meatloaf, biscuit, coleslaw, and potato casserole, and then interviewed Evita, my nineteen-year-old waitress. She said she'd worked at the Lumberton Cracker Barrel for two years and enjoyed it. It's a friendly place and she gets along with her coworkers. "It's like a dysfunctional family," she quipped.

When I told her about the Trump-Cracker Barrel statistic, she didn't seem surprised. "Gun rights, older folks with older ways," she said by way of explaining why these places were attracted to Trump's message. "They're from a generation that stresses an older American way." Evita was right: nostalgia for "an older American way" is evident in every tool, sign, and photograph that adorns the walls of Cracker Barrel restaurants. It was also the subtext of Donald Trump's campaign pledge to "Make America great again."

Alexis, a Lumbee waitress in her thirties, approached me to tell her story. A Robeson County native, Alexis had worked at Cracker Barrel seven years and was now a manager. Alexis pointed to high Obamacare premiums and Trump's "generosity" as the reasons why he won in the county, and why she had voted for him. Asked for specifics about the latter, she offered that Trump had given up his business and pledged to take no salary in the White House. "People appreciate that," she said, adding that she thought Trump was doing a great job.

Overhearing my conversation with Alexis, Danny, the store's head manager, walked over and declared emphatically that he was a Trump supporter. At this point, almost all of the other customers had left, and most of the staff was getting ready to leave for the night. Danny talked as we headed to the doors, through the Old Country Store that sells everything from fried apples to baby clothes. He said I'd be welcome to visit again should I ever return to Lumberton.

The feeling of being welcome is important to everyone, but perhaps especially to those in the Rust Belt, the South, and other places where many people feel ignored or disparaged by a distant elite. They feel excluded from the popular culture and alienated from the rich enclaves around Washington, where too many of society's rules are made. They make a living with their hands or by driving things from one place to another. The people they feel ignore them don't do that.

Comfort food is what people want in places where comforts are hard to come by, places such as Robeson County, where nearly a third of the population lives below the poverty line—where church attendance is sagging, where schools are woefully inadequate, where families are fracturing, and where people are losing their lives to drug addiction and violent crime. In these places, nostalgia for what Evita called "an older American way" is what people yearn for. That's what they believed Trump offered them.

* * *

On subsequent visits to Robeson County, I found more evidence that the county was trending Republican. On a visit in the spring of 2018, I attended the Robeson County Republican Party convention at the Lumberton Lions Club.

Phillip Stephens announced that the local party was just sixty-one voters shy of 10,000 registered Republicans in the county. Stephens later explained that North Carolina's closed primary system means most voters register as Democrats in order to vote in the primaries. Stephens, a former Democrat, said his strategy is to encourage local Democrats to switch to "unaffiliated" as a half-step to becoming a Republican.

After the meeting, I asked Stephens how Trump's support was holding up in the county more than a year into his term. "We have not seen Trump's support die down at all," he said. "But we've seen from Trump supporters anger at the media, who distort what he says and darken everything he does."

Later in 2018, Danny Britt improved on his 2016 election performance, winning reelection with 63 percent of the vote, again pitching in a month before the election when the area was devastated by a hurricane and flooding.[25]

Then came a special election in September 2019 for North Carolina's ninth congressional district. Ballot fraud had marred the initial election nearly a year earlier, which the Republican candidate won by a slim margin, and so a new election was called. Republican Dan Bishop was predicted to win the district, which had been in Republican hands since 1963. He did win, but many analysts failed to grasp why. Lowery dissected precinct-level vote totals in an op-ed for *The Hill* newspaper (where I am an opinion editor), and made a convincing argument that Lumbee voters played a crucial role.[26]

"Many Lumbee feel that the national Democratic Party has simply left them behind as they've embraced more extreme social and economic positions," he wrote. "We're tired of Democratic policies that insult our faith and fail us economically. Democrats' opposition to voter identification laws, support for abortion-on-demand and attacks on religious liberty have alienated many Lumbee." Lumbee, Lowery continued, "hold strong to the values of family and hard work. And at the moment, the Republican Party does a better job of respecting those values."

As for Mark Locklear, I contacted him periodically over the next

State Sen. Danny Britt, Daniel Allott, Jarrod Lowery, and Lumberton City Councilman Chris Howard during relief efforts in the wake of Hurricane Florence in 2018. (Author's personal collection)

three years, asking for his reaction to developments in Trump's presidency or to pick his brain about local political affairs. Whenever I visited Robeson County, Locklear would invite me to drop by his home office for a chat. I'd always check without saying anything to see if the Obama family photo was still perched on his mantle, and it always was.

Mark was always welcoming, even when I showed up at inconvenient times. One day in 2018, I arrived just after he'd discovered that his ATV had been stolen. He graciously chatted with me as he waited for the police to arrive.

When the media lambasted Trump for his response to Hurricane Harvey in 2017, Locklear gave him an A+ grade. "I don't doubt his passion to help the American people," he wrote to me. Locklear grew frustrated at the media's treatment of the new president. "I do wish the media—and I am a CNN freak; I love Anderson Cooper—but I have been swayed to watch now more Fox because of CNN's coverage. ...I say, 'Back off, give the man a chance.'"

Locklear also didn't hesitate to criticize Trump when he felt it was warranted. "Mr. President, please stop the negative tweets," Locklear

Mark Locklear in his home office in Prospect, North Carolina, in 2017. (Jordan Allott)

wrote back to me when I asked what advice he would give Trump at the six-month mark of his presidency. At that point, he gave the president an "A" on policy but lowered his overall grade to a "C" because of Trump's injudicious use of Twitter.

"Oh, my. 'Shit hole countries'? Dan, now I am concerned." That was the brief email message I received from Locklear six months later, after Trump's casual use of that term to describe several less-developed countries. A few months later, he wrote to say that the child separation policy at the border "really pissed me off."

When I met with Mark in the spring of 2018, he again talked about the pendulum, "I can tell you it has certainly swung in a positive direction. Several things have me thinking that." He knew to the dollar how much the tax cut was helping him—$18 on net every two weeks for his wife's job. And he gets 10 cents more per mile for work from the county. All of that equals about $600 a year. That's enough to pay the water bill every month, he said. It reminded me of the previous year, when he had recited to the dollar how much Obamacare was costing him and his family, which had dampened his enthusiasm for Obama.

Locklear said he had grown weary of Trump's cyber saber-rattling with North Korean dictator Kim Jong Un. "I was concerned with the 'Rocket Man' comments," Locklear said. "Is he inciting a war here?" he had asked himself at the time. He had a very personal reason to be concerned. A year earlier, his son, Ethan, had joined the Marines. Ethan is an ammunition technician in the Marine reserves. "When he told us he was going into the Marines, he said he wanted the ultimate challenge,"

Mark said. "He reported on July 10. I cried many a tear. I sent letters every day for fourteen weeks to Marine basic training. He is at school online at UNC Pembroke."

Locklear showed me a portrait of his son. He wept while recounting the fourteen weeks he had been away from his son during basic training and the pride he had felt in seeing him graduate. "These boys would be put on the front lines," Locklear said about the consequences of war with North Korea or another adversary. But just before my visit, the White House had announced direct nuclear talks between Trump and Kim. That gave Locklear a sense of hope.

"Now, looking back, maybe he was doing the right thing," he said about Trump's "hardball approach" with Kim. "Obama was too diplomatic; (Trump) is a straight shooter."

By the fall of 2018, Locklear said of Trump, "I think he's done a good job overall as president." He added that he had not talked to anyone who voted for Trump who had changed their mind, and he thought Trump was on target to win Robeson County again in 2020. "People in my area value common sense over intelligence or book learning," he said. "And that's why they like Trump. He appealed to them at their level. And I just don't think that's going to change…. I haven't made up my mind about whether I'll support Trump again in 2020," Locklear added. "But as of now, I'd vote for him."

* * *

I made my final visit to Robeson County in January 2020, nearly three years after my initial trip. I returned with the goal of answering two questions. First, how was President Trump faring among the county's pivotal Native American voters, and second, how was the economy, which Trump had made the centerpiece of his reelection campaign, affecting people in this impoverished county?

With Locklear's help, I interviewed nearly a dozen Native American residents. At a school board fundraiser in Pembroke, three middle-aged women told me that while they were repelled by some of Trump's conduct, they appreciated what he had accomplished on the policy front. And none responded favorably to my mention of Trump's potential general election opponents, including former Vice President Joe Biden.

At a farm in Prospect, Donovan Locklear (no relation to Mark), a corn and soybean farmer, said he supported Trump's trade war with China. "I think four more years of Trump holding China's feet to the fire, they're going to come to the table and be willing to negotiate even more," the farmer, a registered Democrat, said. "I don't like everything that he does, all the Twitter action. But at the same time, everything he told me he was going to do when he ran for president, he's done." That included Trump's promise to defund Planned Parenthood and his signing of "right-to-try" legislation, which allows gravely ill patients to access experimental medicines. Donovan estimated that 90 percent of farmers would back Trump in 2020.

Donovan's brother Jason, a chiropractor, joined the conversation and began railing about the media's refusal to give Trump credit for his accomplishments. "I don't see anything wrong with putting America first," he said. "I don't see anything wrong with controlling our borders. (Trump) never said anything negative about immigrants. He talked about *illegal* immigrants....The more the media colors what Trump says, the more it makes me want to vote for him again."

Later, I met with Virgil Lowery and McDuffie Cummings, who I was told had a better sense for local politics than just about anyone in the area. "The Democrat party is too left for the grassroots people," said Cummings, who had served as supervisor of Pembroke for three decades. "They've gone with all these liberal ideas. Robeson County is basically conservative. It's a conservative county!"

"You saw it with (Joe) Biden," Virgil said. "He used to be a moderate on abortion. Now he's moved all the way to the left with AOC.... We have a lot of conservative people in this county as far as their morals on homosexuality," Virgil said. "Those kind of issues stirs the folks in this area and causes them all to vote and vote against the Democrats."

"Democrats are just...they're out of sync," Cummings added. "The

Democratic Party is not what the party used to be fifty-five years ago. It's just changed. It went liberal, and it's going to the left farther and farther."

* * *

Before my visit to Robeson County, I asked several of my local contacts to notify me if they ever heard of any "switchers"—that is, people who had voted one way in 2016 but planned to vote another way in 2020. My contacts, among the most well connected people in the county, came up mostly empty. One exception was John, whom I interviewed one evening over dinner at San Jose Mexican restaurant in Lumberton. (He asked that I withhold his last name.) John, a former civics teacher in his late thirties, is a Robeson County native who moved to Northern Virginia before returning with his wife and kids a few years ago to be closer to family.

A conservative Republican, John said he believes there is a moral authority that comes with being president, a moral authority that he felt Trump lacked in 2016. Trump was too much of a "brawler" and "instigator," John said. So on election day, he voted for Republicans in all the down-ballot races but left the presidential contest blank. But John informed me that he had since committed to voting for Trump in 2020.

I asked him what had changed.

"His Twitter account still kills him," he said. "But Trump has actually done what he said he would do." John contrasted Trump's decision to move the US embassy in Israel to Jerusalem with the hollow promises of previous administrations.

"Also on trade policy, they just passed the USMCA—it was like, "Wow! ...The guy told you what he's gonna do, and he did it."

More and more, as Donald Trump's presidency unfolded, I began to hear from Trump's supporters this same sentiment—that Trump has largely done, or at least tried to do, what he promised he would do. I even began hearing it from Trump's critics. "His base is happy because he's done what he told them he'd do," John McNeil, the former head of the county Democratic Party, told me. McNeil acknowledged that the strong economy and the national Democratic Party's leftward shift would be big barriers to Democrats' success locally.

When I asked whether he thought Trump would win the county again, he let out a resigned laugh. "I'm scared of him," he said. "I'm scared of what he will do to our country and to our fundamental values. I'm going to do everything I can do to make sure he does not win. But I don't know if it'll be enough."

Donnie Douglas, editor of *The Robesonian* newspaper, also seemed sure Trump would win in the county again. Douglas believes residents continue to be disappointed with Trump's "boorish behavior" but continue to support his "America first agenda." Douglas said he knows people would "love a viable alternative to Trump but just don't see that at all in the crowd that Democrats have put together…. Yes, I think Trump will win Robeson County again," Douglas concluded. "We love our guns, hate abortion, don't like gay marriage, and on and on, on social issues in which we align with Trump."

My final stop was to see Channing Jones, executive director for the Robeson County Office of Economic Development. When I arrived, Jones, who has worked in manufacturing and academia, told me that the local economy was performing better than it had done in more than a decade. "The economy is doing very well right now," he said.

> I mean, most economic indicators are just tremendous. In November of '19, which is the last snapshot we have, our unemployment rate was 4.9 percent in the county, down significantly from the 6 percent it had hovered around for years. It's the lowest I can remember, and I've been tracking it for twelve years.

Jones stressed that manufacturing was still a crucial part of the local economy—17 percent of the county workforce still works in that sector. But food processing had replaced textiles as the dominant manufacturing industry. As an example, he cited Sanderson Farms, a chicken processor, which arrived in 2017 and invested $115 million in a plant and hired more than 1,000 people.

Jones had also seen growth in new homes, small businesses, and health care facilities over the last three years. "I don't think you can go down many towns in our county and not see a 'Help Wanted' sign somewhere," he said. "In general, if someone is looking for a job, I think they can find it now."

I asked Jones what role, if any, the Trump administration had played in the strength of the local economy.

"Everything with the economy is based upon confidence," he started. "If I gave you a doom and gloom picture, most investors are going to be very hesitant. I think that over the Trump administration, there has been a high level of confidence in the economy. That's been great for our county."

He called the US-Mexico-Canada Agreement (USMCA), which President Trump was scheduled to sign into law that day, "a great thing," mostly because it would lift the cloud of uncertainty that had hung over many industries for years. "I think Trump's appeal is that, whether you like him or not as a person, most people can respect the fact that he said, 'I'm going to do X,' and he's legitimately tried to do it."

But Jones emphasized that the strong economy was only a part of the reason why he felt Trump would win the county and the state. He said that Trump's positions and policies on "some very significant moral issues, faith-based issues," would be the most important factors working in Trump's favor. "Remember, we're in the Bible Belt down here," Jones said. "And it's going to be hard for many people to not think about that when they go to the polls."

7

SALT LAKE COUNTY, UTAH

WHEN PRESIDENT TRUMP issued an executive order shortly after his inauguration halting travel from seven predominantly Muslim countries, it prompted howls of indignation from liberal civil rights groups.[1] But some of the loudest voices of protest came from members of one of America's most conservative organizations—the Church of Jesus Christ of Latter-Day Saints (LDS). Former presidential candidate Mitt Romney, Arizona Sen. Jeff Flake, Utah Gov. Gary Herbert, and other prominent Mormons condemned the order.[2] The LDS church issued a statement implicitly denouncing the administration's move.[3]

Many rank-and-file Mormons also opposed the ban, including Sharlee Mullins Glenn, a children's book author living outside Salt Lake City. She felt that the ban heartlessly singled out Muslims for disfavored treatment. After discovering that many other Mormon women were similarly appalled by the ban, Mullins Glenn launched a Facebook group called Mormon Women for Ethical Government (MWEG).

The page began as a place for Mormon women "to vent frustrations and talk about ideas for saving the country," Mullins Glenn told me. Within two weeks the group had more than 4,000 members. Over the next year, MWEG became part of what could be called the Mormon resistance movement. But unlike the progressive resistance movement that formed in the wake of Trump's election, the women of MWEG weren't marching in pussy hats or calling for Trump's impeachment (at least not yet). In fact, the group's leaders insisted they didn't oppose President Trump at all. Rather, they said they were fighting the dishonesty and callousness they believe define his presidency and the descent into political tribalism they fear will become its legacy.

I found the women of MWEG to be a fascinating case study, highlighting two of the most important questions of the Trump era. First, how would female voters, and particularly well-educated suburban white women, respond to Trump's presidency? Donald Trump won white women voters in 2016, but some polling suggests they might be the voters most likely to abandon the president. Second, in today's hyperpolarized environment, is there any room at all for a group of women who aspire to stand as a bulwark against political tribalism?

I first met several MWEG members at Mullins Glenn's home in Pleasant Grove, about an hour's drive south of Salt Lake City, two days after Christmas in 2017. The women explained that Mormons have a history of being victims of government-sanctioned discrimination.[4] As a consequence, they tend to support accommodating immigration policies. In 2011 majority-Mormon Utah became the first state to establish its own guest worker program.[5] Utah is one of just a handful of states that allow illegal immigrants to drive.[6]

"The travel ban, the refugee, and the immigration issues hit close to home for us," Mullins Glenn said. "We were once refugees, and so we feel very strongly about caring for people who are without a home and making sure families stay together."

"I feel strongly, and our church teaches, that we look after people," said Dalene Rowley, a lifelong Republican-turned-independent who

Members of Mormon Women for Ethical Government (MWEG) in 2017. (Daniel Allott)

worked on immigration policy for MWEG. "And I just feel like wherever people come from, they are part of the human family and we should accept them. And I didn't find that in the Republican Party."

Seventy percent of Mormons identify as Republicans or lean that way—the highest share of any religious group in America, according to a 2015 Pew study.[7] But most Mormons are centrists on immigration. According to a 2016 survey by the Public Religion Research Institute, 45 percent of Mormons believe immigrants strengthen American society, compared to 32 percent of Republicans. Sixty-one percent of Mormons support granting unauthorized immigrants a pathway to citizenship if they meet certain criteria, compared to 52 percent of Republicans.[8]

MWEG advocates for what it calls "ethical immigration reform." In 2017 it published a fifteen-point document outlining its reform priorities, stressing the need for compassion and accommodation in reforming America's immigration system.[9] In an op-ed, Diana Bate Hardy, who led MWEG's immigration committee, criticized the White House's reform framework.[10] President Trump had called for a pathway to citizenship for 1.8 million undocumented immigrants brought to the US as children in exchange for tougher border security measures, including $25 billion for a border wall with Mexico. Trump's plan would have also ended the visa lottery and placed restrictions on family-based migration.[11]

Bate Hardy argued that Trump's plan would "pit one group of immigrants against another ... undermine this country's commitment to basic civil rights and stir up anti-immigrant sentiments."

Several MWEG members described themselves as accidental activists. But all seemed to have embraced their activism with the zeal of the newly converted.

"I was not politically active at all and then found myself in the position where I couldn't do nothing," said Linda Kimball, a Mormon convert who had recently moved to Utah.

"Our motto is we will not be complicit by being complacent," Mullins Glenn added. "We feel we've been awakened."

For several members, the awakening began not with Trump's election but with the ousting of former Utah Senator Bob Bennett. After serving in the US Senate for eighteen years, Bennett, a centrist Republican and a Mormon, became a victim of the 2010 Tea Party revolt. He finished second among delegates at that year's Republican state convention. Bennett blamed his loss on a "toxic ... political environment."[12]

"I looked around and said 'I do not recognize this party,'" Mullins Glenn said about her feelings after Bennett lost. "This in no way represents me or who I am.'" Mullins Glenn had been a lifelong Republican but is now unaffiliated.

Trump's election was the final straw for most of the women. "To see someone elected to the highest office in the land who is the antithesis of (Mormon) values, it was the breaking point," Mullins Glenn said.

Donald Trump finished third in Utah's Republican caucuses in 2016, earning just 14 percent of the vote.[13] Trump went on to win Utah in the general election, but with only 45 percent—an enormous fall-off from the 72 percent that 2012 GOP nominee Mitt Romney, a Mormon, had received, and even from the 62 percent that John McCain had won in 2008.[14]

Evan McMullin, a Mormon conservative, took 21 percent of the vote running as an independent candidate. Very few Utahns were prepared to vote for Hillary Clinton, who captured just 27 percent of the vote. But McMullin's relatively strong performance was evidence that many were looking for a conservative alternative to Trump.

Many Mormons were also repelled by what they saw as Trump's lack of integrity and poor judgment. Mormons commit to living lives of virtue, a concept most Mormons did not associate with Trump. In a poll of Utah voters during the 2016 campaign, just 14 percent felt Trump was a good role model for young people, less than half the 31 percent who considered Clinton a good role model. Sixteen percent of Utahns felt Trump was a moral person, compared to 25 percent for Clinton.[15]

"I just felt like (Trump's) presidency was an affront to women," Catherine Eslinger said. "The way this president speaks to and about women. I'm not saying that there aren't men who aren't upset about that too, but that fuels how we feel. And not just women but how he speaks about minorities, the disabled, there's quite a long list. And we are very sensitive about that, and we couldn't be complacent about that."

Trump's history of sexism was received much differently by Mormons than by other Christian denominations. When the *Access Hollywood* tape was released showing Trump bragging about sexually assaulting women, most Christian conservatives remained silent or offered only mild criticism. But much of Utah's Mormon political leadership withdrew their endorsements of Trump and urged him to step aside. As Salt Lake evangelical pastor Greg Johnson put it to me, "Evangelicals saw the video as sabotage and turned their anger towards Clinton, but most Mormons saw it as proof of Trump's poor character." Trump won a record 81 percent of white evangelical voters, but just 61 percent of Mormon voters.[16]

Mullins Glenn said she had voted for Barack Obama, Romney, and

McMullin in the last three presidential elections. She added that she would have voted for Clinton in 2016 had McMullin not run. Rowley and Kimball both cast their ballots for Clinton, whom they saw as the lesser of two evils.

When I asked the MWEG women to name a Republican politician they admired, John Kasich, then the governor of Ohio, was mentioned more than any other. Kasich ran for president in 2016 as a moderate alternative to Trump.

MWEG believes there is power in a group of Mormon women coming together to enact political change. Mullins Glenn referred to it as "the power of the sisterhood. ...In our church, there is a long tradition of female activism. Utah was the second territory in the union to give women the vote. We draw on that tradition." A year after its creation, MWEG boasted 6,000 members and chapters in most states. Their members spend their time publishing policy positions, open letters, and op-eds; participating in pro-immigrant rallies; and lobbying. "One thing Mormon women know how to do is organize," said Mullins Glenn. She said the group's four active founders make the final decisions on the positions the group takes.

What I found most interesting about the women of MWEG was that despite their strong words about Trump, they insisted that the group was not anti-Trump. "Let me be clear," Mullins Glenn said. "MWEG is a firmly nonpartisan group. We do have members who are registered Democrats, people who voted for Bernie, Clinton, Trump. We cross the political spectrum."

"What we are most concerned about is not Trump *per se*," another member told me. "It's the way he is violating our norms and values."

Some of the women clearly struggled with that distinction. "It's a real internal workout to make sure we are not hating this man," Kimball said. "The results of his actions are what alarm us. But separating them from the person is a real workout."

When I asked the women if they would have started the group if Trump had not been elected, they responded with a chorus of "no's."

"We seek to unify instead of divide," Mullins Glenn said. "We choose love over hate. We seek that common ground where all people of goodwill can agree. And unless an issue is clearly immoral or unethical, we don't touch it."

"Unless there is a clear breach of ethics, then we are not going to deal with it," Eslinger added. "If there is a reasonable argument to be made on either side of an issue, that's not something we worry ourselves with."

But can people of goodwill not differ on the ethics and prudence of temporarily suspending travel and immigration from lawless countries known to be hotbeds of terrorism? Can people who choose love not also support more restrictive immigration policies?

MWEG's focus on Trump and his actions made me wonder: Since the incivility and tribalism that has become a feature of American politics are not exclusive to Trump, would the women of MWEG be willing to call it out when it came from other sources? Would they even be able to identify it if it did? It also seemed odd to me that MWEG refused to take positions on two of the most important ethical and moral issues of our time.

"There are two issues we simply won't go into pro or con, and those two issues are abortion and same-sex marriage." Mullins Glenn said. "Those are two issues that the church has taken a stand on, and so we won't."

I left my first meeting with the women of MWEG wanting to believe they were committed to their stated mission of being "watchdogs against corruption and abuse of power" and "ambassadors of peace who transcend partisanship." But I was not entirely convinced they would be able to remain nonpartisan. A year into Trump's term, polls suggested Mormons' view of Trump had not changed much at all. Gallup found 61 percent of Mormons approved of Trump's job performance.[17] But it was clear MWEG's resistance had only stiffened. When I asked the group to describe Trump's first year in office in one word, members used words like "horrified," "destructive," "disappointment," and "dystopian."

"I'm still having panic attacks," Eslinger said, referring to the effect

Trump's election had on her. "I'm still waking up in the middle of the night."

"He's redefining normal," Mullins Glenn's daughter Erica said. "And that's terrifying to me."

**

The activists of MWEG weren't the only Mormon women grappling with how to respond to the Trump presidency. Mia Love was another. In 2014, Love became the first black Republican woman ever elected to Congress. Representing most of Salt Lake City, the daughter of Haitian immigrants was hailed as the future of a younger, more diverse Republican party.[18] Then Donald Trump came along, and Love was forced into a difficult position. She agreed with many of Trump's policies. In fact, in 2017 and 2018, her votes aligned with the president's policy preferences 96 percent of the time—more than anyone else in Utah's six-member, all-Republican congressional delegation.[19]

But Love hadn't endorsed or voted for Trump in 2016. She had joined other Mormon Republicans in Utah in urging him to step aside after the *Access Hollywood* tape was made public.[20] And she later criticized Trump on select occasions, such as when he defended white nationalists at Charlottesville and when he referred to Haiti and several other poor nations as "shit-hole countries" from which America shouldn't be admitting immigrants.[21] This obviously struck a chord with her personally. Love called the remark "unkind, divisive, elitist" and un-American. She called on the president to apologize both to the American people and to the countries he "wantonly maligned."

In 2016, Trump won Utah's fourth congressional district, which encompasses parts of Salt Lake and three other counties in the middle of the state, with just 39 percent of the vote.[22]

Love's criticism of Trump seemed to be a point of pride. "There isn't anybody in the Republican Party who has called out the president more than I have," she told me when I interviewed her at the Republican National Committee headquarters a few blocks from the US Capitol in the summer of 2018. She acknowledged that some constituents urged her to stop criticizing Trump. But she claimed most said, "Thank you for saying that because I was feeling it too," she said.

Love was in many ways a conventional conservative Republican, earning high marks from all the leading conservative advocacy groups: 100 percent from National Right to Life, 83 percent from the Club for Growth, 93 percent from the Chamber of Commerce, and a solid "A" from the National Rifle Association.[23] [24]

In her two terms in Congress, she had sponsored legislation to combat human trafficking, urged her party's leaders to permanently repeal a medical-device tax that had hobbled medical-technology companies located in her district, and introduced a bill to stop taxpayer money from being used to settle workplace disputes in Congress. Her contribution to the immigration reform debate was called the RAC Act, which would have allowed young, undocumented immigrants who were brought to the United States as children to earn a conditional five-year legal status.

Love's 2018 Democratic opponent was Ben McAdams, the second-term mayor of Salt Lake County. McAdams presented himself as a wonky centrist more interested in fixing local problems such as poor air quality, homelessness, and rampant drug use than in scoring political points. He rarely waded into cultural battles or commented on Trump. His speeches were filled with platitudes about the need for "healing dialogue" and finding "common ground" to enact policies that respect "conscience" while "affording human dignity."

Love portrayed McAdams as a liberal sheep in centrist's clothing. She noted that during his time in the state senate, McAdams had been rated by the *Salt Lake Tribune* as the state's most liberal state senator.[25] She highlighted his ties to Bill and Hillary Clinton, for whom he worked in low-level positions in the 1990s and early 2000s. Love also argued that McAdams, in the House, would become a tool of Nancy Pelosi. McAdams blunted that last line of attack by stating that he would not support Pelosi for House speaker.[26] Utah Democratic Party Chairman Alex Cragun called Love's attacks on McAdams "amateur hour" and claimed that she

Rep. Mia Love and Daniel Allott in Washington, D.C. in 2018. (Author's personal collection)

was all talk and no action when it comes to standing up to Trump. "She says, 'I'm not Trump,' but then goes on and votes for his agenda," he said.

Love saw things differently. "The president doesn't take a vote," she said. "To be honest with you, it's the president who has supported me 96 percent of the time."

Love had broken with Trump on immigration and aluminum and steel tariffs. And she had also bucked party leaders on several occasions, such as when she voted against a $1.3 trillion budget and when she supported the "discharge petition," which would have prompted a debate and votes on a sequence of immigration proposals.

National Democrats targeted her, raising money for McAdams in the hopes that it would be part of a "blue wave" that would wash away the Republican House majority.

Mitt Romney ran for US Senate that year, and Republicans hoped his presence at the top of the ballot in Utah would help drive up turnout. Then again, the last time Romney's name had appeared on a ballot in Utah, when he ran for president in 2012, Love had lost a race for Congress, and McAdams had won his race for mayor.

Heading into the election, polls showed the race to be a dead heat.

When I asked Love whether she would welcome a campaign visit by the president, she said, "I don't need it. I've always been very good on my own."

Then I asked her a question that seemed to catch her off-guard: "Will you support President Trump for reelection in 2020?"

"You know I, I don't know what that's going to look like," she said. "You're going to have to ask me in 2020. You never know." Love's muddled answer reflected her deep ambivalence about Trump. She was being criticized from her left for not being hard enough on Trump, and from her right for criticizing him at all. Love ended up losing her re-election bid by just a few hundred votes. President Trump summed up the political environment aptly the next day at a press conference. He suggested that Love and other Republicans had lost because they did not sufficiently "embrace" him.

"Mia Love gave me no love, and she lost," Trump said. "Too bad. Sorry about that, Mia."[27]

* * *

In the summer of 2018, tiny microbes reacting to changing levels of salinity in Great Salt Lake turned the water half-red and half-blue. It created a stunning visual image—and an apt metaphor for the political changes that are starting to happen in Utah.[28]

If you've never been to Salt Lake City, you might assume that it's a rather conservative, buttoned-up place. It was founded in 1847 by pioneers of the LDS Church, the most heavily Republican-leaning religious group in America. But Salt Lake City is racially diverse and politically progressive. Nearly one in four city residents is Hispanic.[29] In some neighborhoods, two-thirds of school children speak Spanish at home. In recent years Salt Lake City has been ranked as the third most hipster city in the world,[30] one of the queerest cities in America,[31] and the fourth best city for Millennials to live in.[32] Millennials make up nearly half of the city's mortgages, compared to the national average of 9 percent.[33]

Traveling throughout the city during several visits, I met as many non-Mormons—evangelicals, Catholics, Jews, and even a couple of scientologists—as I did Mormons. I also met a whole lot of ex-Mormons. Utah as a whole remains predominantly Mormon, but Salt Lake County, home of the state's capital and largest city, is now majority non-Mormon.[34]

To appreciate how defiantly progressive Salt Lake City is, take the TRAX light rail to Temple Square, the city center and heart of the LDS Church. Church members are forbidden from consuming alcohol. But I counted at least a dozen bars within walking distance of the Temple, including some that mock the Mormon culture with names like the Beer Hive Pub, the Tavernacle, and Ex-Wifes Place. Or drive a few blocks south to Harvey Milk Boulevard and check out the Coffee Garden, Centered City Yoga, or Club Try-angles, which advertises itself as a "high-energy gay bar offering the coldest, cheapest and biggest drinks in town."

"Salt Lake City is extremely progressive," Jennifer Dailey-Provost, who represents Utah's House District 24, told me when we met at Nostalgia Café, a boutique coffee shop and vegan brunch restaurant in downtown Salt Lake City. Every legislative seat in the city is represented by a Democrat. And every mayor since 1976 has been a Democrat, including Jackie Biskupski, the city's first openly gay mayor, who served until January 2020.

Dailey-Provost has a friend who refers to the city as "Berkeley East." Dailey-Provost prefers to call it "a progressive oasis in a vast sea of red. I think most Republicans see it that way, and it drives them nuts that the capitol and (Salt Lake) Temple are both in my district."

One evening in 2019, I attended a house-warming party at the Salt Lake City home of a Democratic activist couple I'd become friendly with. I spoke with nearly two-dozen people that night. Many were former Mormons, and everyone seemed to be a Bernie Sanders-supporting progressive. That shouldn't have surprised me. In 2016, Sanders drew a crowd of 17,000 at a rally in Salt Lake City a few days before winning Utah's Democratic caucuses with 77 percent of the vote.[35] In the

Utah State Rep. Jennifer Dailey-Provost in 2017.
(Daniel Allott)

general election, Hillary Clinton won Salt Lake County by 10 points just four years after Mitt Romney had won it by 20.[36] On Super Tuesday in 2020, Sanders would easily win Utah with 35 percent of the vote.[37]

It has been nearly twenty years since a Democrat won any statewide office in Utah, and more than fifty years since a Democratic presidential candidate won the state. But that sea of red is beginning to recede as young professionals from other states move in to take advantage of Utah's job market, which routinely ranks as the best in the nation. Utah is the country's fastest-growing state. Some of that growth is due to the high birth rate among Mormon families. But much of it comes from young people moving in from out of state, attracted by great jobs, a relatively low cost of living, and Utah's natural beauty.

Salt Lake County's population is projected to rise 50 percent by 2065, according to a University of Utah study. That's an addition of nearly 600,000 people.[38] Many newcomers settle in the metropolitan area that stretches from Ogden to Provo, dubbed Silicon Slopes, where 80 percent of the state's population lives. Home to numerous start-ups and established software companies, medical device manufacturers, and aerospace businesses, it's been ranked as the fourth best metro area in the country for tech jobs. Goldman Sachs, Adobe, and Twitter all have offices there.[39]

Utah Democratic strategist Jim Gonzales sees the influx of people from high-tax, high-cost-of-living states, such as California, as helping Democrats. "They tend to be a little more socially progressive and well educated," he said of the newcomers, adding that these migration patterns help to explain the parts of Salt Lake County where "the red wall may be falling down a little." In 2016, more than 23,000 people moved to Utah from California alone. Few of them were Mormon.[40]

In 2018 Democrats picked up one new state senate seat and five state house seats. But their biggest prize was the fourth Congressional District seat that Ben McAdams narrowly won over Mia Love. McAdams is the first Utah Democrat to win an election for federal office since 2012. Voters also approved two progressive ballot initiatives—one to expand Medicaid, another to legalize medical marijuana.

Gonzales believes Democrats have also benefited from the chaos within the state Republican Party. "The Utah Republican Party is trying to decide whether it's the Trump party or the Romney party," he said. "They haven't come close to deciding that yet." In 2016 Donald Trump became the first Republican in more than half a century not to win a majority of Utah voters. He won less than a third of Salt Lake County voters. Utah Republicans have also been fighting over the structure of their party. A 2014 law known as SB 54 has divided the party. It allows candidates to appear on the ballot by gathering signatures rather than solely through the traditional caucus/convention route.

In 2018, Romney's effort to collect signatures while seeking the Republican nomination for US Senate caused such a backlash among caucus goers that a majority voted for State Senator Mike Kennedy, forcing Romney into a primary.[41] The Utah Republican Party Central Committee fought the law all the way to the US Supreme Court, which declined to hear the case, effectively ending the debate.[42] The fight reportedly bankrupted the state party. The ensuing turmoil caused the state chairman to resign in 2019.

The controversy wasn't received well by rank-and-file Republicans. A survey by Dan Jones & Associates found that nearly two-thirds of Utah Republicans said the infighting had made them less supportive of the Utah Republican Party.[43] When I spoke with Salt Lake County Republican Party Chairman Scott Miller in the spring of 2019, he insisted he wasn't worried about the SB54 controversy. Instead, he was focused on rebuilding the county party, which he says was "apathetic" when he took it over in the summer of 2018. "We'd gotten so used to winning races with minimal effort," he said. "But now that the dynamics of Salt Lake County have changed, we need to change."

Miller was dismissive of local Democrats' recent successes. "I don't think the Democrats are doing anything different than they've ever done. I just think they're getting lucky with the types of people that are moving into the area." Lucky or not, Republicans are slowly losing ground beyond Salt Lake City. Republicans' share of the vote decreased between 2016 and 2018 in twenty-two of the twenty-three Salt Lake County state house races in which both parties fielded candidates. The same thing happened in eight of ten state senate races. Besides lucky demographic changes, Miller blamed the 2018 losses on those two ballot initiatives, which spurred record high turnout. Scott said young voters "came out in droves" to help pass the measures.

But Democratic gains predate 2018. In the state house, for instance, Republican candidates in Salt Lake County lost vote share in more than two-thirds (14 of 20) of eligible races between 2014 and 2016. A couple of years ago, statistician Nate Silver predicted that Utah might be winnable for Democrats as early as 2024. In some ways, Utah "increasingly has the markers of a blue state, meaning high education levels, big tech sector, young population," he said.[44] Silver's prediction seems premature. Most of Utah is still deeply conservative. Then again, if tiny microbes can suddenly change the color of Utah's largest lake to a mix of red and blue, perhaps Democrats can do something similar to the state's political map.

***

As Trump's presidency proceeded, MWEG weighed in with op-eds and official statements. They rebuked the administration for the "unconscionable practice of separating children from their parents at the border"; demanded further investigation into thirty-five-year-old sexual misconduct allegations against Brett Kavanaugh during his Supreme

Court confirmation hearings; and pressed for more witness testimony during President Trump's impeachment trial.[45] When Mitt Romney voted to hear witnesses in the trial, MWEG members hand-delivered a thank-you note, milk, and brownies to the Utah senator's office. They later wrote a letter to Romney thanking him for voting to convict and remove President Trump from office.

Whenever I met with members, they would continue to insist that MWEG was nonpartisan and that, at least in private, their members were having "robust debates" and "tough conversations" on a range of issues and from a variety of perspectives. But while every press statement and op-ed included lofty rhetoric about transcending partisanship, they always directed their ire at Trump and Trump's Republican Party, never at Democrats. And whenever they complimented a Republican, such as with Romney's impeachment vote, it was only when he had broken with his party to side with Democrats.

When I asked members why they hadn't ever criticized a Democrat for unethical or tribal behavior, some of them seemed stumped, as if the possibility had never occurred to them. Others said they expected to do so once a Democrat becomes president. Emma Petty Addams, who became MWEG's executive director in 2019, said their lack of criticism of Democrats was "more of a bandwidth issue," suggesting that the sheer volume of unethical behavior by the Trump administration monopolized their time and resources. To be fair, whenever I asked members to tell me something they felt Trump had gotten right, most had an answer. They would mention the First Step Act, a criminal justice reform bill that Trump had signed into law in 2018, or the taskforce the Trump administration launched to investigate missing and murdered indigenous peoples.

One woman said she appreciated that Trump had overruled his education secretary to restore an annual budget request of $18 million in federal funding for the Special Olympics. "It took all I could do," she said in describing how it felt to write the administration a letter of thanks. "It took courage to do it. I still shudder to think about it now."

In February 2020, a Utah Political Trends poll found that for the first time, a majority of Utah voters approved of President Trump's job performance.[46] The poll also found that 60 percent of active Mormons approved of Trump's job performance. That was consistent with the 61 percent of Mormon voters Trump had won on election day and the 61 percent approval rating he had on the anniversary of his inauguration. But the Utah Political Trends poll showed a sizeable gender gap of 18 points. Just 38 percent of Mormon women approved of the president's job performance. Another poll found 55 percent Mormon approval overall but a gender gap of 11 points.[47] Interestingly, while women were more likely than men to identify as Republicans (68 percent to 63 percent), they were less likely than men to approve of Trump (51 percent to 62 percent).

As the 2020 election approaches, the question for many Mormon women will be tricky. Without a conservative alternative like Evan McMullin on the ballot, for whom will they vote? Will they overlook Trump's character flaws to vote for him? Or will they consider voting for the Democratic nominee, Joe Biden? On my final visit to Utah in February 2020, I spoke separately with more than half a dozen MWEG members. It didn't surprise me that none of them were considering voting for Trump.

Dalene Rowley said she was fond of Elizabeth Warren and that her primary vote for the Massachusetts senator a few days later would be the "first time in a long time that I voted for, and not against, a candidate." Rowley added that she would vote for Vermont Senator Bernie Sanders if he became the Democratic nominee, though the prospect of voting for an avowed socialist was painful for her to imagine. "Ultimately, I would trade the robustness of my 401k for us to be a kinder, gentler nation," she explained.

Melarie Wheat mused about her political transformation since becoming a member of MWEG. She sheepishly told me that she had voted for Texas Sen. Ted Cruz in the 2016 primaries. "What was I thinking?!" she said as she thought back to her earlier vote. Before I had the chance to ask her about President Trump, she revealed that she had cried tears of gratitude when Mitt Romney cast his vote for impeachment. A few days before my visit, Wheat had received a Republican primary ballot in the mail. But she tore it up before mailing it back and requesting a Democratic ballot instead. She said she was open to voting for any of the Democrats except Sanders or former Vice President Joe Biden.

"Old, white men—I'm really done with," she said.

Overall among the women, I found little to no enthusiasm for Sanders or Biden. The names I heard again and again were those of two women who would soon drop out of the race: Warren and Minnesota Sen. Amy Klobuchar.

I also talked to a woman named Shelly Cluff, one of MWEG's most conservative members. Cluff said she was grateful that her involvement with MWEG had challenged her own political biases and allowed her to step out of the conservative echo chamber of her family and friend group in Riverton, a conservative suburb of Salt Lake City. But Cluff also complained that she didn't always feel listened to by other members of MWEG's Facebook discussion groups whenever she voiced a dissenting opinion. Cluff was uncertain how she'd vote in the election, but was certain it wouldn't be for either Trump or Sanders.

Later, she would email to say she didn't think she could vote for Biden either because of his willingness to align with extreme factions of his party. "Religious freedom protections are a big issue to me," she wrote. "And I do not see any part of him standing up for Christians because that's not popular right now."

Most of the women were convinced that Trump would

Sharlee Mullins Glenn at her home in Pleasant Grove, Utah. (Daniel Allott)

be reelected, and that he would perform better among Mormons than he did in 2016. "He has kept his promises," a couple of the women said to explain why many Mormons were turning more decisively toward Trump. Several said they knew friends and family members who in 2016 had reluctantly voted for Trump but now supported him more enthusiastically. "It seems like the attitude in Utah has been, acknowledge the good and ignore the bad," one member said, resignedly.

My last stop in Utah was the home of MWEG's founder, Sharlee Mullins Glenn. Mullins Glenn said that she too was fond of Klobuchar and Warren, but was open to other candidates. "I would vote for anyone that I felt like was reasonable and could listen and could work across the aisle and be respectful and lead," she said.

Then she told me a story that perfectly captures the challenge facing MWEG and anyone else attempting to transcend the partisanship and tribalism that define modern politics.

The *New York Times* had recently published an op-ed Mullins Glenn had written in which she recounted how Trump's election had prompted her to become politically active.[48] In the op-ed, she criticized President Trump for declaring himself to be above the law and instilling fear in the public. She ended the piece by calling the choice between love and the fear represented by Trump "the defining question of our time." The op-ed's original headline, written by a *Times* editor, was, "Why I became an activist against fear." Mullins Glenn felt that headline was "a little lackluster" but that it at least conveyed the main thrust of the piece. But a few hours after the piece had been published, a *Times* editor changed the headline to something quite different: "I am Mormon, and I am fighting against Trump."

As an opinion editor, I understand why the headline was changed. The second headline is much more compelling and certainly more clickworthy. Would the average *New York Times* reader rather read an op-ed by an activist against fear or one written by a Mormon woman who's "fighting against Trump"? That's an easy question: The *Times's* liberal readership would love an op-ed by a member of the most conservative religious denomination in America bashing Trump.

But MWEG has always maintained that it isn't "fighting against Trump." It's fighting against the lawlessness, incivility, and fear they believe are at the heart of his presidency. That nuance may have been lost on the *Times's* editors; it was certainly hard to detect in the op-ed. But it was a crucial distinction for Mullins Glenn and the group she founded.

Mullins Glenn contacted the *Times's* editor and demanded that the headline be changed back. "We are very, very careful to position ourselves as an organization that is for something and not against something," she explained to the editor. "We see ourselves as peacemakers." The editor changed the headline, but by then, the "fighting against Trump" headline had been on *Times's* homepage for a couple of hours, likely seen by thousands of readers. One of those readers was a close family member of Mullins Glenn's, who sent her an angry email, chiding her for adding to the discord.

When Mullins Glenn and I talked about the op-ed and the wrangling over the headline, she still seemed a little frustrated. She had spent a year-and-a-half trying to get a piece published in America's most prestigious newspaper, and was grateful for the opportunity and the overwhelmingly positive response it had generated. But Mullins Glenn felt that the new headline sent exactly the opposite message to the one she wanted to convey. "It violated all of our guiding principles in one headline," she said.

I admired the women of MWEG for aspiring to transcend political tribalism. But I also wondered whether it was a realistic aspiration in a political environment in which almost every institutional force demands that we remain in our tribes and which punishes those like Mia Love who venture outside of them.

8

ERIE COUNTY, PENNSYLVANIA

UNTIL 2016, David Moore had always considered himself politically independent—so independent that he'd never even bothered to vote. But Moore was eager to vote for Donald Trump for president. So was everyone he knew at the plastics shop where he worked. "I know first-hand from just my division, of 125 employees out of three shifts, every single one of us voted for Trump for the same reason," he told me over drinks at an Erie Applebee's early in 2017. "We wanted change."

> We were pretty much standing as a shop saying, "We want to see something different. We don't want the same political promises that don't hold up." And Trump was very, very persistent through his campaigns that he was going to bring that change that a lot of us lower-class working families were trying to find.

Moore didn't agree with Trump on everything; he opposed Trump's proposed border wall with Mexico, for instance. And Moore said that, had he voted in 2012, it probably would have been for Barack Obama. He even gave the former president an "A" grade on performance. That said, Trump's pledge to "make America great again" by renegotiating trade deals and bringing jobs back from overseas made Moore a big fan from early in the campaign. "Myself, and I know my wife, and numerous family members, we were all for Trump from day one."

Moore, once an itinerant youth, settled down in Erie in his early twenties, married, and began working as a roofer, then in manufacturing. In 2012, Moore started off "at the very, very bottom" in the molding division at Plastek Group, a plastics packaging manufacturer and one of Erie's biggest employers. By Moore's count, at least ten established plastics shops in the area had moved abroad during the Obama presidency. "They would come and try to get jobs with us," he said of the laid-off workers. "I think that had a huge influence on why so many of Plastek's employees actually voted for Trump."

In 2016, Moore himself was laid off when Plastek underwent a series of cuts. At the time of our interview, he was doing seasonal contract work, installing sprinkler systems throughout the county. He enjoyed working outdoors again. But with a growing family at home, he knew it wasn't a long-term solution. He was planning to submit his resume to Erie plastics shops, and he seemed confident that he'd soon land a job.

Moore's job loss only reinforced his election day decision. "He's an advocate for the working class and that the politicians haven't listened to them," Moore said of Trump. "If you did not have people in manufacturing, you didn't have people in construction, you didn't have people doing the real hard jobs, our country would not be nothing. I think our voice should be heard a lot clearer, and I've felt that over the years it hasn't."

Trump, Moore said, appealed to the working class on an "'I've been there, I know what you guys have been through' level."

Donald Trump performed well among blue-collar workers like

Moore in 2016: He won 52 percent of voters without a college degree, according to the Pew Research Center, a five-point improvement over Mitt Romney's 2012 performance.[1] Trump even won 52 percent of white union households, a formerly Democratic constituency—the best result for a Republican presidential nominee since Ronald Reagan's landslide in 1984.[2] Trump's strength with working-class voters was crucial in places like Erie County, a faded manufacturing hub that borders Lake Erie to the north, New York to the east, and Ohio to the west.

Four years after Romney lost Erie County by 19,000 votes, Trump won it by 2,000, making him the first Republican presidential candidate to win there since 1984. That 21,000-vote swing (a reversal of 19 percentage points) helped Trump become the first Republican to win Pennsylvania since 1988.[3] Hillary Clinton dominated in Erie City, whose population of 100,000 comprises about one-third of the county's total. But even as she won all of the city's 69 voting precincts, Trump won overwhelmingly almost everywhere else in the county.[4]

Erie has been hit hard in recent decades by the loss of manufacturing jobs and the consequent decline in population as people have moved elsewhere to find better opportunities. More than 10,000 people moved out of Erie County during the six-year period leading up to the 2016 election—a hefty number for a county with fewer than 280,000 residents.[5]

As the 2016 election approached, locomotive manufacturer GE Transportation, then Erie's largest employer, announced it would be laying off 1,500 employees, one-third of its workforce.[6] During the same period, 3,900 refugees and immigrants settled in Erie, including hundreds of Syrian refugees, helping to prop up the shrinking population. But as Erie's economy shifts from manufacturing to a combination of manufacturing and services, education, and health care, some workers are being left out. That's why Trump's pledge to bring back manufacturing jobs resonated so deeply here.

The day after interviewing Moore, I met Todd Sias and his wife Diana at their humble apartment on Parade Street in downtown Erie, just a few blocks from the Lake Erie shore. Before we sat down to talk, Sias showed me some photographs. The printed photos showed Sias, an unemployed forty-four-year-old who immigrated from Mexico as a child, smiling, gesticulating, and having a grand old time at the Erie Insurance Arena on August 12, 2016. That was the day Todd and Diana had witnessed then-presidential candidate Donald Trump holding court in front of some 10,000 admirers. Todd looked in the photo as though he could hardly contain his enthusiasm. "This is me. And I'm wearing my 'Make America Great' shirt," Todd explained. "And I'm happy."

Like Moore, Sias said he had supported Trump "since day one." Sias listed the reasons why he was so enthusiastic about Trump: Trump's pledges to repeal Obamacare, to ban certain refugees from entering the country, and to build a wall between the US and Mexico to keep out illegal immigrants.

I asked Todd whether he was troubled by some of Trump's hard-line positions and harsh rhetoric on immigration. "I know that Trump seems like he's hard-pressed against Hispanics, Muslims, anybody who is not basically an American," Todd answered. "And as well he

Todd Sias in his home in Erie in 2017. (Jordan Allott)

should be. America should be for Americans. I am Hispanic, but I have dual-citizenship, and I filled out the paperwork and got in this country legally."

But the topic that mattered most to Sias and many other Erie County residents was the one Trump zeroed in on that day Sias saw him: trade and manufacturing jobs.

"Would I be good at keeping jobs over here?" he asked the crowd. "You look at this arena, and you see thousands and thousands of people. I think we're going to do great."

Earlier that day, Trump had told the *Erie Times-News* that he'd come to Erie as an ambassador for "the working man and woman." "I'm representing people whose jobs have just been taken away because their companies have left," he said.[7]

Sias had worked in construction and manufacturing for most of his adult life but hadn't found work lately. The day before I met him, he had interviewed at Taco Bell. "I mean, no job is too demeaning when you need food on the table and a roof over your head," he explained. "The thing I like about Trump is, he wants America first," Sias said as Diana looked on. "It seems like we're getting short-ended on all the trade deals. It doesn't seem like we have any growth in the economy, and it seems like we're literally outsourcing all our economy and commerce out of the country."

Perhaps most notable about Trump's presence in Erie was how it contrasted with Hillary Clinton's absence there. Clinton sent all of her top surrogates—husband Bill, daughter Chelsea, and her running mate, Virginia Sen. Tim Kaine—but never set foot in the county herself. "Hillary Clinton wasn't even good enough to campaign for herself," Todd said. "If you're not willing to put in the work, you don't deserve the title."

Maybe Clinton felt she didn't need to show up. As then-Mayor Joseph Sinnott told me later in the week:

(The city of) Erie was a big Clinton area. It always was. They were very, very supportive of Bill Clinton, very, very supportive of (Hillary) Clinton in 2008. But Hillary did not come here. And it was noticed and it was talked about within the party and the voters. And as history now shows, a lot of the folks that you would have expected should have been Hillary voters went the Trump route.

Clinton took this Rust and Snow Belt county for granted, and she paid dearly for it. In places and among people who have felt abandoned and forgotten, hope had been in short supply. And as Todd Sias put it, for many Erie residents, "The hope of (the American dream) is alive again with Donald Trump."

* * *

Following the 2016 election, Erie and other pivotal counties received an avalanche of national media attention, but not necessarily the type of attention their residents felt they deserved. In many of the places I traveled, people would tell me that other journalists had visited, curious about the political changes that had occurred there. Many were wary of out-of-town reporters. Once, when I tried to interview a Hispanic woman in rural Wisconsin, she declined, explaining that a reporter had come through a few weeks earlier and misreported what she had told him. In other cases, residents welcomed the chance to speak with me, sometimes in the hope of dispelling what others had previously reported.

That was the case in Erie, where I met many residents who felt journalists had forced their story into a narrative box. As Sean Fedorko, co-founder of Radius Cowork in Erie, put it about the thrust of the post-election coverage in Erie, "Here's our story about a sad Rust Belt town and the people who are angry about its change, and we just fill in the names."

The subtext was usually that only economic desperation could explain why counties that previously voted overwhelmingly for Barack Obama subsequently voted for Trump. Exhibit A in the media's one-sided treatment of Erie was a documentary produced by CBSN, the streaming video news channel operated by CBS News. Airing a couple of weeks after Trump's inauguration, the twenty-minute documentary was titled, "America: Manufacturing Hope."[8] The video begins with an elderly woman describing how GE Transportation laid off six men, including her brother, who went on to commit suicide. As she tearfully recounts the story, ominous music plays in the background, and on a TV screen nearby, Donald Trump is seen delivering his inaugural address. Erie is referred to as a "sinking ship" that "you'd be crazy not to get off" and as "a community (that) has lost the means to provide for its people."

The video also tells the story of Justin Gallagher, who was about to graduate from a local college. Gallagher tearfully tells of his fear that he'll have to leave Erie because the prospects of finding work at GE, where his father had worked as a principal engineer for thirty-three years, are slim.

The CBS documentary riled a lot of people in Erie. At least half a dozen people across the city mentioned it to me as an egregious act of journalistic malpractice. "The documentary gave Erie a very bad name," said David Moore. It focused on "all the negative of Erie, all the blight, all the violence and didn't reflect how most people here feel about Erie."

There was one particular shot that bothered Fedorko. "It's a really ridiculous (shot) of this decrepit building," Fedorko said with frustration. The thing is, the shot left out what surrounded that building. "To the right is a beautiful new maintained modern one, and to the left is a beautiful brand new sports arena." The depiction of Erie as being in decline was not without merit. Erie had lost half its manufacturing jobs since the 1980s. Whenever I drove along the 12th Street corridor in Erie City, I saw blocks of shuttered warehouses and rusting factories. And every time I visited Perry Square Park and other parts of downtown Erie, I was taken aback by the number of people who appeared homeless, high, drunk, or physically injured in some way. Most of those people appeared to be working-age men.

But the negative portrayal of Erie is incomplete. Erie is more accurately seen as a county in transition, and one with some notable signs of promise. In early 2017, at least three $100 million-plus building projects were beginning in Erie—a $135 million expansion of Erie Insurance that would make room for an additional 600 employees and $100 million-plus expansions of both Erie hospitals, UPMC Hamot and Saint Vincent's. Erie also boasts five universities, including the nation's largest medical school.

Erie's unemployment and poverty rates were only slightly higher than the state and national averages, and the share of adults with a college degree was only slightly lower. Erie was going through the growing pains that usually accompany economic diversification.

Erie residents are quick to list some of Erie's less depressing attributes, including its low cost of living, beautiful scenery, beaches, a symphony, and sports teams, as well as Presque Isle State Park, a sandy peninsula that extends into Lake Erie and is visited by 4 million people annually. Erie's challenge has always been attracting young people, especially college-educated young people who want to build businesses and start families there.

In April 2017, I spoke with six members of the Erie Regional Chamber and Growth Partnership and the Erie Redevelopment Authority, which provides loans to companies that want to expand or relocate to the area. They wanted to make their case that after years of decline, Erie was in the midst of reinvention. Barbara Chaffee, president and CEO of the partnership, said that while a lot of people in Erie talk about the problem of "brain drain," the emigration of well-educated people out of an area, she was seeing what she called "brain gain"—talented Erie residents who move away only to return to start a family and settle down. "It's amazing how many requests we get for, 'I want to come back now. I have a family now. Can you give us some advice on a job or what positions are open?'" she said. "We see a lot of that bounceback."

In the 1950s, more than half of Erie County workers were employed in manufacturing. By 2016, roughly one quarter were. Heavy industry had left and many smaller, family-run firms got bought up by larger companies and moved elsewhere. Some employers were struggling to fill open slots, particularly for skilled positions. That's partly because so many people have left the county, and partly because many who haven't are addicted to drugs and thus unsuitable for employment. The smaller population has shrunk the tax base, straining public services. At one point in 2016, the Erie public school system threatened to close its high schools for insufficient funding.[9]

Almost everybody I spoke with agreed that, despite its decline here, manufacturing would continue to play an important role in Erie's economy. Katrina Vincent, director of real estate for the Erie County Redevelopment Authority, recounted how Lord Corporation, a global aerospace company specializing in shock- and vibration-dampening products, had recently decided against relocating its manufacturing facility away from Erie. Vincent and her team helped Lord, which was founded in Erie nearly a century ago, find a new factory in the county and enticed it to stay through a combination of grants and low-interest loans. "It was a great success," she said. "A loss of 1,100 jobs to this region could have resulted. (But) we were able to work creatively to ensure the company retained their core manufacturing and (research and development) in Erie."

But most people in Erie seem to agree that, even more than manufacturing, the key to Erie's future will be economic diversification. A recent study found that Erie ranked as the 118th most economically diverse medium-sized city in the country out of 144 studied.[10]

"Yes, we've lost hundreds of jobs at GE," said Fedorko, who is in his late twenties. "I don't care. I didn't want to work for them. I don't know anybody my age who says that he wants to work a manufacturing job."

Jake Rouch, vice president of economic development at the Erie Regional Chamber of Commerce, predicted that a generation from now, manufacturing will still be an important part of Erie's economy, but that it will be balanced by stronger medical, education, hospitality, and insurance and professional services sectors.

Erie Insurance, a Fortune 500 company that employs 5,000 Erie

The view of Lake Erie from the beaches of Presque Isle. (Daniel Allott).

Bicentennial Tower in downtown Erie. (Jordan Allott)

residents, had recently hired new employees to build one of the most sophisticated databases in the insurance industry. "We're shifting what kind of city we are," Fedorko said.

County Executive Kathy Dahlkemper talked about the importance of culture in making Erie a more inviting place to work and live. She said Erie is working on making the city more walkable and bike-friendly, and thus more connected. She added that it's important to improve what she calls Erie's "entrepreneurial ecosystem." Entrepreneurialism is seen as a key to Erie's revival. Fedorko's Radius Co-Work provides a "first desk" to remote workers and anyone else who doesn't have office space or wants to connect with others in the city. Each time I visited Radius, I'd see dozens of ambitious young entrepreneurs and contractors working away.

I asked the participants what they saw as their greatest challenge in attracting people to Erie. Fedorko said it comes down to lifestyle and culture. "It's not about better tax credits," he said. "It's not about a special incentive program. It's, is your city a place that talented people want to live?"

Daniel Allott discusses Erie's economic situation with members of the Erie Regional Chamber and Growth Partnership and the Erie Redevelopment Authority in 2017. (Jordan Allott)

Rouch countered that creating good jobs is what's most important. "If I'm a graphic designer and I have six opportunities in Portland, Oregon, but I have one job opportunity in the Erie market, as much as I may love what I see here, I'm probably going to go there because if it doesn't work out with that company, I can move to another," he said. "They may also pay 20 percent more. To me, it's all driven by a job if you get the job opportunities."

Overall, I sensed a cautious optimism about Erie's future.

What does any of this have to do with President Trump? Not much, according to this group—and that's the point. The new president was barely mentioned in our two-hour conversation. The group agreed there were things the federal government could do to help or hinder their progress—lower the cost of college and address infrastructure, for example. But they emphasized that what really matters is local initiative.

"Who the president of the United States is doesn't impact us on a day in and day out basis," Rouch said. "We've got to take care of ourselves. We have to formulate our own solutions."

* * *

Two pernicious narratives have taken hold about how immigrants are treated in America and about how they live their lives once they arrive. The first narrative is that immigrants are unwelcome, discriminated against, and even at risk of harm and death, particularly in rural and Middle America and other places where Donald Trump is popular. This narrative has taken hold on the political left and become almost axiomatic among many journalists. Consider the following headlines:

"Endless fear: Undocumented immigrants grapple with anxiety, depression under Trump" (*USA Today*, Aug. 25, 2019)

"Six immigrants talk about the anxiety of living in Trump's America" (Vox, Aug. 30, 2017)

"On edge in Trump's America" (*Los Angeles Times*, June 30, 2017)

"In Trump's America, immigrants are modern-day 'savage Indians'" (The Conversation, July 16, 2018)

"'It's worse than ever': how Latino Americans are changing their lives in Trump's America" (The *Guardian*, Oct. 7, 2019)

The second narrative is that too many immigrants fail to appreciate the opportunities they have when they arrive in the US, that they are ungrateful, unwilling to assimilate, and interested only in taking advantage of America's generosity. On the right, this narrative has been used as proof that America must scale back immigration significantly.

Both narratives are mostly false. It is true that long-ignored immigration laws are finally being enforced, which means that immigrants who are in the country illegally are at heightened risk of deportation. And you can find examples of casual discrimination against immigrants. It's also true that some immigrants come with malign intentions, and that many fail to adequately assimilate once they arrive.

But I discovered a very different story in talking to immigrants across the country. I talked to high-school-age Central American DACA recipients in rural Wisconsin, Haitian visa-holders in rural Iowa, West African immigrants in West Virginia, Mexican immigrants in southern California, Iraqi immigrants in southeast Michigan, and many more. Far from exposing America's inherent prejudice, their stories reveal its enduring promise. Those I got to know best are Iraqi immigrants Hiba, her sister, Jasmine, and Jasmine's then-husband, Ali.

Erie is home to tens of thousands of refugees and other immigrants. According to one study, no other small American city received more refugees between 2012 and 2016, about 4,000.[11] They have come from places such as Bhutan, Nepal, and Sudan but more recently from Syria and Iraq. In fiscal 2016, 658 Syrian refugees were resettled in Erie. Refugees make up roughly 20 percent of the city's population of

100,000. On my first visit to Erie, I spoke with nearly a dozen refugees and other immigrants. All said they had been welcomed with open arms. And the Erie residents I met, almost to a person, all said they were proud that their community is a top refugee destination. The refugees have been welcomed in part because they're needed. Erie's new residents have helped temper the impact of the county's shrinking population.

Once when I asked the mayor's chief of staff what the federal government could do to make their job easier, his answer was "send us more immigrants." This was understandable since Erie's population had recently dropped below 100,000, making it ineligible for certain federal programs.

Hiba and Jasmine told me their stories over a dinner they prepared of dolma, tepsi baytinijan, fattoush salad, and other Iraqi dishes.

Hiba has lived in the US since 2014 and Jasmine since 2012. They were granted asylum because their male family members had worked as interpreters and in logistics with the US military, which made them targets of the jihadists.

Hiba has a degree in laser engineering. But her initial job in the US was as a cashier at Wal-Mart. She enjoyed it, and made such an impression on her coworkers that some of them cried when she left to take a job as a case manager at Catholic Charities.

Upon arriving in Erie, Hiba and Jasmine were struck by how friendly, polite, and law-abiding Americans are. "This is amazing," Hiba said. "Honestly I get a lot of support, the people here in United States, they're so friendly, so helpful and they are accepting each other, it doesn't matter who you are. They don't treat you based on your race or your background. That's my experience by living here."

"I have a friend who lives in DC, and I tell him I live in Erie," Jasmine said. "He say, 'This is redneck area where nobody likes refugees.' This is not right. I said 'I live there four years and people are so nice, so caring.' Really … I (haven't) met anyone who was against me or didn't like me."

Jasmine recounted being invited to give a talk at a Catholic church in Erie. She was nervous because her English wasn't great and because she's a Muslim who at the time wore a hijab. She was surprised by the response she received. "Oh my God, the reaction I got after that, like I was looking at their faces, they were crying," she said. "Like many women when I was done, they just came and hugged me and said, '(We're) so proud of you, God bless you, if you need anything, (let us know).' This is amazing."

Both women said they often got compliments from women on their head coverings. Jasmine even said she was treated more kindly when she wore her hijab than when she didn't. Jasmine said she understood why Americans are skeptical of some immigrants. She knows some who are entitled and ungrateful, she said. But "(coming to America) is like heaven for me, so you have to appreciate it, you have to work hard for it. And you just have to prove it …. You have to prove yourself to the society."

More than anything, the sisters said they appreciated that America is the land of unrivaled opportunity. "Here, if you work hard, you see the results," Hiba said.

Some readers may find it strange that a county that voted for Trump would be so welcoming to refugees, the fear of whom Trump constantly invokes. That's just one apparent irony for a people and place that defy easy categorization.

During a subsequent trip to Erie, I met Jasmine's husband, Ali, who echoed Hiba and Jasmine's comments about feeling welcomed. In 2012, Ali immigrated to the US with a Special Immigrant Visa, or SIV, after working as a translator and logistician for the US military during the Iraq War. The SIV is granted to Iraqi nationals who provide "faithful and valuable service" to the US government for at least one year and experience ongoing serious threats as a consequence of that work.

During an interview at Ali and Jasmine's home, I learned that both were Trump supporters. Ever since he began running for president, declaring, "Islam hates us," Donald Trump has been dogged by the accusation that he is bigoted against Muslims and immigrants.[12] The Trump administration's so-called "Muslim ban," which the administration attempted to implement in its first year, is considered by many to be the cruelest manifestation of that bigotry. But Jasmine and Ali support Trump—not despite his immigration policies but in part because of them.

When the Trump administration released the first version of its travel ban in January 2017, Jasmine's only quibble was that it left out Saudi Arabia, one of the world's leading state-sponsors of terror. Ali's only objection was that their birth country was ultimately taken off the list of banned countries. The couple had an interesting take on the president's view of Muslims. Ali and Jasmine believe Trump *is* Islamophobic. But they don't blame him or other Americans for fearing Muslims because most Americans hear about Islam only when it involves terrorism.

Jasmine and Ali said they encounter other Iraqis in Erie. Fully employed (Ali as a truck driver and Jasmine as an orthodontic assistant) and raising two children, they were alarmed at the sight of newcomers who exploit America's generous immigration and welfare systems.

"I get annoyed by someone who chose to be here, and they are illegal," Jasmine said. "They know the law, and they break it. And I feel like they are taking advantage. And they have all the benefit and they complain. Why don't you move if you don't like it and are taking all of these benefits? ... Some families, every year they have a new baby, and you ask them why, and they say they want more benefits," Jasmine continued. "You need time to adjust, but there are families living here twenty years and they still get the benefits."

"Oh yeah, they've got Medicaid, food stamps, tax credits, Section 8 housing," Ali added.

Ali and Jasmine said some Iraqi immigrants operate cash-based businesses to keep their tax burden low, helping them qualify for government benefits. "They save the money and then they decide after fifteen years to leave and buy a (nice) house and pay in cash," Ali said. "And that's not right."

"That's what I'll always say," added Jasmine. "Immigrants are not here to visit. If you left your country, you are not here to visit. Most of them, if you ask them, they say, 'Oh, we miss our home country, we wish we could go back.' ... Okay, go back! But they say, 'Oh but there's no power, schools are not great ...'"

Had they been eligible to vote in 2016, Ali and Jasmine said they would have voted for Trump. Ali didn't like everything about the president, especially how he takes credit for rising financial markets. And he hadn't committed to checking Trump's name when he casts his first presidential ballot in 2020. That said, he was "absolutely" happy with Trump's performance thus far and graded him as an "8 out of 10."

Trump earned the same grade with Jasmine, who said she appreciated his determination to put America first on the international stage, even if it risks alienating allies. "Unlike Obama, Trump knows what he wants. If he doesn't like it, he will say it straight in your face."

Hiba Alsabonge and Jasmine Alsabonge at Jasmine's naturalization ceremony in 2018. (Jordan Allott)

In April 2018, after a nearly six-year process, Ali and Jasmine became US citizens. Both said they'd felt a kinship with America long before they recited the Oath of Citizenship. "For me, country is not where you born, it's where you feel home, safe, welcomed, accepted, equal, and protected by law," Jasmine posted on her Facebook page after the ceremony. "Home means the United States for me. This country is in my blood."

While he was proud to become an American citizen, Ali said the ceremony didn't alter an allegiance he's felt deeply since the moment he arrived in the country. "My loyalty didn't change toward the United States since day one and will never change," he said. "So (reciting) the oath just confirmed that."

***

I returned to Erie several times in 2018 and 2019. In 2017 GE Transportation announced it would transfer all locomotive production to Fort Worth, Texas, eliminating hundreds of jobs. The Erie plant would be left to produce prototypes and components. But the company struggled to recruit skilled workers in low-wage Texas, and when demand for locomotives increased, work was sent back to the Erie plant. Hundreds of workers were recalled, and the plant continues to make locomotives. In February 2019, Wabtec Corporation merged with GE Transportation, making it a Fortune 500 company.[13]

Throughout most of Trump's term, Erie's unemployment rate remained at record lows, dropping to under 4 percent in the summer of 2019, and generally tracking slightly above the national rate. As a headline in the *Erie Times-News* put it, "Erie's economy roared in 2018."[14] Erie's GDP rose by 3.1 percent adjusted for inflation. The article found that personal incomes in the county grew 6.1 percent in 2018, up from 2.8 percent in 2017, putting it in the top quarter of counties in the state.

Erie Insurance became the county's largest employer and is gradually turning part of the city into a corporate campus. The region's four universities announced a collaboration called the Innovation Beehive Network to support startup entrepreneurship throughout the county.

The Economic Research Institute of Erie's (ERIE) third quarter 2019 report found an uptick in its Erie Leading Index, a group of ten leading economic indicators.[15] And by the end of 2019, the US Bureau of Economic Analysis (BEA) reported that per capita personal income in Erie County rose by an impressive 6.1 percent between 2017 and 2018, after having risen by 2.8 percent during the previous year. The 6.1 percent rise was higher than the increase in Pennsylvania (5.8 percent) and the nation (4.9 percent).

With election day still a year away, Trump couldn't argue that he had brought blue-collar jobs back—the total number of workers employed in manufacturing in Erie had dropped from 19,400 to 19,100 over the course of Trump's first three years in office.[16] But with the economy as strong as it was, few residents seemed to notice.

Whenever I visited Erie, I'd check in with Jake Rouch and Sean Fedorko to get a sense of Erie's economic situation. Rouch usually talked about the big picture. During a 2018 visit, he stressed that there had to be more honest talk about Erie's future.

You can't just wake up and say, "Erie's going to be a biotech center." If you're going to be a biotech center, you have to have a major research university combined with a hospital, and you'll probably get research. So biotech is probably only going to happen around so many places around the world.

A lot of people know how Pittsburgh has rebounded from the steel mills closing. We didn't have a fatal heart attack like that. What we had was chronic bronchitis. To cure yourself of the chronic bronchitis, you have to stop things; you have to stop smoking and exercise more and eat better and make better mental health decisions. All that stuff is happening in Erie right now.

Local business leaders were pleased with the tax reform law of 2017, Rouch said, while still hoping for a federal infrastructure spending bill.

In 2019 Erie Insurance announced a private $40 million campaign to get more apartments and stores in downtown to attract more young people and businesses. Rouch had noticed more business leaders were stepping up. "Finally, they are investing in their community," he said, citing Erie Insurance as an example. "There are people in Erie who seem both entrepreneurial and civic-minded. They care about their town. They don't like the image it has and want to prove the cynics wrong."

This was something I heard again and again from many civic leaders. A veteran local newspaper reporter, a lifelong Erie resident, told me he was encouraged by the newfound sense of community and solidarity. "You see a lot more collective will to improve things than I've seen in a long time," he told me in 2019 when we met at a local coffee shop.

There used to be a lot of turf battles between agencies. You see a lot of them starting to break down. Because I think people realize we are at a critical point as a community. We have to address poverty, the blight. More people are working together to that end than I've ever seen.

Daniel Allott with Jake Rouch in 2019. (Author's personal collection)

Indeed, in December 2019, the Erie Regional Chamber and Growth Partnership announced that it's hoping to bring at least 2,000 jobs to the area through a $5 million economic development campaign, called Erie Forward, to aggressively recruit new industry, capital investment, and high-paying jobs in the region. Some of the jobs would be in manufacturing, but also food and beverage processing and life sciences.

Fedorko said home prices were finally beginning to rise and noted that Value Momentum, a software company, had opened up a new location in Erie and planned to hire 120 people. And the city had passed tax incentives for homeowners to renovate their homes. Meanwhile,

Radius CoWork had just expanded its businesses. "We've never been busier," Fedorko said.

On politics, Rouch told me in 2019, "I think the percentage of people that voted for Trump the first time that won't vote for him the next is extremely small." Mercyhurst University conducted polls of Erie County throughout Trump's term. Trump's approval rating hadn't budged much at all since the first month after his inauguration.[17]

* * *

One day in June 2018, I met up with Allen Ewanick, one of the 1,500 employees GE had laid off in 2016, at a gastro pub in Millcreek Township, just east of Erie City. "I was a little reluctant to meet with you," Ewanick confessed as he pulled up a chair across from me at a table in the outdoor seating area. "I was like, 'Why does he want to meet with me? I don't have any pearls of wisdom or earth-shattering viewpoint.' But I didn't want to be closed-minded. I think it's important for people to see other people's viewpoints—the average working guy or whatever."

Ewanick, who somewhat resembles Mitt Romney, has lived in Erie since he was five years old. He worked at Kaiser Aluminum for more than three decades and had been a United Auto Workers union member. He left in 2008 and got a job testing locomotives at GE Transportation, where he worked for eight years.

"I loved my job the whole time I worked there," he said. "On the test track, I would take locomotives out and test them. I felt I had the best job at GE. I worked the night shift. We hit a few deer, and coyotes."

Ewanick was sixty years old when he was laid off. "It was a little traumatic at my age," he said. Instead of going back to school or becoming a Wal-Mart greeter, he decided to retire early. Ewanick was on the Trump train early, and he made sure his wife and three daughters got on board too. "I told my three daughters at election time, I said, 'You guys are voting for Trump,'" he said.

They are all very informed about politics. My youngest swears she voted for Trump, and she doesn't lie. I know she was on Hillary initially then stuff started coming out about her, and she said, "Well I don't think that's such a good idea." So I think she voted for Trump by default. But I kept telling them, "When we get there we're voting for Trump. Don't hem-haw around." And my wife, she was all for Trump.

His father's vote took Ewanick more by surprise.

I don't think my dad ever voted Republican before Trump. Voted for Obama. He's retired from GE. He had forty years there. Union guy his whole life. I never thought in a million years that he would be (for Trump). But he was. He kept saying, 'I'm on the Trump train.' Same with my stepmother-in-law. They were fed up. And that's what got Trump into office. People who were just sick and tired of all the BS.

I asked Ewanick to elaborate on the "sick and tired" comment.

Well, when you're in manufacturing basically your whole life, and you're watching company after company after company leave.... And that was one of the reasons I voted for Trump. I won't say it's protectionism. It's just the way he said, "You know what, our country comes first." And a lot of people don't like that attitude. But when your country is struggling, you've got to start looking at bettering your own country.... It's time to take care of our country.

Ewanick suspects very few of his former co-workers voted for Trump, but he knows many farmers who did. They "all went Trump. I mean, signs in their yards. A few years ago I never would have guessed that. But most of the people I knew who voted for Trump were just fed up. Fed up with the pablum that the Democrats have been feeding us." A couple of months before our interview, the Trump administration had imposed import tariffs on steel and aluminum products, prompting retaliatory tariffs from the affected countries.

"I'm all for fair trade, but we had to do something. We can't have this trade imbalance like we've had," Ewanick said, echoing the farmers I talked to in Iowa, Wisconsin, and North Carolina. They had all supported President Trump's hardball trade tactics despite the way it was affecting them. "I think in the long term, (the tariffs are) going to help."

Allen Ewanick in Millcreek Township in 2018. (Daniel Allott)

"I used to vote Democratic," Ewanick confessed. "But the shine on that kind of wore off with Bill Clinton and NAFTA." He noted that every time he was laid off, a Democrat was in the Oval Office. "Obama basically said, 'I'm going to bring the coal industry to its knees,'" Ewanick said. "And a large majority of the locomotives built at GE are BNSF locomotives. And that's mostly what they haul is coal. So when the coal industry dies, the locomotive manufacturing business takes a nosedive."

Social issues also played a big role in the Ewanick's vote. He and his wife staunchly oppose abortion and same-sex marriage; in fact, they are "the two biggest things" that determine their votes. Ewanick said Trump was doing a good job so far and that he anticipated voting for him again absent "a major *faux pas*," such as a reversal on abortion or immigration.

A few days later, I met Dale and Darlene Thompson, who offered a very different perspective. Dale is nearing retirement-age and has large tattoos running down both of his arms. He is a union member and works at a tool manufacturer in Erie. Darlene, a few years younger, is a health care administrator. They invited me to their home in Southeast Erie, where we chatted while sitting on their back patio.

Dale and Darlene loved President Obama and cried watching his inauguration. "On that day, we both turned to each other and said, 'Love won,'" Darlene recalled.

They voted for Bernie Sanders in the 2016 primary, then for Hillary Clinton in the general election, although they both expressed admiration for former Ohio Gov. John Kasich, who ran as a more moderate and less combative alternative to Trump in the Republican primaries. Both expressed shock and horror at Trump's victory but also a curiosity about how it had happened. "On the day he was inaugurated, hate won," Darlene said. "We were physically and emotionally ill for like the first two weeks. We were like, 'Are you kidding me? I couldn't even watch him on TV.' And then Dale was like, 'Dar, we have to watch. We have to know!'"

"And for the life of me, I'm still trying to figure it out," Dale added.

They were astonished to learn that Trump had won the support of many people they know, including most of Dale's coworkers. Dale saw Trump's election as a historical inflection point. "We can't turn America into *Leave it to Beaver* again, which it never was in the first fucking place," Dale said. "And I think we need this exposure of the underbelly of nationalism and white supremacy and hatefulness for everyone to see to launch us into the next era."

"I look at (the Trump era) as the last gasp of the desperate white man's grip on power," Dale went on. "I really do. I don't like his methods. I don't like the fact that he lies. He's white and we're getting our way, so fuck you! Honestly, I don't know if he can be beat in 2020.... This has always been Democratic territory, but they have completely lost touch with working class people. It's not a big secret. And Trump knew that and Trump gave them somebody to blame. It's the Mexican, Chinese, black people."

Despite what they saw as Trump's obvious unfitness for office, Dale and Darlene worried that Democrats still didn't understand the voters they will need to win over to defeat Trump in 2020. "If he doesn't fuck things up too much and the Democrats don't get any more organized with a message than they are right now, then I think he will win again," Dale said.

When I returned to Erie in the summer of 2019, Dale and Darlene were even more anxious about the weakness of the Democratic field. "We need to nominate a candidate that can win, period!" Dale said as we chatted again on their back patio. They responded as I listed some of the other Democratic candidates at the time:

Kamala Harris? "Too radical."

Bernie? "Too damn old, and he can't win."

Pete Buttigieg: "Too gay, for this area."

Julian Castro? "About as exciting as cold oatmeal."

Cory Booker? "Come on!"

Darlene said they were pinning their hopes on a primary challenge to Trump.

"Who could take him on?" I asked.

"I love John Kasich," said Darlene.

"I'd vote for Kasich," Dale said.

Both seemed to think Joe Biden would have the best shot at beating Trump, but the prospect of Biden standing as the lone bulwark between Trump and a second term made them nervous. Dale called Biden a "gaff machine."

"I would be walking on eggshells up until election day if he's the nominee," added Darlene. "Like, what is he going to fuck up now? You know what I mean?"

Dale and Darlene Thompson outside their home in Erie in 2018. (Daniel Allott)

Dale was convinced that his Trump-voting coworkers were

turning against the president. But Darlene was seeing the opposite. "All the Trump voters I know are die-hard," she said. "They're going to vote for him again."

In the year between interviews with Dale and Darlene, one thing had changed, something that I found disconcerting. The first time we chatted, while horrified by Trump's actions, Dale and Darlene were comforted by their assurance that America's institutions were strong enough to withstand Trump's authoritarian tendencies. "He probably won't fuck things up too bad because our institutions have been able to put enough of a check on him," Dale had said then.

But a year later, Dale had become far less optimistic in the strength and resiliency of America's system of checks and balances. When I asked what would happen if Trump won a second term, Dale said, "I think we're done."

"What do you mean?"

"I think we've lost our leadership position in the world," Dale said. "Our allies will know they can't count on us. I just don't know how we recover as a country. I don't know how we get out of this."

As for David Moore, the out-of-work manufacturing worker who said all of his coworkers voted for Trump in 2016, I couldn't get ahold of him for more than two years. Then when I called him in the summer of 2019, suddenly he picked up. He told me that he had just moved away from Erie, not because he couldn't find work there, but because his company had burned down in a fire and was moving operations to South Carolina.

Moore was still very enthusiastic about Trump, saying that he planned to vote for him again. He said he "absolutely" thinks Trump will win Erie County again, and predicted that all the people he knows who voted Trump the first time will do so again. He said that he didn't know any Trump critics who'd changed their minds about him. But he added that he knew of quite a few apolitical people who didn't vote in 2016 who had signaled that they will vote Trump in 2020.

***

I also kept in touch with Hiba, Jasmine, and Ali over the next three years. It was apparent that during that time all three had more fully immersed themselves in the American experience. I spent Memorial Day 2018 at a barbeque Ali and Jasmine hosted in which they were both decked out in red, white, and blue.

Hiba became a US citizen and began a new job as a bank teller. I also noticed that she no longer wore the hijab. In 2019, I learned that Jasmine and Ali had divorced. One weekend in the fall of 2019, I spoke with Hiba and Jasmine over dinner at Bayfront Grille, a restaurant on the bayfront with a stunning view of glimmering Lake Erie.

They again expressed gratitude for the opportunities they had and the lives they were living in America. Jasmine remarked that she no longer has an emotional connection to Iraq and doesn't feel even a tinge of patriotism when she hears the Iraqi national anthem.

Hiba said she feels safe in the US, and appreciated that as a woman she has equal rights and opportunities to men. Jasmine added that that was especially important in her divorce proceedings, which under Iraq's religious laws would have given all the control and rights to the divorcing husband. They both said that they no longer felt Muslim, and that their former faith didn't make much sense to them anymore.

A few weeks later I flew to Milwaukee, where Ali had moved to be closer to his cousin and to begin a new life. We met at an Iranian restaurant on the south side of town. He was no longer working as a long-haul truck driver. I was immediately struck by how much happier and healthier Ali appeared. He smiled and laughed freely during our conversation. Ali was still deeply hurt that his marriage had ended. He became emotional as he recounted the final months of his marriage. Ali, still a practicing Muslim, said Jasmine had complained that he was "too traditional" and "too old country."

"When she walked out, I thought one way—life is destroyed, it has vanished," he said of Jasmine. "But then later on, I realized she did me a favor. She changed me. She make me more care about my daughters."

Daniel Allott and Ali AlAbbasi in Milwaukee in 2019. (Author's personal collection)

Ali said he had enjoyed taking his daughters to Walt Disney World in Florida and was excited about visiting San Francisco with them the following year.

More than anything, Ali seemed hopeful. He had gotten a job as a garbage truck driver two weeks before and was optimistic that he would marry again. He was considering going to college or becoming a stock market analyst. (Ali would become a real estate agent in 2020.)

I wondered whether Ali regretted coming to America because the move had clearly transformed Jasmine. He acknowledged that living in America had put a strain on his marriage. "At one point I did regret it because everything is for the women, I mean the laws," he said, referring to the child support and alimony he's obliged to pay and the scant amount of time he gets to see his daughters.

"But I don't miss Iraq," he said. "I miss the people over there but not the country. That country doesn't mean anything to me. This country right here means more to me. It means everything."

"Are you still glad you came?"

"Oh yes, absolutely. Absolutely, yeah. Nothing can compare to this."

9

VOLUSIA COUNTY, FLORIDA

SANDI HODGDEN WAS IN HER ELEMENT. Standing below an American flag and an immense "Trump 2020 The Sequel—Make Liberals Cry Again" banner, and beside a life-size cardboard cutout of President Trump, the recently widowed mother of two and grandmother of five was attempting to persuade passersby to sign a gun-rights pledge and register to vote.

"Want to sign our Second Amendment petition?" she asked a group of people walking by.

"Sure," a man said.

"Don't need to," said another, motioning toward the cardboard commander-in-chief. "Not as long as we got that guy in the White House."

"Are you registered to vote?" Sandi asked another group.

"Not for him!" several yelled back; others just shook their heads.

"Go Trump!" a woman shouted.

Sandi and her team of volunteers were quite adept at convincing people to write down their names and contact information so that the Volusia County Republican Party could inundate them with election-related messages until election day. They were friendly and energetic but not pushy—unless you happen to have had a strong aversion to President Trump, in which case the mere presence of these women might have been enough to trigger an outburst.

"I wouldn't have anything to do with him if you paid me a million dollars!" a middle-aged woman shouted as she walked by.

"Glad you're here!" another woman yelled.

The volunteers were decked out in Trump gear. One woman wore Trump-themed shoes and earrings; another, a t-shirt with the Betsy Ross flag that said, "Stand up for Betsy Ross."

Sandi pressed a "Trump 2020" sticker on an older man's Marine Corps baseball cap.

"How does it look?" he asked.

"Donald would love it!" Sandi said, beaming.

I was at the Daytona Flea and Farmers Market, a sprawling indoor bazaar with hundreds of booths selling just about anything you'd ever want, and a whole lot more that you wouldn't. Located a mile or so from Daytona International Speedway and across the street from a shooting range, it drew a mostly white, working-class crowd on a Friday afternoon in February 2020. Many were tourists from the Midwest, though several groups of Canadians walked by, looking a little bewildered.

The volunteers tried to enlist my help.

"No, I can't," I said. "I need to stay neutral."

"We won't tell anyone," they said several times before giving up.

As I watched people taking selfies with the cardboard Trump, one of the volunteers explained what had motivated her to volunteer in the president's reelection effort: "I honestly believe, I really do, that everything he does, he does for you and me, not for himself. You and me."

Sandi's booth was not the only Trump-themed station at this market. There was another near the building's entrance, selling Trump apparel. It attracted a steady stream of customers.

There was a sweater that said, "Hell yeah I voted for Trump—And I will again." There was camouflage Trump gear, and a Trump 2020 visor with a layer of fake orange hair resting on top.

And there was a curious number of T-shirts depicting Trump as a cartoon strongman—not as in an autocrat who controls his people by threats and force, but as a circus strongman. There was a shirt with an extremely buff-looking, bare-chested Trump, another which depicted Trump as Superman, and another featuring Trump lifting heavy dumbbells.

I overheard one of the booth's workers complaining that certain items were selling out too quickly.

"That's because people are buying ten at a time," her co-worker responded.

"I think he's going to get elected again," a woman said to her friend as they scanned the merchandise.

"I just don't think we're ready for a Democrat," her friend said. "At least any of the ones running."

Back at the Volusia County GOP booth, Sandi told me about her political evolution—perhaps metamorphosis is a better word to describe her transformation. It's a story I had heard bits and pieces of over the last three years—first when I met Sandi and a group of her friends at a restaurant in 2017, again at a Halloween party she hosted the following year, and then over brunch at her home the year after that.

Sandi Hodgden was born and raised in Wisconsin Rapids, a city of 15,000 people in the geographic center of Wisconsin. Though she grew up in an "unquestionably Democratic" household, Sandi didn't pay much attention to politics until 2007, when Senators Hillary Clinton and Barack Obama ran for president. Sandi had hoped Clinton would become America's first female president. But after Obama won the Democratic nomination, she was equally excited to vote for America's first black president.

Obama's campaign message of hope and change resonated with

Sandi, particularly as it applied to foreign affairs. "Everybody was tired of all the wars," said Sandi, whose late husband, Dave, was a Marine. "Obama was saying, 'Why do we have to fight all these wars? Why? Why do we have to lose all our loved ones?'"

Sandi supports universal healthcare, at least notionally, so she appreciated that Obama promised to reform America's ailing health care system. But, in a story I found to be very common among people who voted for Barack Obama and subsequently for Donald Trump, Sandi was deeply disappointed by the way Obamacare was designed and implemented. She was bothered by Obamacare's new regulations—particularly the individual mandate, which required people to obtain insurance or pay a fine—and the resultant higher insurance premiums.

She was also disappointed that Obama failed to usher in a post-racial America. "It became the total opposite," she said of the contentious racial climate in America while Obama was president. "I couldn't keep up. My own grandkids were accusing me of racism because of a word they felt didn't fall into this political correctness."

By the end of Obama's second term, Sandi felt that Obama "didn't have America's best interests at heart" and that the country was "being brought to her knees with Obama's agenda.... I voted for him with a clear heart and mind—twice in fact. But it was a hard final years until we could vote a new president in."

"I just wanted America back," she said. "We need to speak English and say 'Merry Christmas.'"

Donald Trump immediately caught Sandi's attention when he began running for president, talking about putting America first.

"I knew I had to wake up and help fight for this man," she said. "I was praying I wasn't too late to help make American great again."

Adding to Trump's appeal was his pledge to revitalize American manufacturing. Sandi lived with the memory of losing her job of twenty-three years at Lullabye Furniture, which suddenly closed its factory in Stevens Point, Wisconsin, in 1991 after nearly 100 years of business, laying off about seventy-five workers.[1]

"I loved my job there and couldn't believe this happened," she once wrote to me. "Our livelihoods were destroyed in a day. What the hell?"

Sandi, who had moved to Florida in 2013, started to think about what she could do to assist Trump's nascent campaign. First she registered as a Republican, as did her husband, daughter, son-in-law, and grandson. "We all flipped," she said.

Sandi and a couple of other middle-aged women—self-dubbed "the Trumpettes"—canvassed tens of thousands of homes across Volusia County, Florida, in the lead up to the 2016 election.

When I first met Sandi in 2017, she had already committed to voting for Trump again in 2020. "We don't love him for his mouth," she explained. "We love him for what he's capable of doing."

In the 2018 midterm elections, Sandi volunteered for the campaign of Ron DeSantis, her local US representative who was running for governor of Florida. She didn't feel particularly drawn to DeSantis but was happy to help him because she knew Trump supported his candidacy. Politics took a back seat after the midterms. Sandi focused her attention

Sandi Hodgden (second from right) and the Trumpettes of Volusia County, Florida, in 2017. (Daniel Allott)

on caring for her husband, Dave, who had been diagnosed with late-stage dementia. After Dave's death, Sandi jumped back into her political activism, in part to divert her attention and energy away from the pain of losing her husband. Sandi took on a paid role, organizing for the Volusia County Republican Party.

After Sandi and I had been chatting at the flea market for about twenty minutes, I noticed a line starting to form for pictures with the cardboard commander-in-chief.

A young man walked by.

"Do you want a picture with the president?" Sandi asked.

"Believe it or not, I already have one," he answered.

"Do you want to wear a Trump sticker?" she asked another guy.

"Okay," he said coyly. "But I don't want to get shot."

"You won't," Sandi assured him. "Volusia County is red!"

Volusia County *is* red, but it was blue not long ago. Barack Obama won Volusia County, which encompasses Daytona Beach on Florida's Atlantic coast and the eastern edge of the 1–4 corridor, by five points in 2008 before Mitt Romney won it by one point in 2012. On the strength of increased Republican turnout, Trump won Volusia County by thirteen points in 2016.[2, 3]

Trump's success among the Midwestern transplants like Sandi who populate much of the area helped him win Florida and its twenty-nine electoral votes by just 1.2 percentage points. Trump's victory there foreshadowed victories later on election night in Midwestern states such as Iowa, Michigan, and Wisconsin.[4]

Unlike in the preceding chapters, the questions I address in this chapter aren't specific to Volusia County, but rather to the phenomenon that Sandi Hodgden's political evolution highlights.

Millions of Americans voted for Barack Obama in either 2008 or 2012, or both, and then for Donald Trump in 2016. These voters were crucial to Trump's narrow victory, according to pre- and post-election surveys and voter file data.

The Cooperative Congressional Election Study (CCES), a large survey of more than 64,000 adults, estimated that 6.7 million Obama voters subsequently voted for Trump. Another study found that 9.2 million Americans who voted for Obama in 2012 backed Trump in 2016.[5] Unsurprisingly, Obama-Trump voters are more conservative than other Obama voters. According to the CCES, a majority opposed a path to citizenship for illegal immigrants, and nearly three-quarters supported repeal of the Affordable Care Act (Obamacare). The CCES also found that nearly two-thirds of Obama-Trump voters identified as either Republicans or independents.[6]

The CCES further estimated that Democrats won back about one-fifth of Obama-Trump voters in the 2018 midterm elections, which would amount to a net swing of roughly 1.5 million votes.[7] But there is strong evidence that these voters will return to Trump in 2020. The CCES found that most Trump voters who voted Democratic in 2018 at least somewhat approved of Trump's performance as president. And a November 2019 poll by The *New York Times* Upshot and Siena College found that nearly two-thirds of voters in six battleground states who voted for Trump in 2016 but for Democratic congressional candidates in 2018 planned to return to Trump in 2020.[8]

Throughout Trump's presidency, the media have seemed eager—at times overly eager—to find Obama-Trump voters who regret their vote for Trump and planned to vote another way in 2020. A 2019 *New York Times* story featured life-long Erie County, Pennsylvania, resident Mark Graham, an Obama-Trump voter who said he wouldn't be voting for Trump again in 2020.[9] "If Mr. Trump gets into another four years, where he's a lame duck, it's going to be like adding gasoline to the fire," Graham told the *Times*. Graham's testimonial was so compelling that a progressive political action committee featured his story in an ad that aired across the Erie TV market.

"I don't think Donald Trump cares about the American individual's health care," Graham says in the ad. "He only cares about himself. He doesn't understand life around here."

"I was a Trump voter," Graham says as the ad closes. "But we can't get fooled again."

But it was the *Times's* readers and Erie residents who saw the ad who were getting fooled. A local news outlet contacted the Erie County Elections Office and discovered that Graham was not a disgruntled Trump voter. In fact, he hadn't voted at all in 2016.[10]

George Martin of Detroit, Michigan, in 2019. (Daniel Allott)

I tracked sixteen Obama-Trump voters during my three years on the road. Many of their stories have been featured throughout this book. As of May 2020, all but one of these voters said they were committed to voting for Trump again in 2020.

In the rest of this chapter, I will put their stories in greater context and draw some conclusions about why these voters are sticking with Trump, and what they might do after Trump leaves office.

The Obama-Trump voters I followed fall roughly into two groups, although there is quite a bit of overlap between them. One I call the Policy-Over-Personality (POPs) Trump voters, and the second I call Left-Behind Democrats (LBDs).

The POPs are true independents who acknowledge Trump's flaws but continue to support him, based largely on their agreement with Trump's policy positions, particularly on the economy, as well as their belief that Trump has largely succeeded in enacting his agenda. These voters are more likely to say that they are open to voting for a Democrat for president once Trump leaves office.

Whenever I asked George Martin, a young, black former sailor living in Detroit, to assess Trump's performance, he would run down a list of the president's accomplishments. He credited Trump with reforming the Department of Veterans Affairs, "pull(ing) us out of these endless wars," reining in illegal immigration, and for his stewardship of the economy. "No matter where you stand on Trump," he told me in 2019, "he's gotten a lot done."

"And that's my thing," he continued, "If I want something done, then it's probably going to get done if I vote for (Trump). It's a different kind of politics. It's not about bipartisanship. It's about fulfilling promises. The Democrats will say whatever it is you want to hear and deliver next to nothing."

Martin continued in the same vein when we met in March 2020. "The hard thing about Donald Trump is—and I don't even like saying this, but I'm trying to think—what hasn't he done that he said he was going to do?" he asked while he waited for his band to be called onstage at open-mic night at the New Dodge Lounge in Hamtramck. "Because he has done just about everything that he said he was going to do, and I really tried to think about it from both sides—that's a big deal to me—but I really couldn't think of anything."

I had heard something similar from Cyrus Mazarei when I met him at his sister Michelle's home in Orange County, California, early in 2018. "I like him because he's a doer," Cyrus said, echoing the word many farmers used to describe Trump. Cyrus said then that the only way he wouldn't vote for Trump again would be if he "doesn't keep his promises."

On my final visit two years later, Cyrus said, "(Trump) has exceeded my expectations for his presidency." Cyrus was also sure Trump would win the votes of most of his fellow Iranian-Americans.

"Why are you so sure?" I asked.

"He's kept his promises," Cyrus said. "It's that simple."

Pramit Patel is an American of Indian descent who owns a Best Western hotel in Robeson County, North Carolina. Patel offered nuanced appraisals of Trump's performance whenever I talked to him.

He favored the travel ban that the Trump administration placed on immigrants from lawless countries known to be hotbeds of terrorism in 2017 but felt that more countries should have been included. Patel supported Trump's tax reform law but also expressed concern about Trump's erratic foreign policy. "He has us close to a nuclear war," Patel texted in 2017. "Not sure if this is what we want." But by January 2020, Patel had decided that the bad of Trump's personality was outweighed by the good of Trump's policies. "I think besides the tweets, stupid feuds, name calling, and bad speeches, he has done a great job," he told me. (H)e is doing a lot of the things I thought Obama would do. I will vote for him again."

As I noted above, I call the second group of Obama-Trump voters the Left-Behind Democrats (LBDs). This group is made up of disgruntled former Obama voters who feel the Democratic Party has swung too far to the left, especially on cultural issues such as abortion, guns, immigration, and race.

The LBDs include Joe Wacha from Howard County, Iowa, who voted for Trump because he felt the Democrats were "no longer the party they were thirty years ago." By the fall of 2019, Wacha believed Trump had "accomplished a lot in the last three years" and that "he could have accomplished more if (the Democrats had) worked with him" instead of trying to impeach and remove him from office.

"No, I have nothing good to say about the Democratic Party right now," Wacha said. "I'm still a Trump supporter—nothing's changed there."

Catherine Bolder of Macomb County, Michigan, said that one of the reasons she went from Obama to Trump was the Democrats' lurch to the left, identifying their embrace of late-term abortion and identity politics as two examples.

And Orange County, California, resident Benjamin Yu, a military veteran and Chinese immigrant, appreciated Trump's commitment to free enterprise, traditional patriotism, and enforcement of America's immigration laws.

There was Noel Filla of Trempealeau County, Wisconsin, whose priorities were illegal immigration and health care. She liked that Trump was a businessman with a "backbone that can't be bent" and that he paid attention to people like her. "I definitely feel like he made the rural people feel that they were being listened to and that they were important," she said.

Then there was Jim McCuen, a Volusia County, Florida, resident in his sixties whom I spoke with at length on several occasions. McCuen started his life not as a Democrat but as a "hardcore socialist." Now he describes himself as "libertarian leaning" conservative who believes abortion is "an unparalleled evil." McCuen voted for Obama in 2008 because Republican nominee John McCain seemed to have no clue how to respond when the economy crashed. McCuen is half-Mexican and still has family in Mexico. But he said he was "very happy" with Trump's actions on immigration. He agreed with Trump that many illegal immigrants from Mexico are criminals and rapists, and thought it was crucial that Trump follow through on building a wall on America's southern border.

In late 2018, McCuen railed against outgoing House Speaker Paul Ryan and the inability of Republicans in Congress to work with Trump to get the wall built. "I don't understand why the wall has not been

built," he said. "I think immigration should stop.... Just turn it off." By early 2020, McCuen said he was committed to voting for Trump again in 2020.

The question is, with Obama's vice president, Joe Biden, as the Democratic nominee, how many of these former Obama voters can Democrats hope to win back? My reporting suggests that the answer is very few. None of the sixteen Obama-Trump voters I

Jim McCuen of Volusia County, FL, in 2018. (Daniel Allott)

followed expressed much goodwill toward Biden. And some were quite harsh in their assessments.

"No," Patel texted about whether he'd consider voting for Biden. "I think Trump has his number."

"I would never vote for Biden," Lois Morales wrote in May 2020. "He is just a puppet for the evil people." McCuen said he could not "imagine voting for Biden unless he were running against Pol Pot."

Biden's problem isn't just that his party has moved too far left for many former Obama voters. It's also that Biden himself has moved leftward along with his party. The media have paid a lot of attention to how the Republican Party is changing under President Trump, and before him under the banner of the Tea Party. But big changes have been happening in the Democratic Party too. Joe Wacha lamented that the modern Democratic Party does not resemble the one he knew thirty years ago. But it really doesn't resemble the Democratic Party of ten or twelve years ago, either.

Around the time of Barack Obama's election as president, the Democratic Party began to embrace positions that only a couple of years earlier had been regarded as extreme, even among Democrats. Once-fringe positions on immigration, health care, abortion, race, sexual identity, and climate change suddenly became not only mainstream but almost mandatory for any candidate running for high office within the Democratic Party.

Previously acceptable positions—opposition to same-sex marriage, any restrictions on abortion, and support for at least modest enforcement of immigration law, for example—were now verboten for any Democrat aspiring to lead the party.

Consider immigration. In 2012, the share of white Democrats who supported increasing the number of legal immigrants was 16 percent; six years later, the share was 57 percent.[11] By the time of the 2020 presidential primaries, open borders and no deportations had become a required Democratic position for all the party's presidential candidates. When ten Democratic candidates were asked during a presidential debate in June 2019 to raise their hands if their health care proposals would cover illegal immigrants, all ten quickly raised their hands.[12] It wasn't just that Democrats more and more began to embrace extreme policies. It seemed that the cultural and linguistic paradigm through which Democrats framed politics had shifted.

A writer searched the Lexis/Nexis database (which archives text from media sources) and found that the number of articles mentioning words and ideas such as "diversity," "inclusion," "unconscious bias," "white privilege," "discrimination," and "social justice" began to skyrocket starting around 2010 and 2011.[13] And, according to the Pew Research Center, the share of Democratic or Democratic-leaning registered voters who described their political views as "liberal" or "very liberal" increased from 33 percent in 2008 to 47 percent in 2019.[14] Interestingly, the Pew survey found that almost all of that increase had occurred among whites.

It is white liberals, not minorities, who have dragged the Democratic Party to the left. To take just one example, according to Pew, 80 percent of white liberals felt that racial discrimination was the main reason many black people couldn't get ahead. Only 60 percent of blacks felt that way. And black liberals were nearly twice as likely as white liberals to say that blacks who couldn't get ahead were mostly responsible for their own condition.[15]

Democrats' lurch to the left continued throughout the 2020 Democratic presidential primaries, as candidates proposed and embraced many progressive policies that had not even been on the table just four years earlier. Those included:

- race-based reparations for slavery;

- free college and taxpayer forgiveness of federal college debt;

- free health care for illegal immigrants;

- decriminalization of illegal border crossings;

- wealth taxes;

- withholding tax-exempt status from churches and religious organizations that do not recognize same-sex marriage;

- elimination of all private health insurance in favor of a single, government-run system;

- government confiscation of certain types of guns;

- support for the "Green New Deal," a massive $90 trillion overhaul of America's economy in the name of stopping climate change;

- Defunding of police departments in response to police brutality.

As the 2020 presidential campaign unfolded, even former President Barack Obama was warning the party against moving too far left. "Even as we push the envelope and we are bold in our vision, we also have to be rooted in reality," Obama said. "The average American doesn't think we have to completely tear down the system and remake it."[16] No doubt many of his former voters who subsequently voted for Trump nodded their heads in agreement with that statement.

You wouldn't expect this based on most media coverage of American politics, but an October 2019 poll found that significantly more registered voters think the Democratic Party has moved too far left (47 percent) than believe the Republican Party has moved too far to the right (37 percent).[17]

Joe Biden was seen as the viable "moderate" and "centrist" candidate in the presidential primary race, the one with the best shot at winning independents, former Republicans, and disaffected Trump voters, including those who once voted for a presidential ticket on which Biden's name appeared. But Biden is no longer the moderate he once was. He has moved leftward along with his party, taking several positions to the left of Obama. To name just a few, Biden's health care plan calls for a more aggressive version of the public option than Obamacare had; he's embraced the Green New Deal, and free college.[18, 19, 20]

He has pledged to name former Rep. Beto O'Rourke "to take care of the gun problem" in America.[21] O'Rourke had previously made news for vowing to confiscate legally purchased assault rifles. Biden also changed his long-held support for the Hyde Amendment, which bans the use of federal funds for most abortions, aligning himself with his party's opposition to any restrictions on the procedure.[22]

In April, after Bernie Sanders dropped out of the presidential race and Biden became the nominee-in-waiting, Biden didn't pivot to the center, as nominees typically do. Instead, he moved further left. As a *Politico* story put it, "The day after his last opponent dropped out of the presidential race, Joe Biden took the rarest of turns for a Democratic nominee: to the Left."[23] Biden announced that as president he would lower the Medicare eligibility age from sixty-five to sixty and forgive all student debt for most students.

Biden also seems to be emulating the worst tendencies of his former boss. Many of the Obama-Trump voters I met felt strongly that Obama had apologized too much for America and wasn't a strong enough advocate for the country. Biden has been doing the same thing. In 2019, Biden delivered a speech in Munich on the anniversary of the D-Day invasion in which he called the United States "an embarrassment," specifically citing the Trump administration's immigration policies.[24] This was a dramatic departure from the American tradition of politics stopping at the water's edge. The rule had always been that American politicians would refrain from launching partisan attacks upon each other while speaking on foreign soil to foreign audiences. It's also hard to imagine that this will play very well with the Heartland voters Biden will need to win.

There were three things almost all of the Obama-Trump voters I followed had in common. First, they had all grown embittered as Obama's presidency unfolded, their feelings ranging from mild disappointment to outright contempt. Many felt they'd been duped by Obama, who preached bipartisanship and racial reconciliation but, they believed, governed as a liberal and deepened the racial divide. As Carla Johnson put it, "I bought into the hope and change, which is terrible because he didn't do any of that." Two-time Obama voter Benjamin Yu said that by the end of Obama's presidency, the country seemed to be on a path toward socialism, which he found frightening as an immigrant from communist China—so frightening that he subsequently ran for local office as a Republican.

Jim McCuen said he felt "homicidal" after the bailout of Goldman Sachs during the financial crisis, prompting him to vote for Mitt Romney in 2012; Lois Morales said she "hated" Obama's reliance on constitutionally dubious executive orders, even if she liked some of their outcomes; and George Martin lamented that Obama turned out to be "just a politician—just like every other president we've had." Pramit Patel abandoned Obama in 2012 because Obama's appointees to the National Labor Relations Board made decisions on labor practices and collective bargaining that were harmful to his hotel business. And Cyrus Mazarei felt "buyer's remorse" for his vote for Obama, who he said proved to be a weak commander-in-chief. Cyrus was particularly upset that the Obama administration had abandoned pro-democracy protestors during Iran's short-lived Green Revolution in 2009.

Second, like most Trump voters, Obama-Trump voters deeply resented the idea that race was a factor in their vote for Trump. None of them believe Trump is a racist; in fact, many were quick to blame Obama for the acrimonious racial climate in America. Interestingly, of the sixteen Obama-Trump voters I followed, seven were non-white and two of the whites were married to racial minorities.

Third, most if not all of these sixteen voters felt that the news media are almost comically biased against Trump. Robeson County's Mark Locklear said he began watching more Fox News early in Trump's term because of CNN's slanted coverage of the president. "I say, 'Back off; give the man a chance,'" he told me in 2017.

When Joe Wacha pulled me aside at a Christmas party in Cresco, Iowa, in 2017, he told me how tired he was of the media's constant attacks against Trump, prompting him to embrace the president even more strongly. McCuen told me in 2018 that he thought Trump was performing pretty well, but that it was impossible to know because the media was so biased against him. "How do we know?" he asked, shaking his head. "They're going to attack him no matter what he does.... I don't have any good words for the mainstream media."

* * *

The last time I saw Sandi Hodgden—that is, until her promised visit to Washington, DC, for Trump's second inaugural—was for breakfast at First Watch in Daytona in February 2020. I never quite knew in which group of Obama-Trump voters to place Sandi. She was like most of the Left-Behind Democrats in that she retained no good will for Obama and felt that the Democratic Party had moved too far left on some issues. Then again, she seemed more like a Policy-over-Personality Trump voter when she said things like, "We don't love him for his mouth. We love him for what he's capable of doing."

She also always maintained that she held some liberal views. "I still have some conservative ways, I still have some liberal ways," Sandi once told me. "I still have an open mindedness." Even so, it was difficult for me to imagine her ever voting for a member of a party whose identity is almost entirely consumed by its hatred for and resistance to Trump. Sandi's idea of a fun afternoon is to gather a group of people together to wave Trump campaign signs at passing traffic. But she always emphasized that her loyalty was not to the Republican Party but to Trump. This is something Sandi shared with many other Obama-Trump voters I met.

When Catherine Bolder told me she was committed to voting for Trump in 2020, she added, "I don't know what I'll do after that."

Dave Neubauer was "born a Democrat" and seemed never to have considered changing his voter registration.

Whenever I met with Joe Wacha, he would insist that he was about to change his voter registration from Democratic to Republican, but he never actually did. And although Wacha said he had "nothing good to say" about the current Democratic Party, he would not commit to not voting Democratic in the future. "The thing is, it depends where both parties go," he said at our last meeting. "It's changing so fast that it's hard to say."

At First Watch, I asked Sandi again whether she would consider voting for a Democrat for president after Trump leaves office. "I could," she said. "If I find a Democrat who I believe in, like I do with Trump, then I will vote for him and go fight for him."

10

OF TRUMP AND OF TRIBE

IN THE COURSE OF MY THREE YEARS on the road, I spoke with hundreds of people about President Trump. During in-depth interviews, I had a standard set of questions that I would run through. There was one question that tended to elicit the most revealing responses. If I was interviewing a Trump supporter, I'd say: "Tell me something about the president or his agenda that you oppose or dislike," and if I was interviewing a Trump critic, I'd say: "Tell me something Trump has gotten right or something about him you admire."

This was often the point in the interview when a free-flowing conversation suddenly came to a halt as my subject struggled to think of something—anything—that contradicted his or her overall assessment of the president. Very often, Trump fans just couldn't think of anything he's done wrong. I listened as church-going Christians told me that they just don't believe Trump is a serial adulterer (he is, by his own public admission), congenital liar, and generally a man of low character. Either that or they assumed he'd asked God for forgiveness for his sins, even though Trump himself has said he has never sought forgiveness.

Here's an example of how those conversations usually went. I interviewed a woman named Cathy in the summer of 2018. Cathy had contacted me a few months earlier after watching a documentary film that my twin brother, Jordan, had made about persecuted Christians in the Middle East. When I learned that Cathy lived in Trempealeau County, Wisconsin, one of the nine counties I was studying, I asked her if she'd be interested in chatting the next time I visited. On a Friday night several months later, I arrived at the Historic Trempealeau Hotel on the banks of the Mississippi River. The next day I met Cathy for lunch at Beedles Bar and Grill in Galesville, about ten miles north of Trempealeau.

Cathy was representative of the millions of Christian conservatives who had helped deliver the presidency to Trump. Ardently pro-life and pro-gun, she had supported firebrand Texas Senator Ted Cruz during the 2016 Republican primaries before turning to Trump once he clinched the nomination. Two years later, any reservations she'd had about Trump had disappeared. Here's how part of our conversation went:

DA: "Is there anything about the president you don't like?"

Cathy: "I'm not a big cheerleader for Trump. But I can't think of anything I don't approve of. The tweeting doesn't matter."

DA: "Are there things that bother you as a woman of faith?"

Cathy: "Like what?"

DA: "Well, like his treatment of women, the extramarital affairs and porn star payoffs?"

Cathy: "They haven't proven that that happened. And I didn't follow it because I thought there was more important issues to follow. There are things that need to be accomplished. If he's done it in the past, everyone has had some sort of conversion, and if he has then good for him. Do you want something you've done ten years ago, do you want that brought up, if you confess your sins? Should that prevent you from being a journalist?"

DA: "But do you think Trump is a good person? And do you think it's important that we have a person of solid character as president?"

Cathy: "I think it is. As far as being a good person, I don't know everything he does. As citizens do we know each and every thing that a politician does?"

At this point, I mentioned the *Access Hollywood* tape, a decade-old video published a month before election day. It contained an extremely lewd conversation about women between Trump and television host Billy Bush. At one point in the video, Trump brags that his fame and fortune allows him to "grab (women) by the pussy" and they wouldn't even stop him. This was widely interpreted as Trump acknowledging having committed sexual assault.[1] When the *Access Hollywood* tape was made public, some Republican officeholders withdrew their support for Trump. A few religious leaders also renounced their support, but most remained silent or offered only mild criticism. A month later, Trump won a record share of white church-going voters, including Cathy, a practicing Catholic.[2]

"So if the comments were ten years old," Cathy said, "he could have gone to confession five years later if he was sorry for it."

Then Cathy pivoted to her distrust of the media, questioning their ability to accurately report on Trump. "To tell you the truth, all the headlines you read, I don't know," she said, shaking her head.

I mean, how much is true, and how much is not true? If I'm going to spend all of my time reading every little thing that they said about him, but I couldn't keep my job then. I have an eight-hour (a day) job.... Also, where do I get the facts? How do I know that some story I read isn't biased? I'm at the point now that I don't believe everything I read because I don't know if it's the truth.

I asked Cathy to name some of her news sources. She recited a litany of popular conservative talk show hosts: Rush Limbaugh, Laura Ingraham, Tucker Carlson, and Dennis Prager.

"I like Rush because he has a way of picking you up if you're feeling down about something," Cathy said.

I got turned off of public news with their treatment of (then-Wisconsin Governor) Scott Walker during the recall stuff. You hear all this, what's true if you're hearing one side? What is true? How do you know what's true? I'd have to research myself to find out what's true, because what's being presented might not be true.

I asked Cathy whether she feels similarly compelled to verify what she hears on Tucker and Rush's shows.

"Um, Tucker, the sense that I get from him is that a lot of what I hear is opinion," she said. "But I just find it humorous. Some of the stuff I hear from him I've heard from other sources. Rush, usually if I hear something that sounds strange, I might Google it to find out what else is being said about it. But I might not search that hard."

I don't mean to pick on Cathy. She's hardly alone in her tendency to gloss over Trump's faults, to assume the best of him even against overwhelming evidence, and to cry "fake news" when confronted with information challenging her view of the president. What I found most interesting about Cathy was her assertion at the beginning of our conversation that she did not see herself as a huge Trump fan. "I'm not a big cheerleader for Trump," she had said. And to be sure, Cathy did not come across as a pom-pom-waving Trump supporter. I had a difficult time imagining her donning a red "Make America Great Again" ball cap or joining Sandi Hodgden to wave Trump campaign signs at the passing traffic. But Cathy was clearly a member of the Trump tribe. Perhaps she was less cheerleader than loyal fan—the type of fan who refuses to see any fault in her own team no matter how poorly they're performing on the field.

Other Trump supporters I met found more creative ways to explain away Trump's less edifying qualities.

In 2019, I sat down with Lyman Momeny at his home in American Fork, Utah, a thirty-minute drive south of Salt Lake City. Lyman had moved to American Fork with his wife six years prior and became the owner of an escape room business. Lyman came across as self-assured and convicted in the way many older men are. "I am solidly in the constitutional conservative camp," he said. In many of the interviews I conducted, I felt like I was asking people to ponder questions for the first time, as if they'd never before had an in-depth conversation about politics, values, and culture.

This was definitely not the case with Lyman. He struck me as someone who had thought about most of my questions many times and discussed them with friends. When I asked him whether he was proud to be an American, he immediately said, "I don't think about it in terms of pride. I think about it in terms of gratitude." Then he told me a story he'd probably told a hundred times: His life had started inauspiciously, born to alcoholic parents who had been married five times each. He was grateful that he'd been born in America, the only place "where somebody coming from my station in life could have had the life that I had. I now have six kids and ten grandkids, and we've been very blessed."

Lyman was much less introspective when I asked him whether there was anything Trump had done that he opposes. "Yeah, I can't think of a single thing," was his quick response.

But then Lyman went further, portraying Trump's flaws as part of a brilliant strategy. "Remember, most of the things that people don't like about Trump is all calculated to distract," Lyman offered. "So almost the entire Trump persona is and always was for effect. While people are busy complaining about him, quietly behind the scenes, massive amounts are being accomplished."

Lyman Momeny at his home in American Fork, Utah, in 2019. (Daniel Allott)

The most important finding of my three years on the road was how few people have actually changed their minds about Donald Trump. With rare exceptions, those who supported him on election day 2016 still support him today, and the same is true of those who opposed him. That's not to say that people's views of the president have not changed; but where they have changed, the change has all been in one direction—toward a more extreme and more deeply entrenched conception of the president. This is the product of the increasingly tribalistic nature of American politics.

Tribalism is a way of thinking and behaving in which people are loyal to their group above all else; or, to put it negatively, it's a type of discrimination or animosity based upon group differences. When it comes to Trump and our current politics, tribalism manifests itself in an inability to acknowledge any nuance when assessing the president or his policies. I'm picking on Trump supporters in the above examples. But I found political tribalism was just as common among Trump's critics.

To progressives who couldn't think of a single thing Trump had done right, I'd mention the FIRST STEP Act, a criminal justice reform law Trump championed and signed into law in 2018. Among other changes, it shortened mandatory minimum sentences for nonviolent drug offenses and eased a federal "three strikes" rule—which imposed life sentences for three or more convictions—and issues a twenty-five-year sentence instead. It also gave judges more discretion to depart downward from mandatory minimums when sentencing for nonviolent drug offenses. The law marked the first major reform to our criminal justice system in thirty years, and it had a disproportionate and positive impact on racial minorities, who comprise two-thirds of America's prison population.[3] What's more, the law made changes to the justice system that liberals were advocating for many years before Trump was on the scene and, in most cases, before conservatives had embraced this issue.

Even so, many otherwise well-informed liberals that I spoke with had never heard of it. And perhaps that makes sense. They probably would not have heard much about it if they were watching or listening to their favorite opinion shows on MSNBC, CNN, or NPR. It might have complicated those outlets' uniformly negative characterization of Trump as a vicious and irredeemable bigot. Meanwhile, outlets like FOX News and conservative talk radio barely mentioned it because reforming the criminal justice system has just never been a priority for most conservatives. Even the president was loath to talk about it at first, stating in Fall 2018 that he believed the issue was a political loser.[4]

This only began to change in February 2020, when Trump aired an entire Super Bowl campaign ad focused on this legislative feat. This signaled what could become an aggressive push by his campaign to increase its share of the black vote in 2020. But up to that point, the new law had gone largely unnoticed amid the Mueller-Russia probe, the border caravan crisis, the Ukraine whistleblower scandal, and whatever inflammatory thing Trump had recently tweeted out.

A few months after that new law was enacted, I met up with a young progressive lawyer named Ashleigh at a boutique coffee shop in Long Beach, just south of Los Angeles. Ashleigh came across as thoughtful, well informed, and conscientious—except when it came to anything that challenged her opinion of Donald Trump. When I asked her to name something positive Trump had accomplished, she mused for a few moments over the strong economy and Trump's meetings with North Korean dictator Kim Jong Un before ultimately concluding with a laugh that she didn't want to give the president any credit for that.

"What about the FIRST STEP Act?" I asked.

Ashleigh: "I don't know anything about that (laughter)."

"You didn't hear about it?"

Ashleigh: "No. I feel so ignorant ..."

To her credit, Ashleigh said she would research the law. But then she said something I found typical of many Americans' experiences since the 2016 election.

> You just kind of reminded me that after the election I was really determined to expose myself to the full spectrum of things. And I feel like I've done the opposite. Like even now, I've been so burned out with politics that I haven't even engaged with the primaries. I'm just burned out and I don't have the energy.

Following Trump's election, a newfound desire seemed to spring up among Americans to understand the people on the other side of the political divide. Initially, reporters were deployed to Middle America to discover what had motivated people to vote the way they did. There seemed to be a glimmer of hope that after the most turbulent presidential campaign in recent memory, Americans were ready to engage with one another to unite the country. For me, that hope dissipated soon after I started reporting from across the country. Many people I met had fallen out with friends or family members over politics, or had simply stopped trying to understand those with whom they disagreed. Many had retreated to their ideological bubbles, both in terms of the media they consumed and the people they associated with.

During a trip to Howard County, Iowa, I met a university professor who said he uses President Trump as a filter when deciding whether or not to befriend someone. "If I don't know you and you come out with that Trump shit, I really don't want to get to know you," he said. That's no easy task in a county that Trump won by 21 percentage points and where he still enjoys strong support.

A woman I met began crying as she recalled how political conversations with a group of longtime female friends at her country club had become extremely tense. The tension sometimes erupted into arguments over her exasperation with her friends' unflinching support for Trump. The woman was a Republican, but she couldn't see how her friends could support such a man. The group instituted a "no politics" policy during card nights at the club. Once when she announced, "Spades are trump," another woman got mad and shouted, "There's no politics at the table!"

A woman in Erie County, Pennsylvania, recalled how, right after the 2016 election, a neighbor had confessed that she was grateful so many of the people living around her had put up Trump yard signs. "Now I know who not to talk to anymore," the neighbor had said. A man in Macomb County, Michigan, wrote to say that, "hardly anyone in my family speaks to each other since Trump took office. No more holiday parties. My uncles and I used to go fishing every weekend in the summer. Something we did for fifteen years. That came to an end too."

But no relationship was more revealing of how tribal our politics has become than the friendship between Chris Chilson and his neighbor Todd Mensink, whom I mentioned in Chapter 1. I had first met Chris and Todd in June 2017 at Chris's home in Lime Springs, Iowa, a few miles south of the Minnesota border. When I arrived for our interview, Chris and Todd were sitting in lawn chairs in Chris's back driveway. After

Chris showed me his gleaming Harley Davidson and we cracked open up some beers, we settled in for a lengthy political discussion. Despite having much in common—both are white men in their forties, born and raised a few miles apart—Chris and Todd were a world apart politically.

Chris, a self-described "big, big constitutional guy," voted for Trump in 2016. A former sailor, Chris cares deeply about veterans' health care. For the three years I've been Facebook friends with him, he has posted a daily video of himself performing twenty-two pushups to draw attention to the estimated twenty-two veterans who commit suicide every day.

Todd is a progressive sociology professor. He supported Bernie Sanders for the 2016 Democratic nomination before casting a protest vote for Jill Stein, infuriated by how the "Clintonite Democrats" fixed the primary elections.

Chris, Todd, and I talked about a range of topics—from the low cost of living in Lime Springs to their pride in the town's large municipal pool, which features a water slide. And of course we talked politics. Chris and Todd disagreed about a lot—about the core responsibilities of the federal government, about whether the Democratic Party had moved too far to the left or not far enough, and much more. But Chris and Todd spent a good portion of our discussion debating contentious political issues while also emphasizing whatever areas of agreement they could find. They agreed, for example, that Trump tweeted too much and that cable news deserved criticism for fanning the flames of partisanship.

When Todd was critical of progressives' knee-jerk resistance to Trump's nascent presidency, Chris said he had felt similarly when Republican leaders in Congress took a break-don't bend attitude toward President Obama immediately after his inauguration, seemingly more determined to make Obama "a one-term president" than to give him a chance early on.

As I read over the transcript two years later, I was struck by how many affirming statements were peppered throughout the conversation. "Yeah, I agree."

"That's a good point."

"That's true."

"You're absolutely right." And so on.

Chris and Todd sometimes even finished each other's sentences. At one point, when Chris began talking about the need to eliminate redundancies in the federal government, the following exchange took place.

Todd: "I agree with some of that. A lot of that, actually."

Chris: "Isn't that great? We come at it from two completely (different places), but we can find common ground."

Todd: "That's the only way to be. People take it way too personal."

Chris: "You can be passionate about your opinions, but don't be personal. Just don't do it."

Todd: "You can disagree with somebody and still respect them."

I left my interview with Chris and Todd hopeful that at least these two very opinionated men who resided on opposite ends of the political spectrum

Todd Mensink and Chris Chilson outside Chilson's home in Lime Springs, Iowa, in 2017. (Jordan Allott)

could engage with one another with civility and mutual respect.

But when I returned to Howard County a year later, I discovered that Chris and Todd's friendship had soured. First, I met with Chris and his wife, Sandy, at their home. Over pizza and beers—this time while sitting in lawn chairs in their front driveway—I asked the couple whether any of their relationships had become strained over politics. Here's how that part of the conversation went.

Chris: "You unfriended Todd."

Sandy: "I did unfriend Todd."

Chris: "We were going at it pretty good on something (on Facebook) and (Todd) pulled the Nazi card."

Sandy: "No, (Todd) lit a fire and walked away from it and let people threaten to burn the house and shoot you, and he didn't shut the conversation down."

Chris: "Yeah I guess that was it."

DA: "What was the topic?"

Sandy: "Something political, I don't know."

Chris: "Yeah, that's always what it is."

Sandy: "He threw something out there, and Chris jumped on it."

Chris: "And then a friend of his friends came along and made actual threats."

Sandy: "And I was like, 'Really? Way to light a fire and walk away.' Unfriend! I talk to (Todd) when I see him. I just don't want to … engage with that."

Chris: "I kind of enjoy it. I don't like when it devolves into personal threats, (but) I like lively debate."

Sandy: "Todd apologized for it, but I was like, 'I'm not going to expose myself to that.'"

A few days later, I caught up with Todd. He told me his version of events. Not surprisingly, he remembered things differently. In Todd's telling, his falling out with Chris and Sandy wasn't the result of threats made against Chris by Todd's Facebook friend and Todd's failure to defend Chris. Rather, it was about the very nature of truth.

"Chris and I used to be able to have debates over policy direction," Todd said. "But we agreed on the facts, we just disagreed on what to do with them, where to go."

Now we disagree on facts, and what are facts and what is truth, and the whole fake news. It gets frustrating and now I don't post stuff on Facebook. I haven't probably since October of last year. Because it became so hard, where everything I'm writing has to be backed up by so much. And then they can say, "Well, what about fake news?

That's just your interpretation of the facts." I pretty much just stopped (engaging on social media) because I'm never changing anyone's mind. I'm just banging my head against the wall.

When I learned that Chris and Todd's friendship had cooled, I wasn't surprised that a politically charged Facebook post was at the heart of it. I'd seen how provocative Chris can be on Facebook. His trolling posts make him seem much more unreasonable than he is in person. Despite all of this, Chris and Todd continued to engage with each other on Facebook. One interaction caught my attention.

For several weeks in October 2018, the nation was seized by a terror campaign and investigation into who had sent homemade pipe bombs to thirteen prominent Democrats and Trump critics, including former Presidents Obama and Clinton. When the police arrested Cesar A Sayoc Jr., a fervent Trump supporter who lived in a van plastered with pro-Trump stickers, many Trump supporters were incredulous. On Facebook, Chris mused over the possibility, given credence by Trump, Rush Limbaugh, and others, that the entire episode had been a false flag operation—a conspiracy engineered by liberals to make conservatives look bad ahead of the 2018 midterm elections. By entertaining this idea, Chris and other Trump supporters could disassociate from a member of their own tribe and even place him in the opposing tribe. Chris's refusal to acknowledge that a Trump supporter could have committed the crime incensed Todd. Here's how he responded in a Facebook comment to Chris' post:

> The right will never condemn their own. A 'R' by your name seems to override all integrity and decency. Anything and everything that is wrong is blamed as the Dems faults. Including sending bombs to two former Presidents in some sort of conspiracy theory.

In August 2019, Sayoc was sentenced to twenty years in prison after pleading guilty to sending the pipe bombs.[5]

***

The media deserve a large share of the blame for our deep political divides. Just as politicians win votes by stirring up their base voters, media outlets generate and maintain audiences by playing to people's sense of outrage and grievance. The old newsroom saw about what goes on the front page was that "*if it bleeds, it leads.*" That's still true, but the modern version is something more like, "*if it's going to trigger people, it leads.*" And as the above example illustrates, social media has taken things further. Facebook and Twitter have a unique ability to bring out the worst in us by drowning us in outrage and toxic partisanship, cocooning us in our tribes. Its anonymity allows us to attack other tribes with impunity. A 2017 Pew study found that Facebook posts demonstrating "indignant disagreement" received nearly two times as much engagement as other content.[6]

With Todd and Chris, I couldn't help but wonder whether they would have fallen out absent social media. Given my experiences with them in person, I had to conclude that they would not have. Chris and Todd aren't alone. Politics in the Trump era is bringing out the worst in us. As the headline of a *USA Today* poll put it, "On Trump, we can't even agree on why we disagree. But we assume the worst."[7]

People are purging their friend groups of anyone outside their political tribe. Trump administration officials have been refused service and harassed at restaurants. And it is not uncommon for opinion pieces to appear with headlines such as, "No, we don't have to be friends with Trump supporters." The author of that article argued, "When they go low, stomp them on the head."[8]

A 2017 Pew Research poll found that 35 percent of Democrats said that finding out that a friend had voted for Trump would put a strain on their friendship.[9] Interestingly, only 13 percent of Republicans said the same about learning that a friend had voted for Hillary Clinton. The differential there is striking, suggesting that Trump supporters are at least somewhat more accustomed to hearing or engaging the opposing view—maybe not surprising, given that anti-Trump views are dominant in most mainstream media.

I learned firsthand just how tribal things could become on social media. A few months into my reporting, I launched a Facebook page called "Into Trump's America" with the goal of promoting my articles and videos and perhaps bringing about lively debate about what I was finding as I traveled across the country. Unfortunately, the page immediately became a silo for Trump supporters, with the most tribal ones being the most vocal, showcasing their blind loyalty to Trump. I often posted photos of interview subjects, accompanied by quotes or brief stories about them—sort of like *Humans of New York* for Trump's America. Any pro-Trump post would be liked and shared hundreds or even thousands of times. But if the quote or story was perceived to be even mildly critical of Trump, dozens and sometimes hundreds of commenters would lay siege, often with *ad hominem* attacks. It made me feel awful. On several occasions, I apologized to people I'd interviewed, who I knew would see the comments. I considered closing the page, but I kept it going because I deemed it a useful way to understand the Trump tribe.

One post featured Darryl Howard, a black man in his late twenties whom I had interviewed several times over multiple visits to southeast Michigan. In a post from the summer of 2018, Howard explained his reasons for moving from Macomb County, Michigan, back to his birthplace a few miles south in Detroit. Here's the post:

> I was born in Detroit. My parents moved me to Macomb Township, and we stayed there for fifteen years. And during the last election, I decided that my family would be better off in a new county. We just didn't really feel … I don't want to say we felt unsafe, because we didn't feel unsafe. We felt fine. It was just, I didn't want the ideologies of Trump being portrayed to my kids. My daughter, she was going into the first grade, and they had a mock election in the classroom. It was in kindergarten. Trump won the mock election in her class. That made me think. I didn't want her growing up in this age, in that culture, with his ideologies.

I included a photo I had taken of Howard, smiling at the Renaissance Center in downtown Detroit where we had met for our interview.

As soon as I posted Darryl's photo and quote on the ITA page, the tribal arrows came thick and fast. Here are just a few of the seventy-three responses.

Darryl Howard at the Renaissance Center in Detroit in 2018. (Daniel Allott)

Cathy Zornek: When your ideology takes over your brain, then you're the problem. If you can find a better country and better leader, then leave no one cares, you don't need to broadcast it on Facebook. You won't find a better country than the U.S.A.

Judi Kays Degitz: Just don't come back!

Martha Samudram Rah: Canada or Africa is waiting for you. Green grass there for you.

Gwen Spansel: Good one less disrespectful Socialist, Liberal!!!!!

Barbara Crumpler: Bye Bye you will not be missed

Barbara Tallent: Hope you are already gone , AMERICA has too many of your stinking thinking, bye!

Edward Thrift: Move farther away, maybe another country

Tom Wilson: Buh bye! Neighbors are happy, I'm sure! I know I would be! Now you got you grandstanding moments of fame!

Liz Miller: LEAVE! Go to Russia!!!! Jerk

William A. Brandt: Bye dumbass

Donna Edgerton: Idiot.

Jerome Webster: Treat you child to be a loser also. So sad!

Kevin Sabo: Donald Trump is a better man than you can ever be, regardless of his presidency. He's given to the poor, flown dying young people to surgery around the world free of charge, helped minorities with employment, and hasn't taken a single paycheck yet! Your ignorance is astounding fella. Go to Mexico or Kenya with Hussein.

It would be easy to write off these responses as being all about the inherent racism of Trump supporters. But I have little doubt that if I had posted the same photo of Darryl but with him saying something that reflected well on Trump, it would have generated extremely supportive quotes about Darryl.

How can I be sure? Because when I had posted a photo of Darryl's friend George (a former sailor who's also black) a week earlier with a mildly pro-Trump quote about reforms at VA hospitals, it prompted nearly as many responses, nearly all of them supportive of both Trump and George. Several were of the "May God bless you for your service" variety.

I'd also posted many quotes by white Trump critics, and they generally elicited just as much *ad hominem* vitriol.

So the disgusting reactions to Darryl weren't about race; they were about tribe. To these Trump supporters, the problem with Darryl wasn't his skin color. It's that he opposed Donald Trump. And it was that he opposed Trump so much that he was physically moving away from a place where many Trump supporters lived. By rejecting pro-Trump Macomb County, Darryl had rejected the entire Trump tribe. So now the Trump tribe had to make it clear that they were rejecting him too.

What I found most disconcerting about the responses is how quickly these people rushed to the worst possible conception of Darryl simply because he'd rejected their tribe. Did the commenters care to know that Darryl was a hard-working real estate agent who was trying to help revitalize Detroit while providing for his young family? Did they know that he was a political independent who voted for the Republican presidential nominee in 2012?

It didn't seem to matter to them. All they knew about Darryl was that he had rejected their side, so they went straight into attack mode. *Search and destroy!* If Darryl had overreacted to what life would be like for him and his family in Macomb County after Trump's victory there, these comments probably only reaffirmed his decision to leave. In fact, Darryl himself commented on the post, writing, "Just to clarify. We left because, after the mock election the kids in my daughter's class said they would not play with her because she was brown. Some of the comments here reflect that same mentality. I'm not surprised."

With his move, Darryl was also demonstrating a sort of tribalism—a geographic tribalism that has become more and more common. More people are seeking out places to live near those who think and vote like they do. This long predates Trump. In 2004, journalist Bill Bishop wrote "The Big Sort: Why the Clustering of Like-Minded America Is Tearing Us Apart." But it's happening more and more now. Rural America is increasingly becoming the domain of Republicans and urban America of Democrats. Besides Darryl, several people I spoke to mentioned politics as the primary reason for moving to new areas. It's actually a strange reason to move.

Historically, people have stayed in place, moving only for new jobs or educational opportunities. But today, increasingly, each tribe just wants to give the other a wide berth. Todd Mensink told me in 2018 that he was considering leaving Howard County, Iowa, over politics. Todd said he was heavily invested in his hometown and community, even serving on the Lime Springs town council. But something had changed when he moved back to the area in 2015. It was he who had changed, he explained, not his hometown. His education had made him a different person. He no longer understood his neighbors. He lamented that there was no longer any Democratic presence in the county, and that the people there think that, "everyone's out to milk the system, which is unfortunate because these communities are exactly the ones that need these programs." He planned to move to Waterloo, a relatively diverse, medium-sized city seventy-five miles to the south.

***

Few institutions in America are as tribalistic as its political parties. It's common for politicians to lament today's bitter partisanship and to wax nostalgic for a bygone era when moderates were in abundance and members of Congress mixed frequently and would come together for the good of the country. Even though such lamentations can become tedious, it's true that in this age of tribalism people in politics step outside of their tribes at their own peril.

Braandon Davis found that out when he took over as president of Volusia County Young Democrats in Florida. When I met Davis at a Starbucks a few steps from the shores of Daytona Beach in late 2018, he told me the following story:

> When I first started in a leadership role at this club, as president, I wanted to grow our club. So I invited the mayor of Port Orange to come and speak. I thought it would be a good way for people to find out about the club. The plan was to put it on at one of the local restaurants, and it's a win-win for everybody. But then I got a call from higher ups, or different groups in the DNC locally, and they completely wanted to shut it down because (the mayor is) a Republican even though his son is a VYD (Volusia Young Democrats) member.

Davis explained to me that VYD is under the auspices of the Florida Young Democrats, not under the local Democratic executive committee, which is the organization the caller represented. Still, the warning had been issued. The Democratic official told Davis: "If you do this, we're going to have to shun your club."

"The official really used the word *shun*?" I asked.

"Yes that was the word he used," Davis said. "And I was like, 'You can't (shun us), because we aren't under your umbrella. But what purpose will it serve?' We had a back and forth. Another lady who was running for a position in the local Democratic Party, she said the same thing.... So I held off on this idea," Davis said. "This was my first time being in a leadership role, and looking up and seeing the foot come down on me, it was eye-opening."

The political tribalism infecting our body politic manifests itself in other ways—in Republican politicians going silent or twisting

Braandon Davis at a Daytona Beach Starbucks in 2018. (Daniel Allott)

themselves into rhetorical knots to defend every errant Trump tweet or scandalous remark. This is usually done for fear of facing a primary challenge or being pushed out of office, as many Republican lawmakers have been. They are right to be fearful. Most Republicans have learned that they have little to gain and plenty to lose by criticizing Trump. Many Republicans who have spoken out publicly against Trump are no longer in office.

I already told the story of Mia Love, the Utah congresswoman whose unwillingness to fully embrace Trump may have cost her re-election. But consider also the case of Mark Sanford. A little over a decade ago, Sanford was the extremely popular second-term governor of South Carolina. He was seen as a possible presidential candidate. Then for a week in 2009, he suddenly went missing, and it was revealed that he had secretly traveled to Argentina with state funds to carry out an extramarital affair, leaving his wife and four sons behind. Once the truth was exposed, Sanford stepped down and his political career seemed to be over. But South Carolina voters are a forgiving bunch, and they gave him a second chance. He was voted into Congress four years later in a special election, then cruised to reelection in 2014 and 2016.

Then in 2016, Sanford was critical of Trump, claiming he had "fanned the flames of intolerance" and had a tenuous hold on facts and the Constitution.[10] For this criticism, Sanford drew a primary challenge in 2018 from state legislator Katie Arrington, who embraced Trump and made the primary election a referendum on Sanford's criticism of Trump. Trump endorsed Arrington, tweeting of Sanford, "He is nothing but trouble" and "very unhelpful to me." Sanford lost that primary by five percentage points.

The lesson? You can be forgiven for abandoning your family and your constituents for a mistress halfway across the world; mild criticism of President Trump, however, is unforgivable. And mind you, Sanford was not some vociferous "Never-Trumper." He voted with Trump 89 percent of the time and applauded much of what Trump did. During the 2018 primary contest, he spent close to $400,000 on TV ads in which he told voters that he "overwhelmingly" supported Trump.[11] But it just didn't matter. In the age of tribal politics, any criticism at all is unacceptable. Why give aid and comfort to the enemy?

* * *

Human beings are tribal by nature. And tribalism is connected to feelings of belonging and solidarity, which are inherently good things. But taken to the extreme, tribalism prevents us from perceiving one another accurately. Tribalism means assuming the worst of those outside the tribe—about their intentions and their character. Tribalism means surrendering individual judgment. Tribalism doesn't allow for nuance or context. It's a zero-sum game. It requires complete allegiance to our tribe and complete rejection of other tribes.

Lyman Momeny strained to turn Trump's flaws into a feature. "Remember," he had assured me, "most of the things that people don't like about Trump is all calculated to distract." This allowed Momeny to defend his tribal leader's most glaring flaws. At the same time, when

I asked Momeny whether President Obama had done any good, he managed to turn the one positive thing he could think of into a negative. "I think he pursued the terrorist elements around the world fairly aggressively," Momney said after a long pause. Then he added:

> But I also think he did that so that he could get away with some of the other stuff he did, like the Iran deal. I think his head was always with the Muslim world. I think he favored them. And I think that he went after a few terrorist bad guys so that people could say he was even-handed. Generally speaking, eight years of Obama were a disaster for the country in every imaginable way.

You see what he did there? After giving Obama some credit for something he thought he'd gotten right, Lyman reversed his compliment by accusing Obama of doing it all just to distract from another bad policy. And to emphasize his tribal affiliation, Lyman added that Obama was a terrible president in every conceivable way.

In a tribal culture, those outside the tribe need to be dehumanized. They automatically become our enemies. Meanwhile, those inside the tribe are to be defended at all costs. As a last resort, as with the would-be mail bomber, we might argue that the offender was never really a member of the tribe to begin with; in fact, we convince ourselves that the whole thing was a conspiracy by members of the other tribe. An academic research paper found that 42 percent of the people in each political party view those in the other party as "evil." The researchers even found that nearly 20 percent of Republicans and Democrats agree with the statement that their political adversaries "lack the traits to be considered fully human—they behave like animals." They further found that roughly 20 percent of Democrats and 16 percent of Republicans sometimes think the country would be better off if large numbers of the opposition died.[12]

As I traveled around the country, it didn't take long for me to realize that the tribalism had become so endemic and so toxic that I could accurately anticipate exactly how people would respond to political events as they unfolded. I knew that none of the evangelical Christians and female Trump supporters would have a bad word to say about Trump's Supreme Court nominee Brett Kavanaugh even after multiple accusations of sexual impropriety were reported. I also knew that no matter how high the Dow climbed or how low the unemployment rate fell, many liberals wouldn't give the president any credit at all for the state of the economy. It became very easy to anticipate where people would come down on any issue. Where do you stand on Trump? That's the only question I needed to ask.

By the end of 2019, as President Trump was about to be impeached by the House of Representatives, a poll found that the tribalism of our politics had reached its pinnacle. Ninety-one percent of Republicans approved of the job Trump was doing, while just 6 percent of Democrats said they approved. The 85-point gap was 20 points higher than the gap seen at that point in President Obama's first term.[13]

In February, Utah Sen. Mitt Romney became the first senator to vote to convict a president of his own party in an impeachment trial. For this act of betrayal, Trump attacked Romney in a series of scathing tweets. Several Republicans members of the Utah state legislature proposed bills to recall or censure Romney. And Matt Schlapp, chairman of the Conservative Political Action Committee, withdrew an invitation to the former Republican presidential nominee to address its annual conference. "This year, I'd actually be afraid for his physical safety, people are so mad at him," Schlapp said.[14]

* * *

More than a year passed before I finally got back to Howard County, Iowa. But in November 2019, I met up again with Todd Mensink, who had actually followed through and moved from Lime Springs to Waterloo. We met at a bar on a Sunday night. It was loud because the Green Bay Packers were playing on one of the televisions, and patrons, decked out in green and gold, were cheering the team on. Todd and I sat down at a booth away from the bar, and I asked him about his move to Waterloo. "My heart still belongs in (Lime Springs)," Todd said. "It's where I was born and raised, and I owe a lot to the people of that town, and it's a great community to grow up in."

He stressed that politics weren't the only reason he had moved. The much shorter commute to his job was also part of the calculus. But he reiterated that politics had played an important role. "The Trump election did play a pretty big part in my thinking, too," he said.

> I was definitely (politically) isolated there. When I have DACA students coming to my office, scared, after Trump got elected, asking, 'Am I going to get deported to a place that I haven't been to since I was three months old, that I have no living relatives at, I don't know anything about the country, I don't know anybody there?' What am I supposed to do?

Todd said he didn't spend much time with Sandy Chilson anymore. "The damage was done," he said of the Facebook incident. Things were a little more complicated with Chris.

> Chris and I, we don't really talk all that much anymore since I moved down here. I don't really respond too much on his Facebook stuff anymore because it's pointless. It's not pointless for me and Chris, but it's not just me and Chris. Oftentimes there'd be so many other people that jump on that, and then if I try to explain it, I can't tell you how many times that either I had to or he had to privately message other people and tell them to back off.

"That's the dangerous part about Facebook," Todd continued. "So what I did is, I just quit following him. I don't actually see his posts anymore."

It might seem obvious to some that Donald Trump has caused the current age of political tribalism. But that's not quite correct. Trump did not create the divisions that are tearing our country apart. He embraced and amplified them, certainly. But Trump is more properly seen as a consequence of our tribalism, not its cause. The real causes lie elsewhere, in things that cannot be erased by an impeachment or an election. They're embedded in many parts of American life. Everything about modern politics encourages such tribalism—increasing income inequality, seismic demographic shifts, declining social mobility and the class divide, partisan redistricting, and a badly broken media model that rewards expressions of outrage.

There's virtually no trust in the media or in the capacity of any authority to judge fairly among competing truth claims. As Chris and Todd's story demonstrates, social media amplifies extreme views and keeps people separated in their silos. Surveys show that public trust in nearly every societal institution—from the media and the political system to the courts and organized religion—has plummeted.[15] When trust vanishes, tribalism flourishes.

And there's one other reason for pessimism. It's hard to come to any agreement when the values by which different tribes live are so strikingly at odds. In a 2018 Pew survey, a majority of respondents said that those who disagreed with them about President Trump also probably do not share their values.[16] Only a year earlier, a minority of the public had felt that their political opponents probably did not share many of their values and goals. There are two crucial questions going forward. First, can Americans agree on at least some shared values? And if not, can we live together as a nation of people who embrace values that are at odds with one another?

I met up with Cathy again when I returned to Trempealeau County, Wisconsin, in 2019. As we sat at a picnic table at Perot State Park along the banks of the Mississippi River, I asked her whether she felt forced to pick a political tribe.

"Well, yeah because you're not going to get anywhere if you're not in numbers," she said. "If you have certain values, you're not going to influence anything if you don't have people on your side, especially when you have people that are competing against your values grouping together."

I asked Cathy to identify the people whose values compete against her own. She mentioned people who support gun control and abortion and those who exploit the welfare system.

"If it's going to be tribal, I know the tribe I would stick with because the other one has nothing to offer me," she said. "I guess it's part of survival. I feel like if I'm going to retain my freedom to do what I want, I'm going to have to find other people with the same values, and I'm going to have to stay with them. What choice do I have?"

11

THE FINAL JOURNEY, INTERRUPTED

I MADE MY LAST FORAY into Trump's America in early March 2020. My plan was to spend two weeks traveling through Erie, Macomb, and Trempealeau Counties. I had chosen these three Obama-Trump counties for my final trip because they are located in the three states—Pennsylvania, Michigan, Wisconsin—that had provided Trump with the margin of his electoral college victory in 2016 and that forecasters have predicted will be equally decisive in 2020. By this point, I had developed dozens of reliable contacts in each county. I was eager to get their thoughts one last time on President Trump, the 2020 race, and the state of politics generally. As always, I'd be on the lookout for switchers.

On a sunny Saturday morning, I drove from my home in Northern Virginia and met Jim Wertz at the Erie County Democratic Party headquarters on State Street in Erie. Wertz had been elected county chairman in 2018. He's young and smart, and, as a former Bernie Sanders supporter, he understands the importance of uniting the often-feuding progressive and establishment wings of the party. As Wertz had said after winning the chairmanship, "The first thing we have to do is unify the voters that we have."[1]

I joined Wertz as he canvassed the homes of registered Democrats in a middle-class Erie neighborhood. He wanted to make sure voters were aware of the upcoming primary on April 28 (later postponed to June 2) and a new law allowing mail-in voting. Most of the doors Wertz knocked went unanswered, but a few people responded. At one door, a middle-aged woman appeared and said, "I really don't have time to talk, but I can tell you I'm not voting for Trump," before slamming the door.

At another door, a middle-age man said he was fond of Cory Booker and Barack Obama but unsure about Biden. He also said that while he hates the way Trump uses Twitter, he approved of how the president had handled the economy.

Wertz said something to the effect, "We still have you, right?" speaking of the Democratic Party.

"Yeah, I guess," the guy responded.

At another door, a scruffy millennial answered and informed Wertz that he was enthusiastic about Bernie. Why? Because Bernie was promising "free health care and free tuition," he said. "Well, not free, but you know what I mean."

As we walked, I asked Wertz whether he was concerned that Sanders voters would refuse to turn out on election day if Biden won the Democratic nomination, which the former vice president was on the cusp of doing. Wertz said he was concerned, but he also said that the rift between progressive and establishment Democrats that developed in 2016 had narrowed somewhat: At least Bernie supporters weren't protesting outside the county party headquarters, as they had done in 2016.

Wertz's bigger concern was that national Democrats still seemed to take Erie for granted. He said that Rep. Tim Ryan and former Rep. Beto O'Rourke had visited Erie during the primary season, and that Sen. Elizabeth Warren's campaign had at least returned his phone calls. But none of the other campaigns had visited or engaged. This reminded me of what then-Erie Mayor Joe Sinnott, a Democrat, had told me early in 2017: "Hillary did not come here. And it was noticed and it was talked about within the party and the voters. And as history now shows, a lot of the folks that you would have expected should have been Hillary voters went the Trump route."

"You keep telling us we're important, you keep saying Erie is important," Wertz said with frustration of the Biden and Sanders campaigns and the national party. "But where are you?"

After knocking on a few more doors, Wertz and I drove out to the Erie suburbs. He had been told that Trump flags and banners had started popping up and wanted to check it out for himself. It's easy to dismiss campaign yard signs and flags as measures of enthusiasm for a candidate. Academic researchers have tried to measure the effect; one study calculated that lawn signs are 98.3 percent useless.[2] But many people I talked to across the country said that the sheer volume of Trump signs they saw in 2016—and the scarcity of Hillary Clinton signs—was their first clue that the polling was wrong and that Trump would have more success than the pundits had predicted.

It was early March—still early for most voters to start paying attention to the election. The only Democratic signs I spotted during my trip to Erie were "Tulsi 2020" signs in support of Hawaii Rep. Tulsi Gabbard, who hadn't yet ended her long-shot bid. Wertz knew that the Democratic nominee would likely perform well in the city of Erie (where Clinton won every precinct in 2016)[3] but that the two-thirds of the county's population that lives outside the city proper would be decisive. So that's where we went.

We visited a trailer park in Summit Township, just south of the city. There we saw two or three Trump yard signs, a "Keep America Great" banner, and a couple of "Trump for America" flags.

In nearby Waterford Township, we saw an elderly man wearing a red MAGA hat ambling into a restaurant. Outside one home, we saw a Trump flag with an eagle on it, though it was so tattered that it took us a minute to confirm what the flag said. And just down the road, we

Jim Wertz outside the Erie Art Museum. (Daniel Allott)

saw an enormous Trump flag waving outside a plumbing and excava-
tion business.

Then Wertz, a journalist, had a question for me. He was truly
baffled by the continuing support that Trump enjoyed among church-
going whites and wanted to know whether I had any insight into why.
I explained that Trump's character deficiencies ultimately didn't matter
to most of them because he was delivering on the issues they care about
most—abortion, religious liberty, gun rights, immigration, and so forth.
Wertz still seemed perplexed. It reminded me of the conversation I had
had with him the summer before when he said that many blue-collar
workers had voted for Trump because "they're caught up in what I like
to call the 'non-issues.'"

I asked him what those "non-issues" were.

"The guns and the abortion thing," he said. "It's a heavily Catholic
area."

"But are those *really* non-issues?" I asked. "They're obviously important to those people."

"Well not for those guys they're not non-issues," Wertz said. "I call them 'non-issues' because it's not healthcare, it's not the economy. It's not the things that we really need to be talking about right now."

Wertz's casual dismissal of issues such as guns and abortion spoke volumes. It made me think that Democrats will have a very difficult time winning over rural and working-class white voters unless they come to understand that these "non-issues" matter most to these voters, and that it's pointless to try to convince them otherwise.

That evening, I drove to LongHorn Steakhouse on Peach Street to have dinner with Dale and Darlene Thompson, the progressive couple I had interviewed on several previous trips. In each of our previous chats, Dale had said he strongly suspected that many of the Trump-voting co-workers at the tool shop where he is employed were beginning to turn on Trump. "I'm seeing a lot of regret at work," he said this time, "a lot of people saying, 'What the hell is going on?'" Every time Dale had mentioned his coworkers' regret, I'd asked him if he would be willing to put me in touch with any of them. He had always demurred. This time, however, Dale said he'd immediately call his friend Dave, whom Dale told me was "as far right as I am left." Dale said Dave had told him that he'd had enough of "Trump's lying" and seemed ready to vote against Trump.

So as we waited for our dinner, Dale called Dave and spent several minutes explaining who I was and assuring him that I could be trusted. This reinforced to me how important it is to spend time with people to understand them—to cultivate trust and goodwill with my contacts.

I interviewed Dave the following day. Dave said he had voted for Trump more out of aversion to Hillary Clinton than out of enthusiasm for Trump. Even so, Dave felt Trump had "done a lot of good things that are helping people in need.... If he could just keep his mouth shut and let his record speak for itself." Dave said abortion, religious freedom, and the Supreme Court were his most important issues—the very "non-issues" with which Wertz felt blue-collar voters were unduly preoccupied. Dave didn't have anything good to say about either of the

Democratic frontrunners. Bernie Sanders is too "socialistic," he said. "I have worked too hard for what I have to give it away to someone who refuses to work." And Joe Biden, he said, "doesn't seem to be mentally all there."

Though Dave said he was still undecided about how he'd vote in November, he thought the Democrats were too politically correct and appreciated what he called Trump's "no-nonsense" style. "(Trump) is what the country needs," he said. In short, he didn't quite sound like someone who was about to abandon Trump. In fact, this Dave reminded me a lot of another Dave—Dave Neubauer, the Iowa corn farmer and registered Democrat. In both cases, I had been made aware of a Trump voter who had been complaining about Trump's performance and told that it sure sounded like they were prepared to vote another way. Instead, both Daves turned out to have a lot of positive things to say about Trump and nothing good to say about the Democrats.

* * *

One day, near Perry Square in downtown Erie, I spotted a food truck called Curry Point. I walked over and saw a sign advertising "EXOTIC INDIAN CUISINE" and South Indian specialties, including, kara dosas, shrimp masala, chicken curry, and badam milk. I was a little surprised to see this truck in Erie. Most Indian restaurants in America serve versions of northern Indian cuisine, which tends to be milder. I wondered how this spicy and exotic cuisine was being received in this medium-sized industrial city.

Another food truck on the same block, selling typical American fare, had a long line. There was hardly anyone waiting at Curry Point, which gave me a chance to chat with the proprietor, a man named Sam. Sam told me that his wife, Rijani, actually owned the truck. Rijani, who was studying to become a registered nurse, was at home caring for the couple's four-month old.

"She saved my life," Sam said of Rijani. "She gave me new life after I lost a lot of money (in California during the 2008 financial crisis). "This

Sam, the proprietor of Curry Point Exotic Indian Cuisine, on Perry Square in Erie. (Daniel Allott)

is all hers," he said of the food truck and business. "I want to succeed for her." Sam said it was a challenge to introduce real Indian food to locals. But he still preferred Erie to New York City, his former home, where there was too much competition and too many regulations to succeed in the food truck business.

I told Sam what I was doing in Erie, and he volunteered his opinion. "Trump is a very good guy," Sam said. "He's fixing America." Sam told me he voted for Obama twice but didn't vote in 2016. In 2020, he added, he was prepared to vote for Trump.

As Sam and I were chatting, Erie Mayor Joe Schember walked by. I had interviewed Schember, a former PNC Bank vice president and a Democrat, twice before. He is regarded by many as much more engaged and responsive than his predecessor. Schember has been a constant presence at cultural events in Erie, such as Bosnian Iftar dinners, Nepali gatherings, and naturalization ceremonies. Schember and his staff were always willing to meet with me to share the city's most recent plan to increase cultural diversity, develop the city's downtown and bayfront, and attract more jobs and people to the area. And he was always visible. Once in 2019, I had attended a multicultural arts festival in downtown Erie and spotted Schember dancing along the parade path with an all-female Afro-Brazilian percussion ensemble.

But there is a tension in Erie between the desire to attract more college-educated young people and to incorporate thousands of "new Americans" and the need to address the concerns and challenges of long-time Erie residents. Many of these residents are stuck in a multi-generational cycle of poverty and sometimes feel overlooked or pushed out. Most Erie residents I spoke with had good things to say about Schember. But others worried that he and other city leaders were forgetting those left behind—including the jobless men I would always see roaming around downtown Erie. Schember believes bringing a community college to the city would help immensely, the nearest one being 100 miles south in Pittsburgh.

Erie Mayor Joe Schember. (Daniel Allott)

At the food truck, I asked Schember whether he had tried Sam's South Indian cuisine and whether he liked it. "Yeah," he replied hesitantly. "It was good—but a little spicy."

***

I spoke with several progressive activists on this trip to Erie. At that point, Joe Biden was close to winning enough delegates to secure the Democratic nomination, and I wanted to get a sense for whether the activists thought Sanders supporters would vote for Biden against Trump.

The Cooperative Congressional Election Study estimated that 10 percent of 2016 Sanders primary voters turned to Trump in the general election against Hillary Clinton.[4] A poll in March 2020 found that an even higher share of Sanders supporters—15 percent—said they would back Trump against Biden.[5]

Most of the Erie progressives I spoke with said they would vote for Biden, albeit reluctantly. One activist I interviewed at length was Jasmine Flores, a twenty-six-year-old Sanders supporter who had just been chosen to head the county party's progressive caucus. Half-Mexican and half-Puerto Rican, Flores said that when she graduated from high school a few years ago, she "already knew" that the area colleges and universities were "off limits" to her. And as the oldest of her mother's thirteen children, she seemed to think moving away for school was not an option either. Flores is one of the many Erie residents who could probably benefit from having a community college close to home. Instead of going to college, Flores had spent the last several years working and taking care of her grandmother. Then Flores ran for city council in 2019, an experience she found invigorating, even in defeat.

"Seeing how supportive the community was, and seeing how people were just so willing to write me a check for my campaign made me see how much people want change," she said. Flores said that white residents would sometimes ask her where she was born. They wanted to make sure, not that she had been born in the United States, but that she had been born in Erie. "I don't know what it is, but there's nothing like Erieites, they love other Erieites," she said with a laugh. "And they were like ... 'Where were you born? Here in Erie? Okay, so, you're one of us.'"

Flores seemed resigned to Biden winning the Democratic nomination—and losing to Trump in the general election. "I feel like it was all part of the master scheme to begin with. ... I feel like if we do Biden, we are going to lose to Trump again just because the younger generations don't have anything positive to say about Joe Biden." Flores may have been on to something. An April analysis of polls found Biden leading Trump among eighteen- to thirty-four-year-olds by 14 points—that's

10 points worse than Hillary Clinton performed in an average of polls in the closing days of the 2016 election.[6] I asked Flores whether she would vote for Biden in the general election. "When it comes to November, I guess I will have to step in line and vote blue no matter who, like every other person is force-fed to do," she said. "But how is Biden going to be the best candidate if he can't even do a seven-minute rally without (committing a gaffe)? We have a problem."

"I still feel like a lot of Sanders voters who are not loyal to the Democratic Party will not vote," she continued. "And I feel like you might see some of them even vote for Trump, which is sad to say."

***

A couple of days later, I found myself at Key Note Guitar, a guitar shop in a lonely strip mall on Erie's south side. The thing that I found most daunting during my three years on the road was entering places where I didn't know a soul and trying to build relationships, trust, and goodwill. What I found most gratifying was to see some of those relationships turn into friendships. That's what happened with Ricki Leigh and Trent Mason. I met Ricki, a sixty-something transgender woman who owns Key Note Guitar, at a harmonica concert Trent had invited me to in Upstate New York in 2018. We spent several afternoons and evenings listening to music at Ricki's store, or listening to Ricki play guitar and Trent the harmonica and drinking Aberlour single malt Scotch, Ricki's favorite brand of whisky.

Ricki was born in Erie, a decade younger than the next youngest of seven siblings. Ricki's father was an alcoholic who left the family before Ricki was born, leaving Ricki's mom, a nurse, to raise eight kids. "She worked her tail off just putting food on the table," Ricki once said. "Cared for us all as best she could." As a teenager, Ricki fell in love with the guitar and eventually started performing some local gigs. Eschewing college and the military, Ricki moved to California to play and teach for a couple of years before returning to Erie and buying a house about ten miles south of the city. It was a place where Ricki could get high and jam with friends in the peace and privacy of the countryside. After years of doing various jobs—cutting produce for local restaurants, working at a department store, selling cars and motorcycles—Ricki returned to music, started teaching guitar lessons, and opened the store.

"Every time in life, no matter how bad it got, it always turned around and got better because of music," Ricki once told me. "I'd find a way to make money teaching or working in a music store somewhere." A tattoo on Ricki's left forearm reads, "Music is my religion."

Ricki was very proud of Key Note Guitar and would sometimes send me photos of a new guitar or other musical equipment that had just come in.

I had met Trent at a Memorial Day BBQ hosted by Ali and Jasmine, the Trump-supporting Iraqi couple I featured in Chapter 8. In 2020, Trent began traveling the country, marketing and selling dog toys and seemed to enjoy it. He happened to be back in Erie while I was visiting, so we agreed to meet up.

When I arrived at Key Note, I asked about how business had been. Ricki started complaining about having gone through six employees in the last year-and-a-half. Most were either lazy or addicted to drugs, or both; the promising employees would stay a little while before moving on—a perfect example of Erie's challenges. Trent and his friend Julie soon arrived, carrying a bucket full of mini Fireball bottles and Chinese takeout.

Julie, a lifelong Erie resident, is a local bartender in her thirties. She's a registered independent who said she "dabbles in all the (political) boxes … almost to a fault." Julie was mostly critical of President Trump but allowed that at least his election had shaken up the political system, which she seemed to regard as a good thing. She said her Irish Catholic family had been upset with her after the 2016 election for even suggesting that Trump might do some good. Julie felt that Trump couldn't be trusted because he'd lived such a self-serving life. "How can we trust someone who's always thinking about 'How can I get mine?'" she said.

"I think he's deficient in the qualities needed to be in charge of a group of people and to work for their greater good," she said, adding

Trent Mason, Ricki Leigh, and Daniel Allott at KeyNote Guitar in 2020. (Author's personal collection)

that it frightened her that such a man was in charge during the emerging COVID-19 crisis. Even so, Julie was undecided about how she would vote in 2020.

Trent despised Trump but considers himself politically conservative. Like other Mormons, he seemed most bothered by Trump's mendacity and casual cruelty. "I guess I'm ridin' with Biden," he said with resignation at one point in our discussion.

Ricki, a Bernie Sanders supporter, regularly railed against Trump and in favor of raising the minimum wage to $15 an hour. According to several polls, most small business owners support this. Ricki, Trent, and Julie all appreciated Sanders's willingness to take on the big corporations. Over the two years that I knew Ricki, Key Note Guitar always seemed to be doing fairly well financially. In 2019, Ricki said, "I just bought a second motorcycle because business was so good last year." But whenever I suggested that it was due to a strong economy, Ricki would complain that many Erie residents weren't benefiting and that real wages hadn't increased in a long time. Ricki was certain that a recession was about to hit. This turned out to be prescient because a week or so later the Dow Jones Industrial Average would fall almost 3,000 points. It was the biggest one-day decline in the index's history, as the economy started to shut down as a result of the coronavirus pandemic.

* * *

Looking back, it probably wasn't prudent for me to continue on from Erie to Macomb County. At this point, the first case of the coronavirus had just been confirmed in Michigan, and more than 1,000 cases had been reported across the country. States were beginning to order residents to shelter-in-place. But I wanted to get a few more interviews in, not knowing whether I'd have another chance to travel if the country shut down. So I continued.

I visited Laurie and Rob Rasch at their Detroit-themed memorabilia store near Anchor Bay in New Baltimore. I had written a story about the Rasches and their store the year before. Laurie informed me that after the story was published, they had received several large orders for a ball cap featured in the article. The hat's inscription read "Trump 2020: Elect that MF'er again!" Laurie also told me that their business had grown and that they were in the process of moving into a larger building across the street. I walked over there and met Rob, who told me how much of a hit those Trump hats had become. Some of the memorabilia shows were held in elementary schools, so Rob was reluctant to take the "MF'er" hats in.

> But these parents are coming up to us saying, "Hey, where's the hat, man? My uncle loved that hat for Christmas! My dad loved them!" We just did a show two weeks ago and (the Trump merchandise) outsold our Detroit Pride hats by 35 percent. People were buying more Trump hats. When Trump outsells our product, that's pretty cool.

Rob assured me that he was willing to produce hats for any candidate—Republican or Democrat—but that there just wasn't anywhere near the demand for anyone but Trump. Rob informed me that he didn't know anyone who had supported but since abandoned Trump. In fact, "I've met more people changing to jump on the train, especially after seeing him come to Michigan," he said, referring to a campaign rally that Trump had held in nearby Warren a month earlier.

I asked Rob, who had never voted for president before voting for Trump in 2016, whether there was anything that could happen before election day to make him not vote for Trump.

"No," Rob said flatly. "I'm so happy."

I also met up with Catherine Bolder, the Obama voter-turned-Sanders-voter-turned-Trump supporter, at Parker's Hilltop Brewery in Clarkston, where we had met for two previous interviews. The restaurant was sparse because social distancing measures were starting to be instituted. Catherine floated a conspiracy theory that the Chinese had spread the coronavirus deliberately in retaliation for Trump's tariffs. She predicted that the crisis would be over by mid-April and that Trump would "wipe the floor with" Joe Biden in November.

"Everybody's in love with (the economy)," she said. "Everybody's doing really well."

Catherine and her two sisters had just bought a new house. She also informed me that one of her sisters, Clara, also a two-time Obama voter, was considering a vote for Trump after sitting out 2016. At dinner at Catherine and Clara's home a few nights later, Clara told me that she voted for Obama because she felt it was time for America to have a black president. Clara had a hard time articulating exactly

Rob and Laurie Rasch outside their new store in New Baltimore in 2020. (Daniel Allott)

which of Trump's policies she supported, eventually settling on immigration. But she liked that Trump wasn't a typical politician. Although she wasn't 100 percent committed to voting for Trump, she said she was strongly leaning that way. (Later, in May after the pandemic had been raging for two months, I texted Clara and asked whether she might be tempted to vote for Biden. "Not one iota," she replied. "Mr T has my vote!")

The most illuminating part of my discussion with the Bolders wasn't about politics, but about race and how their family grappled with it. I asked Clara whether Catherine's marriage to her late husband, who was black, had changed her views on race.

"After a while it did," Clara said.

> At first it was, you know, "That's not the way it should be. She's supposed to marry someone of our race, ethnicity." But then I saw how another family member married someone of our race and treated her like a piece of shit. And I saw how (Catherine's husband) treated her like a queen, and I thought, I cannot judge this man's character by his color.

"I was afraid to tell anyone in my family because I thought they'd reject me," Catherine said.

> But then I just got to the point where I didn't care. I remember my mom calling me up and saying, "What will people think?" Well, I said, "When people pay my bills, they can tell me what to do." I think my marriage changed all of my family's view. I was willing to give up my family. I think they ended up loving him more than me because he was a good person. He made me a better person, really.

I also talked to George Martin, the young black Obama-Trump voter I had met earlier in Detroit. George didn't believe Biden would come close to replicating President Obama's success among black voters in southeast Michigan. Black voters he knew had noticed Biden trying to ride Obama's coattails once again, name-dropping Obama at convenient times, especially when talking before black audiences, then distancing himself from his former boss when it suited him, such as on the Obama administration's deportation policy.

Catherine and Clara Bolder. (Author's personal collection)

"Let me put it bluntly," George said:

> In the city of Detroit, voting for the first black president is more important than getting Donald Trump out of office. To see Obama in office, that's to see the black man at the highest. We made it. We can actually do anything in this country. You don't get that by voting Donald Trump out of office. You just don't.

* * *

On March 12, Gov. Gretchen Whitmer shuttered all K–12 schools in Michigan in an effort to slow the spread of Covid-19.[7] On the same day, I joined a group of about 100 Republicans at Enchantment Catering & Banquet in Shelby Township for the Macomb County Republicans' monthly meeting.

In the last chapter on tribalism, I wrote that I knew where just about everybody would come down on any issue of the Trump presidency simply by asking them how they felt about Trump. Even a pandemic, it turned out, was not immune to this tribalism. Revealingly, all of the Democratic meetings I had planned to attend in Michigan had been cancelled. But most of the Republican meetings were still on. At the time, Trump was minimizing the danger from the virus, insisting that it would simply "disappear."⁸ Conservative media were largely following Trump's lead, using words like *hoax* and *hysteria* to describe the virus and the attention surrounding it.⁹

It was clear from the moment I walked into the banquet room for that monthly meeting that no social distancing was going on, even though most of the attendees fell into the over-sixty demographic most vulnerable to the virus's effects. People eagerly shook hands, embraced, and stood and sat close to one another, seemingly unconcerned that a once-in-a-century pandemic was spreading across the world. Some people even joked about it. "You don't have coronavirus, do you?" attendees asked one another with a chuckle before shaking hands or embracing.

I spotted a table at the back of the room, empty except for an older man in a MAGA hat. I sat down, scanned the room, and saw a few familiar faces from meetings I'd attended in previous years. I didn't want them to notice me because, at a meeting the year before, I had mentioned that I was a journalist and they'd nearly forced me to leave. So I tried to keep a low profile. I struck up a conversation with the man in the MAGA hat. He immediately began talking about an incident that had made news two days earlier. Joe Biden had visited a Fiat-Chrysler auto plant in Detroit and gotten into a heated exchange with one of the workers. The worker had accused Biden of wanting to take away his Second Amendment rights.¹⁰

"You're full of shit. I support the Second Amendment," Biden had responded. Don't be "such a horse's ass." Biden had also mistakenly referred to AR-15 rifles as AR-14s.

But the worker wasn't having it. Standing inches from Biden, he told the former vice president that he'd seen an online video claiming that Biden didn't support the Second Amendment. It was an interaction that surely would have made Jim Wertz shake his head. Biden was there to talk about the economy and his record as vice president. "You made me a hero when I was getting a lot of heat for the (auto) bailout, the rescue," he had told the workers a few minutes earlier. But this worker wanted to talk about guns, not about how Biden had supposedly saved his job.

Reinforcing gun enthusiasts' anxiety about Biden, a few days earlier Biden had appeared to pledge to name former Rep. Beto O'Rourke to, in Biden's words, "lead (the) effort" to "take care of the gun problem." O'Rourke, who had just endorsed Biden for president, had become infamous among gun-rights supporters during the presidential debates for pledging to confiscate certain types of guns. "Hell, yes, we're going to take your AR-15, your AK-47," O'Rourke had said on the campaign trail.[11]

Almost everyone I spoke with in Michigan mentioned Biden's confrontation with the autoworker. Many shook their heads at Biden's response. The guy in the MAGA hat at my table was certain that Trump would win reelection because he had done exactly what he promised. "First president since Reagan to do that," he said.

A couple of minutes later, everyone was asked to stand for the Pledge of Allegiance and a prayer, "the most important part of the evening," the emcee said. The woman who said the prayer asked people to pray for President Trump, Vice President Pence, and their advisers. Then she prayed about the coronavirus, asking God to help the country overcome not the virus itself, but rather the "hysteria" surrounding it. I looked around the room and saw people solemnly bowing their heads and a few nodding in approval. Nobody seemed struck at this unusual invocation. *Hysteria* seemed to be the word of the evening: It was uttered at least a dozen times to describe the virus and the atmosphere surrounding it.

Mark Forton, a MAGA-hat-wearing county party chairman, got up to speak next. "Let me first make a few comments about this disaster," Forton, started.

"Hysteria!" someone cried out.

"I'm seventy-three," Forton said, "and I'm not afraid of this thing." Forton claimed that the virus was part of a conspiracy between "communist red China," the Democrats and "half the Republicans and even Wall Street" to "totally disrupt the economy" and "take down Trump."

"That's about it for my chairman's report," Forton said, before assuring people that their Trump yard signs were in the mail.

A series of other club officers, local elected officials, and candidates each got a few minutes at the podium. One of them mentioned Michael Taylor, the Republican mayor of Sterling Heights, who had just endorsed Joe Biden for president. The mention of Taylor's name was like throwing chum into shark-infested waters.

"This guy has got to be excoriated by the party," someone yelled of Taylor.

"He was never a Republican!"

"Get rid of RINOs (Republicans In Name Only)!"

"They gotta go!"

"There are people who come to this meeting who I know are RINOs," someone stood up and yelled. "Get out!"

Then another party leader named Stan Grot got up to talk. He took the vitriol to another level. "Please don't give in to the hysteria by the media," he said. "Panic! Panic!—That's their goal." Then Grot excoriated Fox News contributor and Democratic strategist Donna Brazile, who two days earlier had told Republican National Committee Chairwoman Ronna Romney McDaniel to "go to hell" during an on-air exchange. Romney McDaniel had alleged the Democratic primary process would be "rigged" against Bernie Sanders.[12]

"Donna Brazile, that lying filthy skunk!" Grot yelled. Grot also seemed scandalized that Biden had referred to the autoworker as being "full of shit."

"This guy's running for president with that language?!" Grot said without irony. "Joe Biden is full of shit!" After all that talk of filthy skunks, liars, and shit, Grot urged everyone to go home and say a prayer with their families.

Later, there were candidate speeches and more discussion about the virus hysteria and the evils of socialism. One guy railed against college "being forced down our throats;" another thanked the group for "coming out in the middle of this coronavirus hoax;" a third said, "By the way, this coronavirus, it was made in China—it ain't gonna last."

The whole thing was quite surreal, and also quite sad. These were some of the most vulnerable people. But they didn't seem to care. At this point, whether you took the virus seriously or not was treated as a political act—as a way of signaling which side you were on, which tribe you were in. Whether you felt that the virus was an international pandemic that exposed Trump's unfitness for office or part of a media-created hysteria to weaken Trump ahead of the election depended on where you stood on Trump. And of course there seemed to be no room in between those two extreme views. Part of me understood where these Republicans were coming from. Many Democrats and journalists no doubt did see the pandemic as a chance—perhaps their last chance—to deny Trump a second term in office.

Later on, the wearing of medical masks became a symbol of the political divide over the coronavirus, with liberals wearing masks to signal how seriously they took the pandemic and to demonstrate they were willing to sacrifice personal liberties and convenience to save lives. Some conservatives, meanwhile, refused to wear masks to show that they would not give in to the hysteria surrounding the pandemic or the creeping authoritarianism of the nanny state. The conservative reaction to the virus underscored how little credibility the media has in America. Polling has found that public trust in the media has reached an all-time low and that Republicans are much less likely than Democrats to trust the media.

There's a boy-who-cried-wolf effect that's developed between the media and the public. Conservatives and other Trump supporters have no trust in the media to be neutral arbiters of what is and what is not newsworthy. Virtually every media outlet has an almost comically anti-Trump bias. As Alan Taylor, a Baptist preacher in Robeson County, North Carolina, had put it to me about Trump and the media in 2017:

> I think any time that, with present company excluded, the media comes after him, it makes him stronger. It's like a Godzilla movie. The more he's attacked by the media, the more powerful he becomes because no one believes the mainstream media in flyover country. Everyone can spot it from a mile away. So, whenever they attack him, that makes him stronger.

According to one analysis of Trump's first two years in office, 90 percent of network news coverage of Trump was negative.[13] Late-night comedians and shows such as *Saturday Night Live* heap mounds of abuse on Trump on a daily basis, treatment that is made even more glaring given how sycophantic most of the media were toward Obama. The problem is that if everything Trump does is so terrible, then when Trump does something truly terrible, nobody will notice because the media has no credibility left. Nobody believes a congenital liar, even when he's telling the truth.

Democrats certainly weren't immune from the coronavirus tribalism. A couple of weeks earlier, I had attended a house party with a group of seven or eight Bernie Sanders-supporting progressives in Salt Lake City. It was an enjoyable evening spent with people whom I'd interviewed and become friends with. But my hosts spent part of the evening blaming Trump for his slow response to the pandemic, singling out his naming of Vice President Pence to head up the White House Coronavirus Task Force. They suggested that Pence's religiosity disqualified him from leading the government's response to the public health crisis. They also slammed Trump for closing off travel from China, a move they, like most of the anti-Trump tribe, called bigoted and racist. Joe Biden criticized the president's "xenophobia" and "fear-mongering" in making the decision.

Later, the consensus became that this was one of Trump's better decisions in the early days of the government's response to the pandemic. Biden would later criticize Trump for moving "awfully slow" to close off travel from China.

I don't know whether anyone from that Republican meeting subsequently tested positive for coronavirus or if anyone died from it. But the virus had already been spreading in the area for at least a week. According to a *Washington Post* story, at a bar a few miles south in Detroit the weekend before, at least seven people had been infected and several died.[14] A month later, southeast Michigan would become an epicenter of the virus, with more than 3,100 confirmed cases and more than 200 deaths.

But back at Enchantment Catering & Banquet in Shelby Township, nobody seemed at all concerned. Perhaps the attendees felt that their herd mentality granted them herd immunity from the virus. Near the end of the meeting, an elderly man stood up. "I had coronavirus," he announced solemnly before pausing, for effect. "But I had chicken soup for lunch, so I feel fine!"

12

CONCLUSION

IN MAY, as the COVID-19 pandemic entered its third month and most of the country was sheltering in place, I reached out to my contacts one last time. I wanted to get their opinions about President Trump's performance during the crisis, about Joe Biden, who had become the presumptive Democratic nominee, and about what might happen on election day. I interviewed nearly eighty people from all nine of my counties, this time via phone, email, Facebook Messenger, and text.

It is assumed that Trump's fate will hinge on the public's perception of his handling of the pandemic and the path the virus and economy take in the summer and fall of 2020. But the pandemic hadn't changed many minds among the people I talked to. Each development in the crisis, rather than prompting a reevaluation of the president, had only reinforced whatever view people already held. With few exceptions, Trump's support was unshakeable; his opposition equally so.

To the Trump critics I communicated with, his performance had further exposed how utterly unfit he is to lead the country. Their responses stressed Trump's initial reluctance to acknowledge the severity of the crisis, his promise of early testing that never materialized, and the steady stream of errors, attacks, and bizarre statements during his daily press briefings. Their opinions were perhaps best captured by Narren Brown, a progressive college professor, who began his response to my question about Trump's performance with, "Are you asking me that question in earnest?"

Trump's supporters assessed the president's performance much differently. Most offered some variation of "He has done as well as can be expected under the circumstances." As Geri Mosher of Grant County, West Virginia, put it in a text, "Even though he doesn't always say things the best way, I believe he cares about this country enough that he does and says what he thinks is best at the time."

When I called Mike Gooder late one evening, he was still working at the large plant nursery he owns in Cresco, Iowa. Business was booming as people living under stay-at-home orders began planting home gardens. Mike's friend Ryan Moeller joined Mike, and the three of us chatted on speakerphone. Moeller owns a medium-sized dairy and beef farm that had been hit hard as many of the restaurants and other businesses that typically buy his product remained shuttered. But Moeller did not blame Trump for his dire economic predicament. He believed that the Democrats had paid China to engineer the virus and introduce it into the United States with the hope of torpedoing the economy and Trump's chances for reelection. Moeller believed the conspiracy would backfire and embolden Trump voters' support for the president.

"I don't see any swing against Trump in any way, shape, or form in rural America," Gooder said.

"I've seen a swing *towards* him," Moeller added.

Both men believed Trump had one thing working in his favor: his opponent, Joe Biden.

"Who's going to pull our asses out of this mess?" Moeller asked. "Biden? No! Trump."

Moeller won't be voting for Biden, of course, but I found little enthusiasm for Biden even among those who will. They used words such as "conflicted," "heartsick," "deeply flawed," and the "lesser of two evils" to describe Biden and his candidacy. Many listed Biden's political and personal baggage, and several even said they were holding out hope that Biden would step aside or get pushed aside and that another Democrat would be nominated. And nearly everyone I spoke with raised Biden's apparent cognitive decline and questioned whether he would be able to execute the office of the presidency. Most were convinced he would lose to Trump. Here are a few of those responses—and keep in mind, none of these people are Trump supporters.

"I don't see any enthusiasm for Biden here at all. I don't know a single person who is even bothering to say supportive things about him."

—HEATHER BACH, TREMPEALEAU COUNTY, WISCONSIN

"A vote for Biden only further emboldens the corruption. ... Trump's policies have hurt people I care about. Though I'm not sure Biden would be any better."

—TODD MENSINK, HOWARD COUNTY, IOWA

"Odds are Trump will be reelected because Biden is a profoundly weak opponent."

—JAMES FOUTS, MAYOR OF WARREN IN MACOMB COUNTY, MICHIGAN

"Biden will not have any Chaldean voters because he actually has blood on his hands in destroying Iraq with his disastrous Iraq War vote. ... Many Democratic Chaldeans I know are sitting it out or voting Trump. No, I'm not voting for Biden because he destroyed my ancestral lands and helped pave the way for wiping away Christianity from Iraq."

—JOHNNY ORAM, MACOMB COUNTY, MICHIGAN

"I don't know if Biden has a chance. I would say probably not. I know a lot of the people in Erie liked the fact that Trump came here during the 2016 election, and he also came back after he was president. That direct contact really mattered, and it has stayed with people."

—CHRISTINA VOGEL, ERIE COUNTY, PENNSYLVANIA

"Biden ... excited, no. His age and mental capacity is questionable. Hope to God he picks a great running mate. There was talk that he may pick out members for his cabinet before the election. That may get people excited. Otherwise it just seems he's the guy to vote for if you don't want Trump. That's it. And then there's Tara Reade.... Nothing can come easy for the Democrats ... lol."

—PAUL JERECZEK, TREMPEALEAU COUNTY, WISCONSIN

Note that all of these people live in the crucial Obama-Trump counties and states where the 2020 election will be determined.

A few people had changed their minds about how they intended to vote. When I interviewed Melarie Wheat, a Mormon woman living in Salt Lake City, Utah, in February, she had said she would be willing to vote for any Democrat except Biden or Bernie Sanders. "Old, white men—I'm really done with," Wheat had said at the time. But in May she emailed to say that she had in fact voted for Biden in the Utah Democratic primary after her first two choices dropped out and endorsed him. Now Wheat said she would vote for Biden in the general election, although she qualified her support with paragraphs detailing her misgivings about Biden in light of former staffer Tara Reade's allegation that he had sexually assaulted her in 1993.

Jasmine Flores, the young Bernie-supporting activist in Erie, told me in March that she would grudgingly vote for Biden in the general election. Two months later, she seemed to have changed her mind. "As a Hispanic woman I do not owe my vote to any party," she said. "You earn it, and Biden has not earned my vote as the Democratic nominee, and he has a lot of work to do on the issues to earn my vote."

Flores felt Trump would win the election "hands down" in part because many people she knows believe Trump has taken care of them during the pandemic. "I see a lot of individuals who are not into politics or informed about politics believing (Trump) just gave them $1,200 in stimulus money," she wrote. "They talk about him like he saved us and is generally doing good while in office."

Several Evan McMullin voters I had kept in touch with revealed that they now planned to vote for Trump. A Mormon former CIA officer, McMullin ran for president in 2016 as a conservative alternative to Trump, winning more than 700,000 votes nationwide. One of those voters was Trent Mason, who had told me at Ricki Leigh's guitar shop in Erie that he was resigned to voting for Biden.

"I guess I'm ridin' with Biden," he had said in March. But in a text exchange in May, Trent said he had changed his mind: "In all honesty, I think (Trump) deserves a shot at rebuilding the economy," he wrote. "I want to see if his *policies* can rebuild the economy.... I am just like the majority of the country. We hate Trump but would like to see this economy rebound fast!"

Trent also listed Biden's deficiencies as a candidate: the Tara Reade "nightmare"; "his son making $ in Ukraine"; and Trent's belief that Biden is "close to dementia." "Yeah, I'll vote for Trump," he concluded. "I loathe him, but we have to build this economy."

Trent wasn't alone in believing that Trump would be better at reviving the economy. A poll from early May, when 30 million Americans were out of work, found that 45 percent believed Trump was better suited to create jobs, while only 32 percent said it was Biden.[1]

***

It is the defining irony of the Trump presidency: A president who lies with more frequency and compulsion than perhaps any other president in history has also been arguably the most honest recent president when it comes to delivering on his campaign promises. If Trump wins re-election, it will be because he set a clear agenda and then either achieved or tried to achieve most of it. If Trump loses, however, it will be because his defects of character—his impulsiveness, his inattention to detail, his petty cruelty, and most prominently his routine dishonesty—have turned off many exhausted voters who might otherwise support him. In fact, as I'm writing this, I have just received a text message from Pramit Patel, an Indian-American Obama-Trump voter from Robeson County, North Carolina. The last time we corresponded, in early May, he had told me he was committed to voting for Trump again. But in early June, in the wake of the killing of George Floyd at the hands of Minneapolis police and President Trump's inability to unify or console the nation, Patel texted again. "I don't think I am going to vote this year," he wrote. "Neither candidate possesses the leadership qualities required to be the president of the USA."

The tension between Trump's policies and personality has been a dominant theme throughout this book. It is something Mark Locklear thinks about nearly every day.

Locklear is the Lumbee Native American from Robeson County, North Carolina, whose story I told in Chapter 6. Until Patel texted me, Mark was the only Obama-Trump voter I followed who had not committed to voting for Trump in 2020. Whenever I interviewed Mark, he would describe his feelings for Trump as being like a pendulum swinging from positivity to negativity with every Trump utterance and action. The last time I met up with Mark was in February 2020 at his home office in Prospect, where my journey had started three years earlier. Mark said that he was "not happy with Trump's Twitter account, his bullying," and his "constant lying." It was making Mark question whether he could vote for him. "I just don't know whether I can believe anything he's telling me," Mark said. "I don't know whether he's being honest with me, and that's not a comfortable place to be."

"I don't trust him with my son's life," Mark said of his son Ethan, a young Marine.

I don't trust him with any of our young men's lives. I don't. And I don't like feeling that way. What I see in him right now is that he will do whatever it takes, and sacrifice who he may have to, to come out on top. He's going to have to do some things between now and election day to pull me back across the line.

When I talked to Mark by phone in May, I asked him how he thought Trump was handling the pandemic. "Not at all impressed or satisfied, Dan, I can tell you that," Mark began, again identi-

Mark Locklear holds a framed portrait of his son, Ethan, a Marine. (Daniel Allott)

fying Trump's dishonesty as the source of his dissatisfaction. Mark mentioned Trump's statement in early March that "anybody" who wanted could get tested for the virus. Mark's wife became sick around that time and was unable to obtain a test. "That hit me personally," Mark said.

Mark was driving his truck as we spoke on the phone. He passed a couple of homes that were flying Trump 2020 flags. "Never seen that!" Mark remarked as he drove past the home of someone he didn't know was a Trump supporter.

"I do believe he is going to be reelected," Mark said. "His base is strong. I just don't see where Biden can gain ground.... I'd say the pendulum is in the middle. I am giving Trump from now until election day—whether I mean anything to him or not—to convince me that I can trust him. Because right now, I just don't trust what he is telling me."

***

Despite the unprecedented nature of Trump's presidency, I believe there is recent precedent for how the 2020 election may unfold.

Not long ago, a deeply polarizing president ran for reelection. The opposing party, buoyed by a historic midterm wave election, was confident that they could triumph by zeroing in on what they saw as the incumbent's glaring failures. After flirting with a series of extreme candidates, they settled on the establishment favorite, the safe bet, the candidate nobody seemed very excited about but the one everybody agreed had the best shot at defeating the incumbent. The year was 2012, and the safe bet candidate was Mitt Romney. Romney lost to Barack Obama, who managed to reassemble the coalition that had swept him to victory four years earlier. Obama even increased turnout among his core supporters, who proved to be difference-makers in crucial states.

As I mentioned in Chapter 2, Republicans were surprised that 1.7 million additional black voters turned out for Barack Obama in 2012. But they should not have been. Obama had spent four years fortifying the bond of trust and goodwill with his core constituency. There was no way they would allow him to lose and become a one-term president.

I believe Democrats will be similarly surprised by the turnout Trump receives from his base of white rural, working-class, and religious voters. Many did not vote in the 2018 midterm elections. But they will be back in full force in 2020 because the bond of trust and goodwill that they have with Trump is stronger than ever. They believe this president, despite his flaws, has delivered for them and still has their backs.

The 2020 primaries may have provided a preview of the type of turnout we can expect from Trump voters in November. As the media focused on the Democratic primary race, Trump was piling up unprecedented victories. In the early primary states, Trump surpassed the vote totals that both Barack Obama and George W. Bush had received in their successful reelection bids. In New Hampshire, for instance, Trump received 129,696 votes, more than doubling Obama and Bush's reelection year totals, despite facing only token opposition. Clearly, enthusiasm for Trump still existed; perhaps it had even increased.

As I traveled the country, rural residents would sometimes tell me that they believed there were still many "hidden" and "quiet" Trump voters out there—people who hadn't voted in 2016 but planned to vote for Trump in 2020, or people who didn't identify as Trump supporters but would still vote for him. These voters—who disproportionately reside in battleground states such as Wisconsin, Michigan, and Pennsylvania—tend not to talk to reporters or pollsters or broadcast their support for Trump in any way.

Jon Schultz has had many conversations with these hidden voters. Schultz is a carpenter and high school cross-country couch in Trempealeau County, Wisconsin. A Democrat, Schultz does not support Donald Trump, but he has many friends who do. When I met up with Schultz in the fall of 2019, he was convinced that Trump's hidden support was strong in western Wisconsin. National Democrats still don't understand rural America, he said, but Trump seems to. "There are still a lot of Trump supporters here who haven't voted for him yet," was the way he put it to me.

I heard something similar from Henry and Noel Filla, the Wisconsin farmers I featured in Chapter 2. They said they knew a lot of quiet Trump voters in their community. "It's kind of like, they'll vote for him but they won't admit it," Henry told me about some of his neighbors.

"Yeah there's a lot of that," Noel said.

> We were at the (county) fair the other day, and there was a Republican booth. And the people working there (said) they'll reach out to guys who come by who'll be really quiet because there are other people around. And then when the other people walk away, these guys will speak up and say, "Yeah, I'm a Trump supporter."

"Why would they be quiet about it?" I asked.

"Well, I think it's because people are nervous a little bit because (Trump) does some, you know, erratic things," Henry said. "And because of some of the things he says—it's like, they're ashamed almost. So they don't really want to admit it to people. But in their heart, they feel he's right."

ACKNOWLEDGMENTS

THIS BOOK WOULD NOT HAVE BEEN POSSIBLE without the generous assistance of many people. Eric Kampmann and Al Regnery at Republic Book Publishers believed in this book and saw the importance of investing in a kind of deep journalism that seems to have gone out of fashion.

David Freddoso provided superb editing and welcome advice. Jimmy Finkelstein, Bob Cusack, Frank Craig, and my colleagues at *The Hill* were patient and supportive throughout. Hugo Gurdon and my former colleagues at the *Washington Examiner* launched me on this journey under the banner of The Race to 2020 reporting project.

My twin brother, Jordan Allott, joined me during much of the first year of this journey and was an invaluable sounding board. He also took most of the wonderful photos featured in the book. Gary Bauer provided valuable advice and support. And Emily Leayman, Nicole Rizkallah, and Deirdre McQuade each helped with research, planning, and photography at various stages.

Many family members, friends, and colleagues offered encouragement, advice, and inspiration at just the right moments during the long journey. I'd like to especially thank: Laurel Allott, Richard Allott, Susan Dreghorn, Susan and Phillip Jones, Carol Klein and the Denkenberger family, Rayhan Asat, Bannaros Atichattumrong, Gisela Diaz, Andrew Doran, Chieu Duong, Christine Guluzian, Ana Raquel Heredia, Monica Herman, Elnaz Nazemi, George Neumayr, Johnny Oram, Anjelica Tan, Leslie Walton, Mike Walsh, and Theresa Kelly Winters, Chris Wright.

I am grateful for the hundreds of people I met on the road who invited me into their homes, communities, and lives. I would especially like to thank Mike and Rachel Gooder and their family, Ali AlAbbasi, Hiba and Jasmine Alsabunji, Bo Biggs, Catherine and Clara Bolder, "the unsinkable" Danny Britt, Karina Brown, Chris and Sandy Chilson, Cindi Corbin, Henry and Noel Filla, Joe Heim, Sandi Hodgden, Darryl Howard, Laura Hubka, Ken and Paul Jereczek, Cathy Kulig, Ricki Leigh, Mark Locklear, Eddie Lopez, Jarrod Lowery, Sharlee Mullins Glenn, George Martin, Trent Mason, Michelle Mazarei, Todd Mensink, Geri and Ed Mosher, Jason Passmore, Jake Rouch, Brenda Sams, Jon Schultz, Spiff Slifka, Phillip Stephens, Dale and Darlene Thompson, Mitch and Angel Vice, Bryan Ward, and Jim Wertz.

ENDNOTES

INTRODUCTION

1   Jill Abramson, "Will the Media Ever Figure Out How to Cover Trump?", *Washington Post*, February 3, 2019, https://www.washingtonpost.com/opinions/will-the-media-ever-figure-out-how-to-cover-trump/2019/02/03/b74e8774-266a-11e9-90cd-dedb0c92dc17_story.html.

CHAPTER 1

1   AP, "2016 Iowa Presidential Election Results," *Politico*, https://www.politico.com/2016-election/results/map/president/iowa/; "2012 Iowa Presidential Results," Politico, last updated November 19, 12, https://www.politico.com/2012-election/results/president/iowa/.

2   Thomas Frank, *What's the Matter with Kansas?* (New York: Metropolitan Books, 2004).

3   Alan S. Gerber et al. "Self-Interest, Beliefs, and Policy Opinions: Understanding How Economic Beliefs Affect Immigration Policy Preferences," *Political Research Quarterly* 70, no. 1 (January 6, 2017): 155–71, https://doi.org/10.1177/1065912916684032.

4   Susan A. Cohen, "Abortion and Women of Color: The Bigger Picture," *Guttmacher Policy Review* 11, no. 3 (Summer 2008), https://www.guttmacher.org/sites/default/files/article_files/gpr110302.pdf.

5   Mark Weinraub, "Trump's Tariff War Threatens to Erode Support of Farmers," Reuters, June 18, 2018, https://www.reuters.com/article/us-usa-trade-agriculture/trumps-tariff-war-threatens-to-erode-support-of-farmers-idUSKBN1JE2X2.

6   Alexander Mallin, "As Trump Visits Iowa, Farmers Warn 'Patience Is Wearing Thin' on Tariff Fight," ABC News, July 26, 2018, https://abcnews.go.com/Politics/trump-visits-iowa-farmers-warn-patience-wearing-thin/story?id=56837609.

7   Dan Balz, "Loyalty, Unease in Trump's Midwest," *Washington Post*, May 10, 2018, https://www.washingtonpost.com/graphics/2018/national/trump-voters/.

8   Laura Hubka, "We Are Not the Ones We Were Waiting For," *Bleeding Heartland* (blog), October 8, 2017, https://www.bleedingheartland.com/2017/10/08/we-are-not-the-ones-we-were-waiting-for/#.WdwK6AG2_78.facebook.

CHAPTER 2

1   Election Center 2008, "National Exit Poll," CNN, https://www.cnn.com/ELECTION/2008/results/polls/#USP00p1.

2   Sam Roberts, "2008 Surge in Black Voters Nearly Erased Racial Gap," *New York Times*, July 20, 2009, https://www.nytimes.com/2009/07/21/us/politics/21vote.html.

3   U.S. Bureau of Labor Statistics, "Unemployment Rate—Black or African American," FRED: Federal Reserve Bank of St. Louis, updated June 5, 2020, https://fred.stlouisfed.org/series/LNS14000006.

4   Corey Dade, "Obama's Most Vocal Black Critics Dial Back Attacks as Election Year Begins," NPR, January 13, 2012, https://www.npr.org/sections/itsallpolitics/2012/01/13/145188135/obamas-most-vocal-black-critics-dial-back-attacks-as-election-year-begins.

5   Dan Balz and Ted Mellnik, "Census: Black Voted at Higher Rates Than Whites in 2012," *Washington Post*, May 8, 2013, https://www.washingtonpost.com/politics/census-blacks-voted-at-higher-rates-than-whites-in-2012/2013/05/08/7d24bcaa-b800-11e2-b94c-b684dda07add_story.html.

6   Katrina Trinko, "Ryan on Election: 'The Surprise Was Some of the Turnout,'" National Review Online, November 13, 2012, https://www.nationalreview.com/corner/ryan-election-surprise-was-some-turnout-katrina-trinko/?itm_source=parsely-api.

7   Paul Steinhauser, "Poll: Obama Makes Big Gains among Black Voters," CNN, January 18, 2008, https://www.cnn.com/2008/POLITICS/01/18/poll.2008/index.html.

8   Humeyra Pamuk and P.J. Huffstutter, "Trump's Trade War Looms over Divided U.S. Farms Belt ahead of Vote," Reuters, November, 1, 2018, https://www.reuters.com/article/us-usa-election-farmers/trumps-trade-war-looms-over-divided-u-s-farm-belt-ahead-of-vote-idUSKCN1N65TL.

9   Tara Golshan, "Trump's Trade War with China Is Hurting Farmers, but They Won't Abandon Him—Yet," Vox, September 9, 2019, https://www.vox.com/2019/9/9/20757042/trump-trade-war-china-farmers-iowa-2020.

10 News Editor, "Farm Futures Survey: Farmer Support for Trump Slipping," American Ag Radio Network, August 13, 2018, https://americanagnetwork.com/2018/08/farm-futures-survey-farmer-support-for-trump-slipping/; Scott Perry, "Trump Speaks to Farmers, Via Phone, at Farm Progress Show in Decatur," *Herald & Review*, August 28, 2019, https://herald-review.com/business/agriculture/trump-speaks-to-farmers-via-phone-at-farm-progress-show/article_987fbd42-c28c-588f-8d86-17dc3eae5868.html.

11 Elena Schneider and Catherine Boudreau, "Dems Fear Another Rural Wipeout Will Reelect Trump," *Politico*, August 20, 2019, https://www.politico.com/story/2019/08/20/democratic-primary-rural-outreach-1469005.

12 Megan Casella, "Farmers Are Losing Money Thanks to Trump—but They Still Support Him," *Politico*, November 1, 2018, https://www.politico.com/story/2018/11/01/trump-farmers-trade-900623.

13 "USDA Announces Details of Support Package for Farmers," USDA website, July 25, 2019, https://www.usda.gov/media/press-releases/2019/07/25/usda-announces-details-support-package-farmers.

14 "USDA Announces Coronavirus Food Assistance Program," USDA website, April 17, 2020, https://www.usda.gov/media/press-releases/2020/04/17/usda-announces-coronavirus-food-assistance-program.

15   Jerry Hagstrom, "Trump Tells Perdue to 'Expedite' Aid to Farmers," *The Fence Post*, April 10, 2020, https://www.thefencepost.com/news/trump-tells-perdue-to-expedite-aid-to-farmers/.

16   Election Results 2008, "Wisconsin: Presidential County Results," *New York Times*, December 9, 2008, https://www.nytimes.com/elections/2008/results/states/president/wisconsin.html.

17   Ken Belson, "Election 2012: Wisconsin," *New York Times*, https://www.nytimes.com/elections/2012/results/states/wisconsin.html?mtrref=www.google.com&gwh=69C403FD5E4094ED2BF471D77F96AA59&gwt=pay&assetType=REGIWALL.

18   Erin Gloria Ryan, "Trump Is Banking on Wisconsin Being Racist Enough to Go Red for the First Time Since 1984," *Daily Beast*, November 1, 2016, https://www.thedailybeast.com/trump-is-banking-on-wisconsin-being-racist-enough-to-go-red-for-the-first-time-since-1984.

19   The New York Times, "Wisconsin Presidential Race Results: Donald J. Trump Wins," *New York Times*, August 1, 2017, https://www.nytimes.com/elections/2016/results/wisconsin-president-clinton-trump.

20   Frank Newport, "Americans Big on Idea of Living in the Country," Gallup, December 7, 2018, https://news.gallup.com/poll/245249/americans-big-idea-living-country.aspx.

21   AP, "Farm Population Lowest Since 1850s," *New York Times*, July 20, 1988, https://www.nytimes.com/1988/07/20/us/farm-population-lowest-since-1850-s.html.

22   "Fast Facts about Agriculture and Food," American Farm Bureau website, accessed June 12, 2020, https://www.fb.org/newsroom/fast-facts.

23   Julia Mitric, "As Farmers Age, They Face the Challenge of Finding Successors to Take Over," Marketplace, May 21, 2019, https://www.marketplace.org/2019/05/21/as-farmers-age-they-face-the-challenge-of-finding-successors-to-take-over/.

24   Hope Kirwan, "Wisconsin Lost Record-Breaking Percent of Dairy Farms in 2018," *Wisconsin Public Radio*, December 7, 2018, https://www.wpr.org/wisconsin-lost-record-breaking-percent-dairy-farms-2018.

25   Colleen Kottke, "Wisconsin Continues to Lead U.S. in Farm Bankruptcies," Wisconsin State Farmer, January 31, 2020, https://www.wisfarmer.com/story/news/2020/01/31/wisconsin-continues-lead-u-s-farm-bankruptcies/4625866002/.

26   Patricia Cohen, "The Struggle to Mend America's Rural Roads," *New York Times*, February 18, 2020, https://www.nytimes.com/2020/02/18/business/wisconsin-roads.html?action=click&module=Top%20Stories&pgtype=Homepage.

27   Katherine J. Cramer, *The Politics of Resentment: Rural Consciousness in Wisconsin and the Rise of Scott Walker* (University of Chicago Press, 2016), 63.

28   Cramer, 59

29   Jack Shafer and Tucker Doherty, "The Media Bubble Is Worse Than You Think," *Politico*, May/June 2017, https://www.politico.com/magazine/story/2017/04/25/media-bubble-real-journalism-jobs-east-coast-215048.

30   Jose A. Delreal and Scott Clement, "New Poll of Rural Americans Shows Deep Cultural Divide with Urban Centers," *Washington Post*, July 17, 2017, https://www.chicagotribune.com/nation-world/ct-rural-americans-poll-urban-divide-20170617-story.html.

31   Schneider and Boudreau, "Dems Fear Another Rural Wipeout Will Reelect Trump."

32   Stephen Dinan, "Court Orders Restoration of DACA Program," *Washington Times*, February 13, 2018, https://www.washingtontimes.com/news/2018/feb/13/court-orders-full-restoration-daca-program/.

33 Reuters, "Nancy Pelosi Says Trump Wants to 'Make America White Again,'" *Guardian* (UK), July 9, 2019, https://www.theguardian.com/global/video/2019/jul/09/nancy-pelosi-says-trump-wants-to-make-america-white-again-video.

34 U.S. Census Bureau (2014–2018), *Hispanic or Latino Origin by Specific Origin American Community Survey 5-Year Estimates*, Census Reporter: Arcadia, WI, https://censusreporter.org/data/table/?table=B03001&geo_ids=16000US5502500&primary_geo_id=16000US5502500.

35 Nathan Hansen, "Despite National Tensions, Arcadia Embraces Diversity, *La Crosse Tribune*, April 9, 2017, https://lacrossetribune.com/news/local/despite-national-tensions-arcadia-embraces-diversity/article_a1b9a828-5a2f-5b40-b15b-2bf57e01fd55.html.

36 Ryan, "Trump Is Banking on Wisconsin Being Racist Enough to Go Red for the First Time Since 1984."

37 Lucy Madison, "Romney on Immigration: I'm for 'Self-Deportation,'" CBS News, January 24, 2012, https://www.cbsnews.com/news/romney-on-immigration-im-for-self-deportation/.

38 U.S. Census Bureau (2014–2018), *Hispanic or Latino Origin by Specific Origin American Community Survey 5-Year Estimates*.

39 U.S. Census Bureau.

40 U.S. Bureau of Labor Statistics, "Unemployment Rate in Trempealeau County, Wisconsin," FRED: Federal Reserve Bank of St. Louis, updated June 3, 2020, https://fred.stlouisfed.org/series/WITREM1URN.

41 Joint Economic Committee, "Rural DACA by the Numbers," https://www.jec.senate.gov/public/_cache/files/e02f2015-ab3a-47aa-aa6f-215a1db74986/rural-daca-by-the-numbers.pdf.

CHAPTER 3

1 Time Staff, "Here's Donald Trump Presidential Announcement Speech," *Time*, June 16, 2015, https://time.com/3923128/donald-trump-announcement-speech/.

2 Quick Facts: Santa Ana City, California, United States Census Bureau, July 1, 2019, https://www.census.gov/quickfacts/santaanacitycalifornia.

3 Wikipedia, s.v. "1984 Presidential Election in California," last edited May 21, 2020, https://en.wikipedia.org/wiki/1984_United_States_presidential_election_in_California.

4 Quick Facts: Orange County, California: United States Census Bureau, July 1, 2019, https://www.census.gov/quickfacts/orangecountycalifornia.

5 Joel Rubin, "O.C. Whites a Majority No Longer," *Los Angeles Times*, September 30, 2004, https://www.latimes.com/archives/la-xpm-2004-sep-30-me-census30-story.html.

6 United States Census Bureau, Data USA: Orange County, California, https://datausa.io/profile/geo/orange-county-ca#demographics.

7 "Top Orange County Public Schools," *Public School Review*, accessed June 12, 2020, https://www.publicschoolreview.com/california/orange-county.

8 Chris McGinnis, "Could John Wayne's Racist Views Lead to Airport Name Change?," *SFGate*, September 30, 2020, https://www.sfgate.com/travel/article/John-Wayne-racist-airport-14480305.php.

9 Jordan Graham, "Late Vote Count Confirms Irvine Mayor Don Wagner Will Be New County Supervisor," *Orange County Register*, March 18, 2019, https://www.ocregister.com/2019/03/18/late-vote-count-confirms-irvine-mayor-don-wagner-will-be-new-county-supervisor/.

10 Election 2016: California Results, *New York Times*, August 1, 2017, https://www.nytimes.com/elections/2016/results/california.

11   Adam Nagourney, "A Democratic Rout in Orange County: Cisneros's Win Makes It Four,"
     New York Times, November 17, 2018, https://www.nytimes.com/2018/11/17/us/politics/cisneros-
     orange-county-democrats.html.

12   Michael R. Blood and Stephen Ohlemacher, "Democratic Sweep in California Raises GOP
     Suspicion," Associated Press, November 30, 2018, https://apnews.com/3cfd93f7859149809949b
     d611287154e.

13   "How Groups Voted in 1992," The Roper Center, https://ropercenter.cornell.edu/how-groups-
     voted-1992.

14   Hansi Lo Wang, "Trump Lost More of the Asian-American Vote Than the National Exit Polls
     Showed," National Public Radio, April 18, 2017, https://www.npr.org/2017/04/18/524371847/
     trump-lost-more-of-the-asian-american-vote-than-the-national-exit-polls-showed.

15   Adam Nagourney and Robert Gebeloff, "In Orange County, a Republican Fortress Turns
     Democratic," *New York Times*, December 31, 2018, https://www.nytimes.com/2018/12/31/us/
     orange-county-republicans-democrats-demographics.html.

16   Nagourney and Gebeloff.

17   Alexandra DeSanctis, "Virginia Governor Defends Letting Infants Die," National Review
     Online, January 30, 2019, https://www.nationalreview.com/corner/virginia-governor-defends-
     letting-infants-die/.

18   Jordain Carney, "Chants of 'USA' after Trump Says, 'America Will Never Be a Socialist
     Country,'" *The Hill*, February 5, 2019, https://thehill.com/homenews/house/428648-chants-of-
     usa-after-trump-says-america-will-never-be-a-socialist-country.

19   Congressional Leadership Fund memo, accessed June 12, 2020, https://www.
     congressionalleadershipfund.org/wp-content/uploads/2019/03/How-We-Win-The-House-
     Back-3.5.19.pdf.

20   Carlos Echeverria-Estrada and Jeanne Batalova, "Chinese Immigrants in the United States,"
     Migration Policy Institute, January 15, 2020, https://www.migrationpolicy.org/article/chinese-
     immigrants-united-states.

21   "Democrats and Republicans Aren't Just Divided. They Live in Different Worlds," *Wall Street
     Journal*, September 19, 2019, https://www.wsj.com/graphics/red-economy-blue-economy/.

22   Luis Noe-Bustamante, Abby Budiman, and Mark Hugo Lopez, "Where Latinos Have the
     Most Eligible Voters in the 2020 Election," Pew Research, January 31, 2020, https://www.
     pewresearch.org/fact-tank/2020/01/31/where-latinos-have-the-most-eligible-voters-in-the-2020-
     election/.

23   Eli Lake, "Why Obama Let Iran's Green Revolution Fail," Bloomberg, August 24, 2016, https://
     www.bloomberg.com/opinion/articles/2016-08-24/why-obama-let-iran-s-green-revolution-fail.

24   Jordan Graham, "Orange County Will Switch to Vote Centers in 2020, a Move Aimed at
     Boosting Turnout and Cutting Costs," *Orange County Register*, February 26, 2020, https://www.
     ocregister.com/2019/02/26/orange-county-will-switch-to-vote-centers-in-2020-a-move-aimed-
     at-boosting-turnout-and-cutting-costs/.

25   Orange County Registrar of Voters, Election Data Central, accessed June 12, 2020, https://
     www.ocvote.com/datacentral/.

26   Kurt Snibbe, "Why Orange County Is the New Blue," *Orange County Register*, August 9, 2019,
     https://www.ocregister.com/2019/08/09/why-orange-county-is-the-new-blue/.

CHAPTER 4

1   Michigan Results: Election 2016, *New York Times*, August 1, 2017, https://www.nytimes.com/elections/2016/results/michigan.

2   Chad Selweski, "Macomb One of Three Counties Nationwide That Won It for Trump," *Politically Speaking*, December 23, 2016, https://www.politicscentral.org/macomb-one-three-counties-nationwide-won-trump/.

3   Story Hinckley, "Warning Signs for Trump in a Famous Swing County," *Christian Science Monitor*, August 21, 2019, https://www.csmonitor.com/USA/Politics/2019/0821/Warning-signs-for-Trump-in-a-famous-swing-county.

4   "What Is the Airbnb Cancellation Policy for Stays?," Airbnb Help Center, accessed June 12, 2020, https://www.airbnb.com/help/article/149/what-is-the-airbnb-cancellation-policy-for-stays.

5   John McWhorter, "Racist Is a Tough Little Word," *Atlantic*, July 24, 2019, https://www.theatlantic.com/ideas/archive/2019/07/racism-concept-change/594526/.

6   "49% of Democrats Think TRUMP VOTERS ARE RACIST," Rasmussen Reports, July 31, 2019, https://www.rasmussenreports.com/public_content/politics/general_politics/july_2019/49_of_democrats_think_trump_voters_are_racist.

7   Geoffrey Skelley, "Just How Many Obama 2012-Trump 2016 Voters Were There?" *Sabato's Crystal Ball*, UVA Center for Politics, June 1, 2017, http://centerforpolitics.org/crystalball/articles/just-how-many-obama-2012-trump-2016-voters-were-there/.

8   Ashley Jardina, "The White Backlash to 'Crying Racism': How Whites Respond to Calling Racial Preferences Racist," presented at the Annual Meeting of the American Political Science Association, 2017, https://drive.google.com/file/d/1ZYEtGiXCQlCG9cQaM-1sxjjWpiKSAyny/view.

9   Edward Isaac-Dovere, "How the Democrats Took Back Michigan," *Atlantic*, November 18, 2018, https://www.theatlantic.com/politics/archive/2018/11/how-democrats-won-big-michigan-midterms/576043/.

10   David Eggert, "Michigan Election: Gretchen Whitmer In Follows Wakeup Call for Dems," *Oakland Press*, November 25, 2018, https://www.theoaklandpress.com/news/state/michigan-election-gretchen-whitmer-win-follows-wakeup-call-for-dems/article_c544117e-f0f4-11e8-97d0-f336e98455b0.html.

11   Joel Gehrke, "Biden Tells Europeans in Munich That America Is 'an Embarrassment," *Washington Examiner*, February 26, 2019, https://www.washingtonexaminer.com/policy/defense-national-security/biden-tells-europeans-in-munich-that-america-is-an-embarrassment.

12   Kirk Pinho, "Macomb County Outlook: A Slow Recovery, Pockets of Growth," *Crain's Detroit Business*, January 18, 2015, https://www.crainsdetroit.com/article/20150118/NEWS/301189972/macomb-county-outlook-a-slow-recovery-pockets-of-growth.

13   Lauren Gibbons, "A Look Back at President Trump's Previous Visits to Michigan," MLive.com, April 25, 2018, https://www.mlive.com/news/erry-2018/04/306a6e24eb935/a_look_back_at_president_trump.html.

14   *Orange County Register*, "Ford, Criticized by Trump, Cancels Plans to Build Mexican Plant," Orange County Register, January 3, 2017, https://www.ocregister.com/2017/01/03/ford-criticized-by-trump-cancels-plans-to-build-mexican-plant/.

15   Wikipedia, s.v. "List of Michigan Locations By Per Capita Income," last edited April 16, 2020, https://en.wikipedia.org/wiki/List_of_Michigan_locations_by_per_capita_income.

16   United States Census Bureau, Quick Facts: Oakland County, Michigan, July 1, 2019, https://www.census.gov/quickfacts/oaklandcountymichigan

17   United States Census Bureau, Quick Facts: Macomb County, Michigan, July 1, 2019, https://www.census.gov/quickfacts/macombcountymichigan.

18   CNN Politics: 2016 Exit Polls, updated November 23, 2016, https://www.cnn.com/election/2016/results/exit-polls.

19   Josh Landon, "Full Speech Video: Trump Holds Rally in Sterling Heights, Fox News, November 6, 2016, https://www.fox2detroit.com/news/full-speech-video-trump-holds-rally-in-sterling-heights.

20   Elaina Plott, "Infrastructure Week Became a Joke. Now It's for Real," *Atlantic*, May 3, 2019, https://www.theatlantic.com/politics/archive/2019/05/trump-and-democrats-hope-strike-infrastructure-deal/588616/.

21   Alex Szwar, "Macomb County Has Largest Manufacturing Jobs Increase in Nation," *Macomb Township Chronicle*, February 12, 2019, https://www.candgnews.com/news/macomb-county-has-largest-manufacturing-jobs-increase-in-nation-112006.

22   Aaron Rupar, "New congress member creates stir by saying of Trump: 'We're going to impeach this motherfucker!'" Vox, January 4, 2019, https://www.vox.com/policy-and-politics/2019/1/4/18168157/rashida-talib-trump-impeachment-motherfucker.

23   Nate Cohn and Claire Cain Miller, "They Voted Democratic. Now They Support Trump," *New York Times*, November 26, 2019, https://www.nytimes.com/2019/11/26/upshot/democratic-trump-voters-2020.html.

24   "Abortion Trends by Gender, Gallup, accessed June 12, 2020, https://news.gallup.com/poll/245618/abortion-trends-gender.aspx.

25   Chaldean American Chamber of Commerce: Community Overview, accessed June 12, 2020, https://www.chaldeanchamber.com/community-overview/.

26   Ariana Brockington, "Members of Iraqi Religious Minority Who Supported Trump Detained by ICE," NBC News, June 28, 2017, https://www.nbcnews.com/news/us-news/members-iraqi-religious-minority-who-supported-trump-detained-ice-n777696.

27   Julia Edwards Ainsley and Matt Spetalnick, "Trump Says He Will Order 'Safe Zones' for Syria," Reuters, January 25, 2017, https://www.reuters.com/article/us-usa-trump-syria-safezones-idUSKBN1592O8.

28   Justin Fishel, "ISIS Has Committed Genocide, Obama Administration Declares," ABC News, March 17, 2016, https://abcnews.go.com/US/secretary-state-john-kerry-declare-isis-committed-genocide/story?id=37713938.

29   "Remarks by President Trump at the 2018 Values Voter Summit," WhiteHouse.gov, October 13, 2017, https://www.whitehouse.gov/briefings-statements/remarks-president-trump-2017-values-voter-summit/.

30   Mahita Galanan, "Trump Says He Met with the President of the Virgin Islands. But That's Him," *Time*, October 13, 2017, https://time.com/4982458/donald-trump-president-virgin-islands/.

31   Jon Huang et al., Election 2016: Exit Polls, *New York Times*, November 8, 2016, https://www.nytimes.com/interactive/2016/11/08/us/politics/election-exit-polls.html.

32   Claire Cretien, "President Trump: Our 'Religious Heritage' Will Be Cherished, Protected, and Defended,'" LifeSite, October 13, 2017, https://www.lifesitenews.com/news/trump-ahead-of-schedule-on-protecting-religious-liberty-conscience-rights.

CHAPTER 5

1   Alan B. Krueger, *Where Have All the Workers Gone? An Inquiry into the Decline of the U.S. Labor Force Participation Rate*, Brookings Papers on Economic Activity, September 7–8, 2017, https://www.brookings.edu/wp-content/uploads/2017/09/1_krueger.pdf.

2   American Addiction Centers Editorial Staff, "First Responders Worry about Accidental Fentanyl Exposure," Drubabuse.com, accessed June 12, 2020, https://drugabuse.com/first-responders-worry-about-accidental-fentanyl-exposure/.

3   DEA Strategic Intelligence Section, "National Drug Threat Assessment," Drug Enforcement Administration, December 2019, https://www.dea.gov/sites/default/files/2020-01/2019-NDTA-final-01-14-2020_Low_Web-DIR-007-20_2019.pdf.

4   Nana Wilson et al, "Drug and Opioid-Involved Overdose Deaths—United States, 2017–2018," *Morbidity and Mortality Weekly Report* 69, no. 11 (March 20, 2020): 290–97, https://www.cdc.gov/mmwr/volumes/69/wr/mm6911a4.htm.

5   Max Blau, "STAT Forecast: Opioid Could Kill Nearly 500,000 Americans in the Next Decade," STATNews.com, June 27, 2017, https://www.statnews.com/2017/06/27/opioid-deaths-forecast/.

6   http://wonder.cdc.gov, "Drug Overdose Mortality by State," Centers for Disease Control and Prevention, National Center for Health Statistics, last reviewed April 29, 2020, https://www.cdc.gov/nchs/pressroom/sosmap/drug_poisoning_mortality/drug_poisoning.htm.

7   Hanna Kozlowska, "A Horrifying Statistic That Conveys the Sheer Scale of the US Opioid Crisis, September 28, 2017, *Quartz*, https://qz.com/1089723/the-opioid-crisis-is-so-bad-west-virginia-has-spent-nearly-1-million-on-transporting-corpses/.

8   Dan Levin, "Teaching Children How to Reverse an Overdose," *New York Times*, February 23, 2020, https://www.nytimes.com/2020/02/23/us/opioids-tennessee-narcan-training.html?referringSource=articleShare&fbclid=IwAR3GF0FEvJ7CQOBuB8_fy3MeEqqQkikeN0NC5-AHOp5MzYp2VKi7uJjlbRA.

9   Eric Eyre, "Drug Firms Poured 780M Painkillers into WV amid Rise of Overdoses," *Charleston Gazette-Mail*, December 17, 2016, https://www.wvgazettemail.com/news/legal_affairs/drug-firms-poured-780m-painkillers-into-wv-amid-rise-of-overdoses/article_99026dad-8ed5-5075-90fa-adb906a36214.html.

10 WHSV Newsroom and Associated Press, "West Virginia Attorney General Sues Grant County Pharmacy over Painkillers," WHSV, December 22, 2016, https://www.whsv.com/content/news/West-Virginia-Attorney-General-sues-Grant-County-pharmacy-over-painkillers-407964895.html.

11 "Remarks by President Trump on Combatting Drug Demand and the Opioid Crisis," Whitehouse.gov, October 26, 2017, https://www.whitehouse.gov/briefings-statements/remarks-president-trump-combatting-drug-demand-opioid-crisis/.

12 "HHS Commits $144.1 Million in Additional Funding for Opioid Crisis, HHS.gov, news release, September 15, 2017, https://www.hhs.gov/about/news/2017/09/15/hhs-commits-144-million-in-additional-funding-for-opioid-crisis.html.

13 "CDC Awards #28.6 Million to Help State Fight Opioid Overdose Epidemic, APhA, CDC news release, September 6, 2017, https://www.pharmacist.com/article/cdc-awards-286-million-help-states-fight-opioid-overdose-epidemic.

14 Department of Justice Office of Public Affairs, "Department of Justice Awards Nearly $59 Million to Combat Opioid Epidemic, Fund Drug Courts," United States Department of Justice, Justice News, September 22, 2017, https://www.justice.gov/opa/pr/department-justice-awards-nearly-59-million-combat-opioid-epidemic-fund-drug-courts.

15   "The Underestimated Cost of the Opioid Crisis," Council of Economic Advisers, November, 2017, https://www.whitehouse.gov/sites/whitehouse.gov/files/images/The%20 Underestimated%20Cost%20of%20the%20Opioid%20Crisis.pdf.

16   2016 West Virginia Presidential Election Results, *Politico*, December 13, 2016, https://www. politico.com/2016-election/results/map/president/west-virginia/.

17   "Overdosed," (2019), https://www.imdb.com/title/tt7391064/.

18   "President-Elect Trump's Remarks on Opioids," Advocates for Opioid Recovery, October 16, 2015, https://www.opioidrecovery.org/president-elect-trumps-remarks-on-opioids/.

19   "Remarks by President Trump in State of the Union Address," Whitehouse.gov, February 4, 2020, https://www.whitehouse.gov/briefings-statements/remarks-president-trump-state-union-address-3/.

20   "President Donald J. Trump Has Dedicated His Administration to Fighting Back Against the Opioid Crisis," Whitehouse.gov, Fact Sheets, September 5, 2019, https://www.whitehouse.gov/ briefings-statements/president-donald-j-trump-dedicated-administration-fighting-back-opioid-crisis/.

21   Marianna Sotomayor, Trump Signs Sweeping Opioid Bill with Vow to End 'Scourge' of Drug Addiction," NBC News, October 14, 2018, https://www.nbcnews.com/politics/congress/trump-signs-sweeping-opioid-bill-vow-end-scourge-drug-addiction-n923976.

22   "U.S. Opioid Prescribing Rate Maps," Centers for Disease Control and Prevention: Opioid Overdoses, https://www.cdc.gov/drugoverdose/maps/rxrate-maps.html.

23   "CPB Enforcement Statistics Fiscal Year 2020," U.S. Customs and Border Protection, https:// www.cbp.gov/newsroom/stats/cbp-enforcement-statistics.

24   "Life Expectancy Increases in 2018 as Overdose Deaths Decline along with Several Leading Causes of Death," Centers for Disease Control and Prevention, National Center for Health Statistics, news release, January 30, 2020, https://www.cdc.gov/nchs/pressroom/nchs_press_ releases/2020/202001_Mortality.htm.

25   German Lopez, "The Rise in Meth and Cocaine Overdoses, Explained," Vox, January 30, 2020, https://www.vox.com/policy-and-politics/2020/1/9/21055113/opioid-epidemic-stimulants-cocaine-meth-drug-overdose-death.

26   Associated Press, "Feds Allow Use of Opioid Funds to Stem Meth, Cocaine Surge," CBS News, January 21, 2020, https://www.cbsnews.com/news/feds-allow-use-of-opioid-funds-to-stem-meth-cocaine-surge/.

27   Vincent J. Felitti, MD, FACP, et al, "Relationship of Childhood Abuse and Household Dysfunction to Many of the Leading Causes of Death in Adults," *American Journal of Preventive Medicine* 14, no. 4 (May 1, 1998): 245–58, https://doi.org/10.1016/S0749-3797(98)00017-8.

28   "West Virginia: 2015: Teen Births," County Health Rankings & Roadmaps, accessed June 15, 2020, https://www.countyhealthrankings.org/app/west-virginia/2015/measure/factors/14/ data?sort=sc-3.

29   "Grant County, West Virginia Demographics Data," Town Charts, accessed June 15, 2020, https://www.towncharts.com/West-Virginia/Demographics/Grant-County-WV-Demographics-data.html,

30   "Children in Foster Care in West Virginia," The Annie E. Casey Foundation Kids Count Data Center, accessed June 15, 2020, https://datacenter.kidscount.org/data/tables/6243-children-in-foster-care#detailed/2/50/true/870,17/any/12987.

CHAPTER 6

1   "North Carolina Poverty Rate by County," index mundi, accessed June 15, 2020, https://www. indexmundi.com/facts/united-states/quick-facts/north-carolina/percent-of-people-of-all-ages-in-poverty#map.

2   Robeson County Homicide Assault Death Statistics, LiveStories, accessed June 15, 2020, https://www.livestories.com/statistics/north-carolina/robeson-county-homicide-assault-deaths-mortality.

3   Claire Galofaro, "A Trump County in NC: Residents Weigh Racial Divides," *News & Record* (Greensboro, NC), December 5, 2017, https://www.greensboro.com/ap/north_carolina/a-trump-county-in-nc-residents-weigh-racial-divides/article_28a8a9d0-c2d2-59aa-bba0-bc6f2ce601c6.html.

4   Bob Shiles, "Democrats on Decline, Unaffiliated Surging in Robeson, *Robesonian* (Robeson County, NC), October 15, 2017, https://www.robesonian.com/news/103802/democrats-on-decline-unaffiliated-surging-in-robeson.

5   "Election Results 2008: North Carolina: Presidential County Results," *New York Times*, December 9, 2008, https://www.nytimes.com/elections/2008/results/states/president/north-carolina.html.

6   Stephanie Strom, "Election 2012: North Carolina," *New York Times*, https://www.nytimes.com/elections/2012/results/states/north-carolina.html?mtrref=www.google.com&gwh=C9838FACD F69D51A0CEDC4DE6C2AE4D7&gwt=pay&assetType=PAYWALL.

7   "Data USA: Prospect, NC," accessed June 15, 2020, https://datausa.io/profile/geo/prospect-nc/#demographics.

8   "11/08/2016 Official General Election Results—Robeson," North Carolina State Board of Elections, accessed June 15, 2020, https://er.ncsbe.gov/contest_details.html?election_dt=11/08/2016&county_id=78&contest_id=1001.

9   "North Carolina Presidential Race Results: Donald J. Trump Wins," *New York Times*, August 1, 2017, https://www.nytimes.com/elections/2016/results/north-carolina-president-clinton-trump.

10 Jim Morrill, "Election Exposes NC Urban and Rural Fault Lines," *Charlotte Observer*, November 18, 2016, https://www.charlotteobserver.com/news/politics-government/article115779373.html.

11 "Quick Facts: Robeson County, North Carolina," United States Census Bureau, accessed June 15, 2020, https://www.census.gov/quickfacts/fact/table/robesoncountynorthcarolina/INC110218.

12 Associated Press, "Converse Closes Chuck Taylor Plant," *Billings Gazette*, May 30, 2001, https://billingsgazette.com/business/converse-closes-chuck-taylor-plant/article_aa78045e-5e0e-5bd4-bf02-ef7033bc27c5.html.

13 Catherine Pritchard, "20 Years after Passage, NAFTA Shadow Lingers," *Fayetteville (NC) Observer*, January 18, 2014.

14 Stephen Gandel, "Donald Trump Says NAFTA Was the Worst Trade Deal the U.S. Ever Signed," *Fortune*, September 27, 2016, https://fortune.com/2016/09/27/presidential-debate-nafta-agreement/.

15 Michael Luo, "Memo Gives Canada's Account of Obama's Campaign Meeting," *New York Times*, March 4, 2008, https://www.nytimes.com/2008/03/04/us/politics/04nafta.html.

16 Donald J. Trump, *Crippled America: How to Make America Great Again* (New York: Simon & Schuster, 2016).

17   "Quick Facts: Robeson County, North Carolina," United States Census Bureau, July 1, 2019, https://www.census.gov/quickfacts/robesoncountynorthcarolina.

18   "Judge Doesn't Expect Opt-Outs on Gay Weddings," Robesonian, June 20, 2015, https://www. robesonian.com/news/463/judge-doesntexpect-opt-outson-gay-weddings.

19   "11/08/2016 Official General Election Results—Robeson."

20   "Britt Leads Republican Charge," *Robesonian* (2016), accessed June 15, 2020, https://www. robesonian.com/news/93377/britt-leads-republican-charge/amp.

21   "Quick Facts: Robeson County, North Carolina."

22   Scott Bigelow, "Schools Next to Last in Local Funding," *Robesonian*, February 3, 2018, https:// www.robesonian.com/news/107386/schools-next-to-last-in-local-funding.

23   Dave Wasserman, "Donald Trump won 76% of counties w/ a Cracker Barrel & 22% of counties w/ a Whole Foods—a 54% gap. In '92, gap b/t same counties was 19%," Twitter, November 9, 2016, https://twitter.com/Redistrict/status/796425128359972864.

24   Jeff Zeleny, "Obama's Down on the Farm," *The Caucus* (*New York Times* blog), July 27, 2007, https://thecaucus.blogs.nytimes.com/2007/07/27/obamas-down-on-the-farm/, no longer accessible.

25   Allen Turner, "Danny Britt Wins Reelection to N.C. Senate," *News Reporter* (Whiteville, NC), November 9, 2018, https://nrcolumbus.com/danny-britt-wins-reelection-to-n-c-senate/.

26   Jarrod Lowery, "Why My American Indian tribe Voted Republican in NC's Special Election," *The Hill*, September 12, 2019, https://thehill.com/opinion/campaign/461146-why-my-american-indian-tribe-voted-republican-in-ncs-special-election.

CHAPTER 7

1   "Lawsuits Related to Trump's Muslim Ban," ACLU website, accessed June 15, 2020, https:// www.aclu.org/other/lawsuits-related-trumps-muslim-ban.

2   Dan Nowicki, "Sens. John McCain, Jeff Flake Slam President Trump's Refugee Ban," azcentral, January 29, 2017, https://www.azcentral.com/story/news/politics/azdc/2017/01/29/sen-john-mccain-slams-president-donald-trumps-refugee-ban/97213920/.

3   Tad Walch, "LDS Church Issues Statement after Trump Orders Ban on Refugees," *Deseret News*, January 28, 2017, https://www.deseret.com/2017/1/29/20605059/lds-church-issues-statement-after-trump-orders-ban-on-refugees.

4   Hunter Schwarz, "138 Years Ago, the Controversy over Travel Bans and Religion Was about Mormons from Europe," CNN, January 30, 2017, https://www.cnn.com/2017/01/30/ politics/1879-mormon-travel-ban/index.html.

5   Julia Preston, "Utah Republicans Adopt Alternative Approach on Immigration," *New York Times*, March 7, 2011, https://www.nytimes.com/2011/03/07/us/07utah.html.

6   "States Offering Driver's Licenses to Immigrants," National Conference of State Legislatures, February 6, 2020, https://www.ncsl.org/research/immigration/states-offering-driver-s-licenses-to-immigrants.aspx.

7   "A Deep Dive into Party Affiliation," Pew Research Center, April 7, 2015, https://www.people-press.org/2015/04/07/a-deep-dive-into-party-affiliation/.

8   Betsy Cooper et al., "How Americans View Immigrants, and What They Want from Immigration Reform: Findings from the 2015 American Values Atlas," PRRI, March 29, 2016, https://www.prri.org/research/poll-immigration-reform-views-on-immigrants/.

9   MWEG (Mormon Women for Ethical Government), "2019 | Official Statements," *MWEG in the News*, accessed June 15, 2020, https://www.mormonwomenforethicalgovernment.org/mweg-in-the-news.

10 Diana Bate Hardy, "Take Action Now to Help Dreamers," *Washington Examiner*, February 28, 2018, https://www.washingtonexaminer.com/take-action-now-to-help-dreamers.

11 Roberta Rampton and Susan Cornwell, "Trump Seeks $25 Billion for Border Wall, Offers 'Dreamer' Citizenship, Reuters, January 28, 2018, https://www.reuters.com/article/us-usa-immigration-whitehouse/trump-seeks-25-billion-for-border-wall-offers-dreamer-citizenship-idUSKBN1FD2UU.

12 Kristina Wong and Rachel Martin, "Tea Party Power: Who's Next after Bennett?" ABC News, May 9, 2010, https://abcnews.go.com/Politics/2010_Elections/tea-party-movement-unseats-bennett-ahead-republican-incumbents/story?id=10598877.

13 "Utah Caucus Results," *New York Times*, March 22, 2016, https://www.nytimes.com/elections/2016/results/primaries/utah.

14 The New York Times, "Utah Presidential Race Results: Donald J. Trump Wins," *New York Times*, August 1, 2017, https://www.nytimes.com/elections/2016/results/utah-president-clinton-trump.

15 Robert Gehrke, "While Mormons Nationally Stuck with Trump, in Utah He Lagged," *Salt Lake Tribune*, November 18, 2016, https://archive.sltrib.com/article.php?id=4573783&itype=CMSID.

16 Gehrke.

17 Thomas Burr, "National Poll: 61 Percent of Mormons Approve of President Donald Trump—Highest of Any Religious Group," *Salt Lake Tribune*, January 12, 2018, https://www.sltrib.com/news/politics/2018/01/12/national-poll-61-percent-of-mormons-approve-of-president-donald-trump-highest-of-any-religious-group/.

18 Associated Press, "Mia Love Is Congress' First Black Republican Woman," *USA Today*, November 5, 2014, https://www.usatoday.com/story/news/politics/elections/2014/11/05/mia-love-first-black-republican-woman-congress/18523515/.

19 "Tracking Congress in the Age of Trump," FiveThirtyEight, updated May 18, 2020, https://projects.fivethirtyeight.com/congress-trump-score/mia-b-love/.

20 Daniel Woodruff, "Some Utah Republicans Dump Trump in Light of Video, Others Don't" KUTV, October 7, 2016, https://kutv.com/news/local/utah-lt-gov-says-leaked-video-makes-it-that-much-easier-not-to-support-trump.

21 Abigail Abrams, "'The President Must Apologize': Haitian-American GOP Rep. Mia Love Slams Trump's 'Shithole Countries' Comment," *Time*, January 11, 2018, https://time.com/5100217/mia-love-donald-trump-shithole-remark/.

22 Bryan Schott, "Trump, Clinton Underperformed in Utah's Four Congressional Districts in 2016," UtahPolicy.com, March 28, 2017, https://utahpolicy.com/index.php/features/today-at-utah-policy/12770-trump-clinton-underperformed-in-utah-s-four-congressional-districts-in-2016.

23 Calvin Freiburger, "Utah Rep. Mia Love Hammers Dem Opponent for Backing Same-Sex 'Marriage,'" LifeSite, September 5, 2018, https://www.lifesitenews.com/news/utahs-mia-love-hammers-dem-opponent-for-backing-same-sex-marriage.

24 "NRA Endorses Mia Love for U.S. House in Utah's 4 Congressional District," NRA-ILA, October 12, 2016, https://www.nraila.org/articles/20161012/nra-endorses-mia-love-for-us-house-in-utah-s-4th-congressional-district.

25 Adam Brown, "Who Is REALLY the Most Conservative Utah Legislator?" *Utah Data Points*, May 9, 2011, http://utahdatapoints.com/2011/05/who-is-really-the-most-conservative-utah-legislator/.

26 Roll Call Staff, "Here Are the 15 Democrats Who Didn't Vote for Pelosi as Speaker," *Roll Call*, January 3, 2019, https://www.rollcall.com/2019/01/03/here-are-the-15-democrats-who-didnt-vote-for-pelosi-as-speaker/.

27 Benjamin Wood, 'Love Gave Me No Love': President Trump Slams Utah Rep. Mia Love in Post-Election News Conference, Says She Lost," *Salt Lake Tribune*, November 7, 2018, https://www.sltrib.com/news/politics/2018/11/07/love-gave-me-no-love/.

28 Herb Scribner, "Video: Stunning Footage Shows Contrast in Color of the Great Salt Lake," *Deseret News*, September 13, 2018, https://www.deseret.com/2018/9/13/20653399/video-stunning-footage-shows-contrast-in-color-of-the-great-salt-lake.

29 "U.S. Census Bureau: Quick Facts, Salt Lake City, Utah," July 1, 2019, https://www.census.gov/quickfacts/saltlakecitycityutah.

30 Mike Anderson, "Salt Lake City ranks 3rd Most 'Hipster City,'" KSL.com, April 14, 2018, https://www.ksl.com/article/46299916.

31 Amelia Robinson, "Dayton the Queerest (Unexpected) City in America," Dayton.com, January 12, 2015, https://www.dayton.com/lifestyles/dayton-the-queerest-unexpected-city-america/SUfAamIno2Xe0FqfEZQQzH/.

32 "Mayflower & Livability's Top Ten Cities for Millennials on the Move," accessed June 15, 2020, https://www.mayflower.com/newsroom/top-10-millennial-cities-salt-lake-city-ut.

33 Jim Weiker, "Millennials Gain Clout in Urban Housing Markets," GoErie.com, January 25, 2020, https://www.goerie.com/entertainmentlife/20200125/millennials-gain-clout-in-urban-housing-markets.

34 Matt Canham, "Salt Lake County Is Now Minority Mormon, and The Impacts Are Far Reaching," *Salt Lake Tribune*, December 9, 2018, https://www.sltrib.com/religion/2018/12/09/salt-lake-county-is-now/.

35 Daniel Strauss, "Sanders Wins Utah," *Politico*, March 23, 2016, https://www.politico.com/story/2016/03/sanders-wins-utah-221136.

36 "Utah Presidential Race Results: Donald J. Trump Wins."

37 Lisa Riley Roche, "Sanders Wins Utah In Final Presidential Primary Results," KSL.com, March 24, 2020, https://www.ksl.com/article/46734152/sanders-wins-utah-in-final-presidential-primary-results.

38 Pamela S. Perlich et al., "Utah's Long-Term Demographic and Economic Projections Summary," Kem C. Gardner Policy Institute, University of Utah, research brief, July 2017, https://gardner.utah.edu/wp-content/uploads/Projections-Brief-Final-Updated-Feb2019.pdf.

39 Joel Kotkin, "Best Cities for Tech Jobs," *Forbes*, https://www.forbes.com/sites/joelkotkin/2012/05/17/the-best-cities-for-tech-jobs/#3a162ef932a3.

40 "Top 10 Places Californians Call Home in 2018," February 20, 2018, *Outside the Box* (blog), https://www.tsishipping.com/blog/moving/top-10-places-californians-now-call-home-2018.

41 Daniel Allott, "Meet the 'Plain Old Guy' Who Could End Mitt Romney's Political Career," *Washington Examiner*, June 13, 2018, https://www.washingtonexaminer.com/opinion/meet-the-plain-old-guy-who-could-end-mitt-romneys-political-career.

42   Bob Bernick and Bryan Schott, "Supreme Court Rejects Appeal over SB54, Meaning Utah's Law Allowing Candidates to Gather Signatures Stands . . . for Now," UtahPolicy.com, March 4, 2019, https://utahpolicy.com/index.php/features/today-at-utah-policy/19630-supreme-court-rejects-appeal-over-sb54-meaning-utah-s-law-allowing-candidates-to-gather-signatures-stands-for-now.

43   Bob Bernick, "Poll shows Utah GOP infighting in angering party members," UtahPolicy.com, February 15, 2019, https://utahpolicy.com/index.php/features/today-at-utah-policy/19451-poll-shows-utah-gop-infighting-is-angering-party-members.

44   Herb Scribner, "Could Utah Become a Blue State? Why Expert Nate Silver Says It Already Is," *Deseret News*, May 24, 2017, https://www.deseret.com/2017/3/24/20608907/could-utah-become-a-blue-state-why-expert-nate-silver-says-it-already-is.

45   MWEG (Mormon Women for Ethical Government), https://mormonwomenforethicalgovernment.org/press/media-releases/.

46   Bryan Schott, "For the First Time, a Majority of Utah Voters Approve of President Trump," UtahPolicy.com, February 4, 2020, https://kutv.com/news/local/for-the-first-time-a-majority-of-utah-voters-approve-of-president-donald-trump.

47   Jana Reiss, "Trump's Mormon Problem Continues, New Study Shows," *Salt Lake Tribune*, February 4, 2020, https://www.sltrib.com/religion/2020/02/04/jana-riess-trumps-mormon/.

48   Sharlee Mullins Glenn, "Why I Became an Activist against Fear," *New York Times*, February 19, 2020, https://www.nytimes.com/2020/02/19/opinion/mormons-religion-trump.html.

CHAPTER 8

1   Alec Tyson and Shiva Maniam, "Behind Trump's Victory: Divisions by Race, Gender, Education," Pew Research Center, November 9, 2016, https://www.pewresearch.org/fact-tank/2016/11/09/behind-trumps-victory-divisions-by-race-gender-education/.

2   Timothy Noah, "Does Labor Have a Death Wish?" *Politico*, November 7, 2017, https://www.politico.com/magazine/story/2017/11/07/labor-movement-trump-betrayal-215796.

3   "Pennsylvania Presidential Race Results: Donald J. Trump Wins," *New York Times*, August 1, 2017, https://www.nytimes.com/elections/2016/results/pennsylvania-president-clinton-trump.

4   Kevin Flowers, "Final Erie County Vote Totals Shed Light on Trump's Win," GoErie.com, November 20, 2016, https://www.goerie.com/news/20161120/final-erie-county-vote-totals-shed-light-on-trumps-win.

5   Gary Weiss, "Erie County's Population Shrinks for Fourth Straight Year," GoErie.com, March 23, 2017, https://www.goerie.com/news/20170323/erie-countys-population-shrinks-for-fourth-straight-year#.

6   Jim Martin, "A Year of Challenges for Erie's GE Plant," GoErie.com, November 6, 2016, https://www.goerie.com/news/20161106/year-of-challenges-for-eries-ge-plant.

7   Nico Salvatori, "Trump Draws 8,000-Plus to Erie Campaign Rally," GoErie.com, August 13, 2016, https://www.goerie.com/news/20160813/trump-draws-8000-plus-to-erie-campaign-rally.

8   CBS News, "America: Manufacturing Hope," *CBSN Originals*, March 2, 2017, https://www.youtube.com/watch?v=ynGdIhpWrLs.

9   Kevin McCorry, "In Erie, a Microcosm of Pennsylvania's Struggle for Education Equity," WHYY, July 21, 2016, https://whyy.org/articles/erie-public-schools-a-district-on-the-brink/.

10   Richie Bernardo, "Cities with the Most and Least Diversified Economies, WalletHub, May 3, 2018, https://wallethub.com/edu/cities-with-the-most-least-diversified-economies/10852/#size.

11   Lisa Adams, "Erie Refugee Surge Featured in Wall Street Journal Article," *Erie News Now*, updated March 7, 2017, https://www.erienewsnow.com/story/34629549/erie-refugee-surge-featured-in-wall-street-journal-article.

12   Theodore Schleifer, "Donald Trump: 'I Think Islam Hates Us,'" CNN, March 10, 2016, https://www.cnn.com/2016/03/09/politics/donald-trump-islam-hates-us/index.html.

13   "Wabtec Completes Successful Merger with GE Transportation," Wabtec Corporation, February 25, 2019, https://www.wabtec.com/press-releases/8803/wabtec-completes-successful-merger-ge-transportation.

14   Jim Martin, "Erie Economy Roared in 2019," GoErie.com, January 10, 2020, https://www.goerie.com/business/20200110/erie-economy-roared-in-2018?utm_source=SFMC&utm_medium=email&utm_campaign=Newsletter%20Dynamic%20Ads&utm_content=GTDT_ERI&utm_term=011020.

15   "Erie Leading Index: 3rd Quarter 2019 Report," *ELI: Erie Leading Index* 32 (Fall 2019), https://eriedata.bd.psu.edu/sites/default/files/2019-12/ELI%20%2332%20-%202019.Q3%20-%20FINAL.pdf.

16   "All Employees: Manufacturing in Erie, PA," FRED: Federal Reserve Bank of St. Louis, https://fred.stlouisfed.org/series/ERIE542MFGN.

17   Trip Gabriel, "I Gave the Other Guy a Shot," *New York Times*, October 7, 2019, https://www.nytimes.com/2019/10/07/us/politics/trump-democrats-pennsylvania-.html.

CHAPTER 9

1   "Lullabye Furniture Closing Is No Bedtime Story," *Journal-Times*, March 18, 1991, https://journaltimes.com/news/national/lullabye-furniture-closing-is-no-bedtime-story/article_d695d161-8897-556f-bef2-9814fd333c28.html.

2   "Election Results 2008: Florida," *New York Times*, December 9, 2008, https://www.nytimes.com/elections/2008/results/states/florida.html.

3   The New York Times, "Election 2012: Florida," *New York Times*, https://www.nytimes.com/elections/2012/results/states/florida.html?mtrref=www.google.com&gwh=09D4E2BFE3EBD39D5E7C6A2582B4C189&gwt=pay&assetType=PAYWALL.

4   The New York Times, "Florida Presidential Race Results, Donald J. Trump Wins," *New York Times*, August 1, 2017, https://www.nytimes.com/elections/2016/results/florida-president-clinton-trump.

5   "Cooperate Congressional Election Study," Harvard University, https://cces.gov.harvard.edu/.

6   "Cooperate Congressional Election Study."

7   "Cooperate Congressional Election Study."

8   "Cohn and Miller, "They Voted Democratic. Now They Support Trump" (see chap. 4, n. 23).

9   Gabriel, "I Gave the Other Guy a Shot" (see chap. 8, n. 17).

10   "Man Who Appeared in Anti-Trump Ad Didn't Vote in 2016," yourerie.com, December 5, 2019, https://www.yourerie.com/news/local-news/man-who-appeared-in-anti-trump-ad-didnt-vote-in-2016/.

11   Thomas B. Edsall, "Trump Has a Gift for Tearing Us Apart," *New York Times*, December 11, 2019, https://www.nytimes.com/2019/12/11/opinion/trump-immigration.html.

12 Matthew J. Belvedere, "Health Care for Undocumented Immigrants May 'Haunt' Dems against Trump, Says Ex-Sen. Evan Bayh," CNBC.com, July 1, 2019, https://www.cnbc.com/2019/07/01/health-care-for-undocumented-immigrants-may-haunt-dems-against-trump.html.

13 Zach Goldberg, @ZachG932, "1/n Spent Some Time on LexisNexis over the Weekend . . . ," Twitter, May 28, 2019, https://twitter.com/ZachG932/status/1133440945201061888.

14 "White Democrats, Those with College Degrees More Likely to Describe Their Views as Liberal," Pew Research Center, January 17, 2020, https://www.pewresearch.org/fact-tank/2020/01/17/liberals-make-up-largest-share-of-democratic-voters/ft_2020-01-17_demdideology_02/.

15 "Thomas B. Edsall, "The Democrats' Left Turn Is Not an Illusion," *New York Times*, October 18, 2018, https://www.nytimes.com/2018/10/18/opinion/democrat-electorate-left-turn.html?login=smartlock&auth=login-smartlock.

16 16. Emma Newburger, "Obama Warns Democrats against Going Too Far Left: 'We Have to Be Rooted in Reality,'" CNBC.com, November 16, 2019, https://www.cnbc.com/2019/11/16/obama-warns-democrats-against-going-too-far-left.html.

17 Chris Cillizza, "Half of Americans Think the Democratic Party Has Moved Too Far Left," CNN, October 24, 2019, https://www.cnn.com/2019/10/24/politics/democratic-party-left-liberal-q-poll/index.html.

18 Joe Biden, "Health Care," Biden President, accessed June 15, 2020, https://joebiden.com/healthcare/.

19 Dino Grandoni and Jeff Stein, "Joe Biden Embraces Green New Deal as He Releases Climate Plan," *Washington Post*, June 4, 2019, https://www.washingtonpost.com/climate-environment/2019/06/04/joe-biden-embraces-green-new-deal-he-releases-climate-plan/.

20 Jennifer Epstein, "Biden Adopts Free Public College Plan in Response to Sanders," Bloomberg, March 15, 2020, https://www.bloomberg.com/news/articles/2020-03-15/biden-adopts-free-public-college-plan-in-response-to-sanders.

21 Victor Morton, "Biden Says Beto O'Rourke to Lead Gun-Control Push: 'The Country Needs You'" *Washington Times*, March 3, 2020, https://www.washingtontimes.com/news/2020/mar/3/joe-biden-beto-orourke-lead-gun-control-push/.

22 Katie Glueck, "Joe Biden Denounces Hyde Amendment, Reversing His Position," *New York Times*, June 6, 2019, https://www.nytimes.com/2019/06/06/us/politics/joe-biden-hyde-amendment.html.

23 Marc Caputo, "Leftward Ho! Biden Pivots to Progressives," *Politico*, April 9, 2020, https://www.politico.com/news/2020/04/09/biden-progressives-sanders-178073.

24 Katherine Hignett, "Joe Biden Says Trump's Brutality to Refugees Is an 'Embarrassment' and That Americans Know That's Not Right,'" *Newsweek*, February 17, 2019, https://www.newsweek.com/joe-biden-immigration-europe-nato-donald-trump-1334094.

CHAPTER 10

1 Tim Alberta, "'Mother Is Not Going to Like This': The 48 Hours That Almost Brought Down Trump," *Politico*, July 10, 2019, https://www.politico.com/magazine/story/2019/07/10/american-carnage-excerpt-access-hollywood-tape-227269.

2 Jonathan Swan, "How Trump Won with Evangelicals—and won big," *The Hill*, November 13, 2016, https://thehill.com/blogs/ballot-box/presidential-races/305665-how-trump-won-with-evangelicals-and-won-big.

3 John Gramlich, "The Gap between the Number of Blacks and Whites in Prison Is Shrinking," Pew Research Center, April 30, 2019, https://www.pewresearch.org/fact-tank/2019/04/30/shrinking-gap-between-number-of-blacks-and-whites-in-prison/.

4 Gabby Orr and Daniel Lippman, "Trump Snubs Jared Kushner's Signature Accomplishment," *Politico*, September 24, 2019, https://www.politico.com/story/2019/09/24/trump-kushner-criminal-justice-snub-1507285.

5 Benjamin Weiser and Ali Watkins, "Cesar Sayoc, Who Mailed Pipe Bombs to Trump Critics, is Sentenced to 20 Years," *New York Times*, August 5, 2019, https://www.nytimes.com/2019/08/05/nyregion/cesar-sayoc-sentencing-pipe-bombing.html.

6 Jonathan Haidt and Tobias Rose-Stockwell, "The Dark Psychology of Social Networks," *Atlantic*, December 2019, https://www.theatlantic.com/magazine/archive/2019/12/social-media-democracy/600763/.

7 Susan Page and Merdie Nzanga, "Poll: On Trump, We Can't Even Agree on Why We Disagree. But We Assume the Worst," *USA Today*, June 21, 2018, https://www.usatoday.com/story/news/2018/06/21/poll-trump-we-cant-agree-why-we-disagree/720698002/.

8 Talia Lavin, "No We Don't Have to Be Friends with Trump Supporters," *Forward*, June 12, 2018, https://forward.com/opinion/402990/no-we-dont-have-to-be-friends-with-trump-supporters/.

9 "Since Trump's Election, Increased Attention to Politics—Especially among Women," Pew Research Center, July 20, 2017, https://www.people-press.org/2017/07/20/since-trumps-election-increased-attention-to-politics-especially-among-women/.

10 Andy Kroll, "Rep. Mark Sanford: Trumpism Is a 'Cancerous Growth' in the Republican Party,'" *Rolling Stone*, June 15, 2018, https://www.rollingstone.com/politics/politics-features/rep-mark-sanford-trumpism-is-a-cancerous-growth-in-the-republican-party-628833/.

11 David Weigel, "Rep. Mark Sanford Loses Primary to Pro-Trump Challenger," *Washington Post*, June 12, 2018, https://www.washingtonpost.com/politics/2018/live-updates/midterms/live-primary-election-results/rep-mark-sanford-predicts-hell-primary-to-pro-trump-challenger/?arc404=true.

12 Thomas B. Edsall, "No Hate Left Behind" *New York Times*, March 13, 2019, https://www.nytimes.com/2019/03/13/opinion/hate-politics.html.

13 Gerald F. Seib, "In Impeachment, Tribalization of Politics Becomes Almost Complete," *Wall Street Journal*, December 16, 2019, https://www.wsj.com/articles/in-impeachment-tribalization-of-politics-becomes-almost-complete-11576507724.

14 Aris Folley, "CPAC Chairman Says He Would Fear for Romney's Safety at Conservative Gathering," *The Hill*, February 10, 2020, https://thehill.com/blogs/blog-briefing-room/news/482288-cpac-chairman-says-he-would-fear-for-romneys-safety-at/.

15 "Confidence in Institutions," Gallup, accessed June 15, 2020, https://news.gallup.com/poll/1597/confidence-institutions.aspx.

16 Alec Tysons, "Disagreements about Trump Widely Seen as Reflecting Divides over 'Other Values and Goals,'" Pew Research Center, March 15, 2018, https://www.pewresearch.org/fact-tank/2018/03/15/disagreements-about-trump-widely-seen-as-reflecting-divides-over-other-values-and-goals/.

CHAPTER 11

1 Hannah McDonald, "Jim Wertz Elected Erie County Democratic Party Chairman," *Erie Reader*, June 12, 2018, https://www.eriereader.com/article/jim-wertz-elected-erie-county-democratic-party-chairman.

2 Phillip Bump, "Sorry Campaign Managers: Lawn Signs Are Only 98.3 percent Useless," *Washington Post*, December 29, 2015, https://www.washingtonpost.com/news/the-fix/wp/2015/12/29/sorry-campaign-managers-lawn-signs-are-only-98-3-percent-useless/.

3 Kevin Flowers, "Final Erie County Vote Totals Shed Light on Trump's Win," GoErie.com, November 20, 2016, https://www.goerie.com/news/20161120/final-erie-county-vote-totals-shed-light-on-trumps-win.

4 Danielle Kurtzleben, "Here's How Many Bernie Sanders Supporters Ultimately Voted for Trump," NPR, August 24, 2017, https://www.npr.org/2017/08/24/545812242/1-in-10-sanders-primary-voters-ended-up-supporting-trump-survey-finds.

5 William Cummings, "Poll: 15% of Sanders Supporters Will Vote for Trump If Biden Is Nominee; 80% Would Back Biden," *USA Today*, March 30, 2020, https://www.usatoday.com/story/news/politics/elections/2020/03/29/bernie-sanders-supporters-vote-trump-over-biden-poll/2936124001/.

6 Harry Enten, "Joe Biden Has a Young Voter Problem," CNN, April 16, 2020, https://www.cnn.com/2020/04/16/politics/biden-young-voters/index.html.

7 Sarah Leach, "Parents Brace for Monthlong School Closures," March 13, 2020, *Holland (MI) Sentinel*, https://www.hollandsentinel.com/news/20200313/parents-brace-for-monthlong-school-closures.

8 Tom McCarthy, "'It Will Disappear': The Disinformation Trump Spread about the Coronavirus—Timeline," *Guardian* (UK), April 14, 2020, https://www.theguardian.com/us-news/2020/apr/14/trump-coronavirus-alerts-disinformation-timeline.

9 Jeremy W. Peters, "Alarm, Denial, Blame: The Pro-Trump Media's Coronavirus Distortion," *New York Times*, April 1, 2020, https://www.nytimes.com/2020/04/01/us/politics/hannity-limbaugh-trump-coronavirus.html.

10 William Cummings, "You're Full of S***': Joe Biden Gets in Heated Gun Control Debate with Detroit Plant Worker," *USA Today*, March 10, 2020, https://www.usatoday.com/story/news/politics/elections/2020/03/10/joe-biden-gun-control-exchange-auto-plant-worker/5011344002/.

11 Kate Sullivan and Eric Bradner, "Beto O'Rourke: 'Hell, Yes, We're Going to Take Your AR-15, Your AK-47,'" CNN, September 13, 2019, https://www.cnn.com/2019/09/12/politics/beto-orourke-hell-yes-take-ar-15-ak-47/index.html.

12 Quint Forgey, "Donna Brazile to Ronna McDaniel: 'Go to Hell'" *Politico*, March 3, 2020, https://www.politico.com/news/2020/03/03/donna-brazile-ronna-mcdaniel-go-to-hell-119492.

13 Rich Noyes, "Networks Trashed Trump with 90% Negative Spin in 2018, But Did It Matter?" NewsBusters, January 15, 2019, https://www.newsbusters.org/blogs/nb/rich-noyes/2019/01/15/networks-trashed-trump-90-negative-spin-2018-did-it-matter.

14 "The Coronavirus Was Spreading. The parties Went On. Now Comes the Pain," *Washington Post*, April 9, 2020, https://www.washingtonpost.com/national/the-coronavirus-was-spreading-the-parties-went-on-now-comes-the-pain/2020/04/09/39bdbe1e-7908-11ea-a130-df573469f094_story.html.

CHAPTER 12

1   Chris Kahn, "Biden's Edge Evaporates as Trump Seen as Better Suited for Economy, Coronavirus Response, Polls Shows," Reuters, May 5, 2020, https://www.reuters.com/article/ us-usa-election-poll/bidens-edge-evaporates-as-trump-seen-as-better-suited-for-economy- coronavirus-response-poll-shows-idUSKBN22I005.